A survey of streets, buildings
and residents in a part
of Camden

Streets and Characters of West Hampstead and Cricklewood

by Dick Weindling & Marianne Colloms

edited by
David Hayes

designed by
Eve Barker

published in London
by Camden History Society

CAMDEN
HISTORY
SOCIETY

Diagram of the nine Areas

Streets and Characters of West Hampstead and Cricklewood

© DICK WEINDLING and
MARIANNE COLLOMS 2021
ISBN 978 1 913213 04 6

Printed and bound in Great Britain
by The Ludo Press Ltd, London

*Front cover: West Hampstead Fire Station
(photo: Caroline Sharp)*

This book is one of a series of fifteen that survey the history of all parts of the London Borough of Camden. The first Camden History Society book that covered the area west of Finchley Road under the title The Streets of West Hampstead was published in 1975 and revised in 1992. Reaching from a northern boundary with Barnet, the western boundary followed the line of Cricklewood Broadway, Shoot-up Hill and Kilburn High Road before turning east after a short stretch of Maida Vale across to St John's Wood, which formed the boundary with Westminster City Council.

The many changes that have occurred since 1992, notably the redevelopment of derelict railway land, brown field sites and industrial buildings, has necessitated splitting the district into two books, covering the streets that lie north and south of the Jubilee line. This, the first and completely reworked book, takes in the northern neighbourhoods. The area south of the Jubilee line will be covered in a companion volume, Streets and Characters of Kilburn and South Hampstead.

The western and eastern boundaries are unchanged. The western follows an ancient division between the parishes of Willesden and Hampstead, now the Boroughs of Brent and Camden, running up the middle of the Kilburn High Road. The eastern boundary is Finchley Road, a much more recent creation. It took Colonel Henry Eyre four

attempts before an 1826 Act of Parliament allowed him to lay down the line of Avenue Road and Finchley (New) Road, which opened in 1830.

This book is divided into nine areas; beginning with Area 1 covering both sides of Shoot-up Hill north to the Crown at Cricklewood and ending with Area 9 which looks at Finchley Road, north from the Underground station as far as the Hendon Way.

The main road through Kilburn follows the track of the Roman road later called Watling Street, much used by pilgrims en route to St Albans. West End (later called West Hampstead), was an isolated village connected to Kilburn by West End Lane and Mill Lane. A few large mansions stood alongside small cottages whose inhabitants were frequently poor.

When Hampstead Cemetery was created in 1876 it stood in open fields but as London expanded, the large houses were demolished and their estates sold off and today's streets were laid out by developers and builders. Many of them became very rich and then went into bankruptcy with the peaks and troughs of the market. The housing generally catered for comfortably off, lower middle-class residents and there were fierce local fights to preserve the decreasing supply of open land for public use. Several neighbourhoods developed parades of shops that comprehensively catered

for the needs of nearby residents. Before large-scale development got underway, the area was crossed by three railway lines that cut across fields and boundaries, in many cases forcing street plans to adapt to the tracks. A feature of later development was the mansion flat block, a way of maximising the potential of a building site.

We have looked at both the history of the streets and the interesting mix of characters who lived here. These include two Nobel laureates, the physicist Joseph Rotblat and the writer Doris Lessing. A soldier awarded the Victoria Cross, Allan Ker, and a West Indian cricketing legend Sir Learie Constantine. Actors including Joan Collins and Burt Kwouk, as well as current residents Emma Thompson, Greg Wise, Jim Carter and Imelda Staunton. Musicians such as Dusty Springfield, Brian Jones, Joan Armatrading, Jack Bruce, Sir Adrian Boult and Benjamin Britten. Keats' beloved Fanny Brawne, the writer Evelyn Waugh, and film director and Monty Python member Terry Gilliam. And, of course, the huge number of permanent residents buried at Hampstead Cemetery, including many famous people from all walks of life.

We are grateful for the assistance of staff at Camden Local Studies & Archive Centre (CLSAC), especially the Senior Archivist Tudor Allen. Particular thanks go to our editor David Hayes, and to Steve Job for his expert customisation of the street maps.

Contents

List of illustrations

Image credits

1, 4, 8, 9, 11, 17, 24, 30, 32, 41, 45, 46, 47 Marianne Colloms
2 © The Powell-Cotton Trust
3 National Library of Scotland (Creative Commons)
5, 13, 14, 15, 29, 40 Camden Local Studies & Archives Centre
6, 12, 16, 18, 19, 20, 21, 22, 26, 28, 33, 34, 36, 42, 43, 49, 50 Wikimedia Commons
10 © Caroline Sharp
25, 48 Jean Smith
27 Caroline Kwouk
31, 39 Dick Weindling
35 J S Farley, Monumental Masons
37, 38 Jenny Miles
44 EMI archives

Historical Overview

The area covered by this book once formed part of the parish of Hampstead, which stretched across Hampstead Heath to Highgate and south as far as the borders of St John's Wood and Chalk Farm.

The linear village of Kilburn straggled northwards along both sides of Kilburn High Road, from today's Maida Vale. This well-used main road encouraged many taverns; the cottages, some doubling as shops, were interspersed with mansions standing in substantial grounds. Ten horse-bus and coach services ran to Kilburn by 1840. Beyond Shoot-up Hill, the small settlement of Cricklewood was clustered close to the junction with Cricklewood Lane.

By contrast, West End Lane wound its way through the fields to enter the village of West End which took its name from its geographical position, namely west of the main settlement of Hampstead. At its heart was West End Green, where the Lane turned sharp right to climb the hill to Frognal. Like Kilburn, West End also had a mix of mansions and cottages. But unlike its neighbour, West End was so quiet that locals reported hearing the guns of Waterloo and much later, the chimes of Big Ben. The seclusion was disturbed for a few

days in late July every year when a fair was held. It attracted hundreds of Londoners but grew too large to effectively police and after violence broke out in 1819 it was suppressed.

Although the neighbourhoods of West End and Kilburn were quite different, the surrounding countryside provided ample scope for wealthy people to build a new home or extend an existing property, sometimes creating a substantial estate in the process. The new gentry class predominated, men who had made their money by working rather than inheriting it from their parents. At the time, the district was in the country but close enough to Town to permit commuting.

The area was originally the property of just a few landowners. Fields bordering Finchley Road and Crediton Hill were owned by Sir Thomas Maryon Wilson, whose family had been Lord of the Manor of Hampstead since the mid-eighteenth century. Under the legal terms of his inheritance, he was only permitted to grant a maximum lease term of twenty-one years. Other families in the same situation usually managed to overcome this difficulty. One way was for the owner to join forces with an adult son and acting together, they could then make agreements for the

usual 99-year lease term. But Sir Thomas remained a bachelor and the other course of action, namely an Act of Parliament, was consistently denied him. This resulted in a forced suspension of building operations over a wide area of the Hampstead parish that lasted until his death in 1869. The new owner and his son cooperated to overcome the restriction.

Often called Shoot-up Hill farm, the largest acreage in the area was owned by the Powell-Cotton family whose family home was Quex Park in Kent. Its fields bordered east on Hampstead Cemetery, west on Shoot-up Hill and Cricklewood Broadway, extending almost as far as Cricklewood Lane. In 1773 John Powell bought the 112 acres as an investment and for many years the farm followed the usual pattern of such properties with absentee landlords, being rented out to produce an income. Captain Henry Perry Cotton succeeded his uncle John Powell Powell in 1849; the later amalgamation of the two surnames gave rise to the more commonly encountered form of Powell-Cotton.

The 46 acres of West End Farm extended north from West End Green as far as Hampstead Cemetery and Finchley Road. It was bought in 1755 and descended through the Flitcroft family. South of the Green, the Ripleys inherited their land which reached from West End Lane across to Kilburn High Road in the eighteenth century.

In 1775 Old West End House was acquired by Thomas Wildman who bequeathed it to Maria Beckford. Its land straddled Iverson Road with a field some distance away, later the site of Hillfield Road. Other landowners were relative newcomers: in the late 1830s the Burgess family bought land that reached from Fortune Green Road as far as Burgess Hill and Finchley Road. The Potters arrived at West End and built an iron foundry in the 1860s, and added to their property portfolio whenever the opportunity arose. There were also a handful of mansions with substantial grounds bordering West End Lane.

The transformation of Kilburn and West End into suburban neighbourhoods took many years. Fields and footpaths eventually disappeared under rows of streets and houses, but it was a complicated process. The willingness or the ability of an owner to sell their land and whether economic conditions were favourable to house building were most important. The London building booms of 1825 and 1868 (as well as the subsequent collapse of the market), made their mark. Public transport might support or could even be used to promote new building, but on its own was never the sole reason behind a development. However, the deep scars made by the various rail lines that crossed the district were another matter. They had a definite effect by dictating the direction new roads could or could not take. While Hampstead parish lay in the path of several companies seeking to establish a metropolitan terminus, the earliest rails were laid down well in advance of local customers. The Hampstead Junction Railway (today London Overground) opened in 1860 but the passenger traffic did not merit a West End Lane station until 1888. The Midland (today Thameslink) arrived in 1868, the line exiting a tunnel at Finchley Road, running across the fields to curve north and pass on to a large depot and sidings at Cricklewood. It opened a station on Iverson Road in 1871 but its main impact on West End was a physical one. The formerly level ground was excavated to create a deep cutting that altered the landscape forever; it was this carving up of their properties rather than any new transport provision that contributed to the decision of some landowners to sell up. In the case of old West End House, its fields were crossed by the tracks of the Hampstead Junction and Midland, breaking up the property and reducing the value of the mansion. The Ripley's fields were among the worst affected by railway building. The Hampstead Junction was carried across the Kilburn end of their land on an embankment leaving six acres isolated south of the line. Far worse was to come when the Midland line was built right through the centre of the property.

The early developments were conspicuous for the amount of land bought by Land Companies, organisations specifically created to provide cheaper housing. The process got underway of diverting field paths into new roads, open drains and streams, often insanitary and smelly, into covered sewers. The inexorable process of suburbanisation was underway. Despite several false or slow starts, there was clearly a growing awareness of new opportunities.

West End clung to its village like atmosphere well into the 1890s. The contemporary OS map shows a district of two halves: to the west of the Lane, house building was well underway, while to the east, the continuing existence of several large houses and extensive grounds right in the heart of the community, gave it a distinctly rural feel. These soon fell into developer's hands but not before an unsucssful campaign to preserve some as park nd. Today Kilburn and West Hampstead are ot well provided with public open spaces. As opulation numbers rose and houses covered n ever-increasing area, it became an nportant issue and hard battles were fought o secure West End Green and Fortune Green.

The supporting infrastructure developed: laces to worship, schools, libraries, a emetery and many shopping parades. Building could take place in fits and starts, or n sections of a street at different times, early ouses were often named, either individually r as part of a terrace. Shops were frequently grouped in parades which were abolished when a road was renumbered throughout. The old name of West End lingered on but the 1879 opening of West Hampstead station on the Metropolitan line (today Jubilee) was highly significant, as one of the first examples of the use of the present-day name for the locality.

The properties built in this part of Kilburn and West Hampstead were for the most part aimed at the middle and upper-working classes. Terraces predominated with the area around West End Green conspicuous for the number of mansion flats. It took Londoners a while to accept the idea of flat dwelling, but the benefits of amenities such as lifts, porters, and later central heating, won many over. A fair amount of poverty had always existed, limited to a degree by the generosity of better off members of the community, charitable organisations or religious groups. But in the days before any State assistance, the poor were largely on their own. Cheap accommodation in mews above stables was eagerly sought, while the newly built houses in some Kilburn streets were divided into flats or rooms from the outset. Families ate, slept, cooked and washed in a single room in overcrowded and insanitary conditions. The special needs of this neighbourhood were acknowledged when the Palmerston Road public baths and wash house opened in 1886, although this came about as the result of philanthropic and not local authority intervention.

Building was largely complete by the time WWI broke out and continued spasmodically during the war years. The northern extremities of the Powell-Cotton land and parts of Finchley Road were completed post-war. The 1930s were conspicuous for the number of applications to demolish large houses and replace them with blocks of flats. So many were approved, that some observers felt there was a danger that Hampstead would be swamped by these new builds. But these larger houses, often on main roads, were increasing seen as too big and expensive for a single family. The alternative to demolition was to divide them into rooms or flats for rent which became home to many young musicians and actors.

In the 1930s, the council cleared over three acres on Shoot-up Hill and had plans for redeveloping the Kilburn Vale area, but the only local authority housing to be completed prior to WWII was the Westcroft Estate off Westbere Road, officially opened in 1935.

WWII bombing caused some significant and collateral damage to property. 1940 and 1944 were particularly bad years for civilian fatalities, and a substantial number of the deaths occurred in West Hampstead and Kilburn. The post-war years saw Hampstead Council using some bomb sites for local authority housing, such as Dennington House on the corner with Dennington Park Road. Until then, the damaged buildings were the contemporary equivalent of an adventure playground for children in the 1950s. They could also play unsupervised in the street outside their home: there were few cars, little traffic and walking to school was the norm as was using public transport, both unaccompanied. After the 1960s and early 1970s when many houses remained in multiple occupation, properties began to be sold for 'development', which involved creating self-contained flats that were sold rather than rented. This process is referred to as 'gentrification' as it displaced less affluent residents.

The railway invasion of this area north of the Jubilee line had an unexpected effect in recent years. There were few sites available to create municipal housing and the sell-off of council property that began under Margaret Thatcher only made matters worse. Reusing derelict land was one option. 14 acres of disused sidings north of Maygrove Road had been blighted by proposals to build the Motorway Box in the sixties (see p 29) and were finally purchased by Camden Council as the site for the West End Sidings estate. After much argument and false starts that included plans for mixed residential/commercial use, a second area of sidings north of Finchley Road underground station was privately developed as the O2 shopping centre. Most recently, further disused railway land between the Overground and Underground lines was used to build seven blocks of flats. Elsewhere, regeneration has involved conversion of office blocks to residential use. The high street has fewer shops but many more eating places. Railway stations have been and are being rebuilt to accommodate more passengers as West Hampstead has grown in importance as a transport hub.

The multitude of events and colourful characters you will find in this book shows how wrong Pevsner's *London* (1952) was to conclude, 'West Hampstead need be visited only by those in search of Victorian churches. The houses and streets require no notice'.

Street names explained

Names for which there is no clear explanation are o▮

Achilles, Ajax Agamemnon,	heroes of the Trojan War; nam▮ assigned, for reasons unknow▮ three of the local 'Greek roads
Alvanley	1st Baron (d.1804), Chief Justice of the Common Pleas and Hamp stead resident
Asmara	the capital of Eritrea**
Barlow	William Henry, civil engineer wh built the train shed at St Pancra
Berridge,	Richard, benefactor of the Natio Society, whose Berridge House was on the site of the Mews
‡ Besant	Sir Walter, novelist and historia▮ who lived in Frognal Gardens
Beswick,	pottery manufacturer ¶
Brassey,	Thomas, civil engineering contrac▮ who worked on part of the Midla Railway's extension to London
Burgess,	Henry Weech, local landowner a▮ resident
Burrard,	Sir Harry Paul, director of Natio Standard Land, Mortgage & Inve ment Co.
Cannon,	Charles, wealthy merchant and creator of Cannon Hill
Cholmley	Lodge was previously on the sit▮ of the flats
Cricklewood,	village on the road to St Albans
Crown:	probably Royal Crown Derby, porcelain manufacturers ¶

† Dent de lion, medieval owners of Garlinge (q.v.) Castle

Doulton Royal, ceramic manufacturer ¶

Dresden, makers of porcelain ¶

Ebbsfleet, near Sandwich, Kent*

Finchley, destination of the turnpike road opened in 1829

Fordwych, from Fordwich (sic), a small town in east Kent*

Fortune green, open space, the origin of its name name unknown

‡ Galsworthy, John, novelist and playwright, who lived in Admiral's Walk

Garlinge, near Margate*

Gondar, walled city in Ethiopia*, but not visited by Major Powell-Cotton until well after the road was named

Hall oak, the manor farm stretching south from Hampstead Village (though not as far west as the Sidings Estate)

† Heysham, Lancashire ferry port, an important Midland Railway destination

Hillfield, name of a sloping local meadow

‡ Horton, Rev. Robert F, minister of Lyndhurst Road Congregational Church, Hampstead

‡ Howard: probably Frank Geere Howard, thrice Mayor of Hampstead 1921-25

Ingham, Edward, Secretary of National Standard Land, Mortgage & Investment Co.

Liddell, Charles, consultant engineer to the Midland Railway

Lithos, Greek for 'stone'; road built on site of parish stoneyard

Manstone, from Manston (sic), a village near Quex Park*

‡ Marnham, Herbert, Baptist stockbroker & philanthropist, Mayor of Hampstead 1925-26

Medley, John Edward, developer

Menelik II, Emperor of Ethiopia**

Mill: Shoot-up Hill windmill, to which Mill Lane led

Minster, village of Minster-in-Thanet*

Minton: Mintons, pottery manufacturers ¶

Orestes, son of Agamemnon, q.v.

Parsifal: Wagner's opera premiered in London in 1882; road built the next year

Ranulf Peverell, a Hampstead landowner listed in Domesday

Richborough, near Sandwich, Kent*

Rondu, gorge on river Indus in Kashmir**

St Cuthbert's, local parish church

Sandwell, large house on the site of the Crescent

Sarre, village on the Isle of Thanet*

Skardu, city and valley in Kashmir**

Somali: relating to Somaliland**

Spode, makers of bone china ¶

Ulysees, hero of Homer's epic poem The Iliad; name of another local 'Greek road'

Wedgwood, makers of china and porcelain

Weech, middle name of local landowner Henry Burgess

West End, settlement on the western side of Hampstead parish

Westbere, village in east Kent*

Westcroft, Cricklewood farm, later a home for horses

Worcester, Royal, makers of porcelain ¶

---

* place name connected with the Powell-Cotton family, who lived at Quex Park, Kent and were important land owners in that county and in our area

** place visited by the explorer Major Percy Powell-Cotton

† superseded street name

‡ one of five roads named after Hampstead worthies, on Hampstead Council's Westcroft Estate, across the Camden-Barnet border

¶ street names on the Lymington Road Estate, popularly known as the Potteries Estate, have no local association.

NW2, the Powell-Cotton estate

Shoot-up Hill, Cricklewood Broadway as far as the Crown pub, Fordwych Road, Minster Road, Westbere Road, and their various offshoots

The boundary between the Boroughs of Brent and Camden (formerly Willesden and Hampstead) runs up the middle of **SHOOT-UP HILL**. Originally part of the Roman road to St Albans and beyond, the Hill is part of Hampstead's oldest thoroughfare. Variously referred to as Watling Street or Edgware Road, Shoot-up Hill appeared as such on Rocque's map of 1746, although the name was officially sanctioned only in 1899. From 1710 the highway was maintained by a Turnpike Trust. A short-lived tollgate on the brow of the Hill, which had been relocated north from Kilburn High Road in the mid-1860s, was removed in 1872 after tolls were abolished.

On the Camden side of the main road is a large area originally owned by the Powell-Cotton family. Until the late 1860s, the only buildings on this section of Shoot-up Hill were the farmhouse serving the Powell-Cotton fields (p 7) and three cottages inside its yard. The Hill was developed with comfortable, predominantly detached properties intended for well-off middle-class residents, professional

men or merchants, and initially not numbered but named. Some of the houses were replaced by private blocks of flats before WWII and more have been demolished since, often redeveloped as local authority housing schemes.

Between Garlinge and St Cuthbert's Roads (p 14) is the long west frontage of the **Templar House Estat**e. A 3.4 acre site here was partly cleared for municipal flats before the outbreak of WWII. The Estate was developed after the war in three stages. The four blocks of 112 flats comprising **Templar House** itself were designed by Frank Scarlett, and work began on 30 April 1951 with an estimated cost of £291,000 for land and buildings. The Estate was officially opened by the Princess Royal on 4 November 1954. It takes its name from the Knights Templar, who owned the land in the Middle Ages.

Today, considerable imagination is needed to envisage this stretch of the Hill lined with Victorian villas. Joseph Acworth was living in 1891 at Sheldmont (later No.14 Shoot-up Hill). He was a photographic chemist who set up the Imperial Dry Plate Company in Ashford Road, Cricklewood. The firm became very successful and in 1917 Acworth sold it to Ilford, the large photographic company. Around 1903 Joseph and his wife Marion moved across the road to Thornbank (No.35).

They visited Egypt several times and became fascinated by the early civilisation. In 1939 Marion donated their collection of 600 pieces of Egyptian scarabs and bronzes to the British Museum as the Acworth Collection. Joseph died on 3 January 1927 as a very wealthy man, leaving £562,026 to his children, worth around £28 million today.

Oakfield (later Nos.20-22) and The Firs (No.24) were the first new houses to be built on the Camden side, by 1866. This early speculation was the work of George Verey (p 14). Jack Barnato Joel (1862 -1940) lived at The Firs from 1900 to 1902, before moving to Grosvenor Square. He was one of three brothers who became millionaires from their ownership of diamond and gold mines in South Africa. From 1931 he was Chairman of Johannesburg Consolidated Investment Co. Ltd. Also a major racehorse owner and breeder, Joel died at his home in St Albans.

In September 1882, the local paper promised that 'a handsome structure' was to be built on the southern corner of St Cuthbert's Road. Thomas Bate, a local developer and estate agent, was responsible for commissioning two houses here. Eversholt (No.26 Shoot-up Hill) and Mount Edgcumbe (No.28) were completed in 1883 to the design of architect Edward Arthur Heffer. The style was old English/Tudor; Mount Edgcumbe ad embattled towers seventy feet high, plus turret and a spire. In 1928, it became a branch of Pitman's Commercial College. onald Proyer, who lived in Ulysses Road 73), was sent there by his parents soon fter WWII broke out. It was an Air Raid recautions (ARP) post during the war and adly damaged by an air raid. Ronald said, Ve students turned up for class one morning find a smouldering ruin, the teachers ending us off with messages for our parents. have a vivid memory of an incendiary bomb mbedded halfway into a pavement slab its ail fin neatly sticking up, the pavement vhite-scorched around it. It surprised me hat a paving slab could burn'.

Over on the Brent side of the Hill all the riginal houses have been demolished. At he lower end, a V1 flying-bomb landed on 5 August 1944, destroying Nos.5-9, and lamaging many other properties north of Kilburn Station. Thirteen people were killed. Converted into residential flats in the late 1990s, the large red-brick **Jubilee Heights** was designed by Eric Bedford as Telephone House, headquarters of the North West London telephone area, and built on the site of the bombed houses and adjacent properties in 1953.

Further up the Hill on the same side, Mon Abri (No.27) was for many years the home of Señor Manuel Garcia, a famous singing teacher who taught the soprano Jenny Lind, popularly known as 'the Swedish nightingale'. Garcia invented the laryngoscope, which became a valuable diagnostic tool. On his 100th birthday he was decorated by King Edward VII as Honourable Commander of the Victorian Order. Garcia died at Mon Abri on 1 January 1906. A later resident was Frederick Beesley, who died here in 1928, having previously lived in what is now Mortimer Crescent, Kilburn. He worked for Purdey, the famous Mayfair gunmakers, before setting up his own gun-making business off Pall Mall, in 1879. Beesley guns are now highly prized collectors' items.

Two consulting chemists, Donald Willoughby West and Leonard Angelo Levy, were living at No.31 in 1934 when they registered patents for the production of X-ray fluorescent screens. Half the patent was assigned to Ilford Ltd.

A surviving house on the Camden side, beyond Kingscroft Road (p 15), is **No.38**, originally named Tan-y-Bryn, meaning 'beneath the brow of the hill' in Welsh. Soon after the Gollancz family moved in, Rabbi Samuel Marcus Gollancz, cantor of the Hambro Synagogue in the City, died there in May 1900. His son Israel (later knighted) took over the property, sharing it with his sister and brother. Israel was a scholar of early English literature and Shakespeare, a lecturer at Cambridge and professor of English at King's College London, 1905-30. He moved across the road to No.15 around 1915, but members of his family continued to live at No.38 to at least 1929.

The large houses, some on very generous plots, encouraged developers to focus on Shoot-up Hill in the 1920s and '30s, where they could buy up and demolish the properties and replace them with blocks of residential flats. At the time, this practice was common to many other roads in Hampstead. In 1935 and again the following year, Hampstead Council objected to the demolition of Nos.50 and 52 but the LCC agreed the developer's plan for a block of flats, today's **Fordwych Court**.

No.54, on the brow of the Hill and on the corner of Mill Lane, was demolished and replaced by **Hillcrest Court**. Tenants first appeared here on the electoral roll in 1936. Flat No.20 was rented by Joe Collins, a theatrical agent in partnership with Lew Grade. Joe married Elsa Bessant in 1932 and set up home off Maida Vale, and daughter Joan Collins was born the following year. The family moved to the newly built Hillcrest Court and daughter Jackie was born around the corner in a nursing home in Fordwych Road (p 15). The Collins family soon departed, returning to Maida Vale. Joan [1] has had a long and successful career in films and Jackie (d.2015) became a best-selling novelist. The

1 Joan Collins

Collins' neighbour in Flat No.5 was violinist and band leader Max Jaffa who moved out in 1938. Jaffa got his big break in 1929 with weekly BBC radio broadcasts. His Palm Court style was very popular and in 1960 he did a summer season at Scarborough which he repeated for a record 27 years.

Two streets run east off Shoot-up Hill, on either side of the Templar House Estate, to meet Fordwych Road (p 15). The more southerly is **GARLINGE ROAD**. All the odd-numbered Victorian properties on the north side of the road have been replaced by modern housing. **Garlinge Court** flats, at the east end, date from the mid-1970s. Nearer the Hill is **Chevington** designed by David Hyde-Harrison and completed by 1970. A six storey block of flats was suggested for the 1.1 acre site but Hyde-Harrison worked out he could build a low rise 2-storey terrace, that maximized light and space, with sun terraces and private gardens. He believed the design should be based on the car and each home was provided with a garage.

In 1910, George Probyn Coldstream, a physician and surgeon, moved into **No.10**, one of the surviving villas on the road's south side. He took over from Dr Alfred Tilly, a medical practitioner at that address since at least 1885. Coldstream ran his surgery from the house, calling down the prescriptions to his

pharmacist through a speaking tube. In 1937 he left for Cannon Hill (p 107), where he lived until his death in 1950. His son William Coldstream became a well-known artist.

The southwest corner of Garlinge Road has been redeveloped as **Caesar House** and **Claudius Court** (Genesis Housing Association). The roadway at the junction with Shoot-up Hill is now closed to vehicular traffic.

ST CUTHBERT'S ROAD was originally known as Dent de Lion Road. Off the south side a service road leads through the Templar House Estate towards **Chelsea Crescent**, the last part of the Estate to be developed. Approved in 1998, the curved terrace of twelve low-rise properties backs onto gardens of houses in Fordwych Road.

Close to the junction of St Cuthbert's and Kingscroft Road was the site of Shoot-up Hill Farmhouse. Set back from the main road, this was home to the tenant farmer of the Powell-Cotton fields until the early 1850s, when George Verey, part owner of the Kilburn Brewery, turned it into a private house and renamed it The Elms. Henry Perry Cotton [2], who succeeded to the Powell-Cotton estate in 1849, was the black sheep of the family. His marriage was unhappy and after his wife's death in 1868, he married his mistress Charlotte. The couple had been living together for some years. After Verey left the property ound 1872, Henry moved in, renaming the house Kingsgate Lodge, and he stayed there until 1877. The years he spent at the Lodge with his new family were particularly happy, and Henry left specific instructions that he wanted to be buried at Hampstead Cemetery rather than in the family vault in Kent. Around 1883, St Cuthbert's Road cut through the grounds of the Lodge. A series of fairly short-term lets ensued, the usual pattern preceding the demolition of a mansion such as this.

In 1911, permission to build **KINGSCROFT ROAD** across the remaining garden area was granted, and the house was finally demolished late that year or early the next. Most of the Edwardian houses were built by T H Perkins and Co., who were also responsible for completing the St Cuthbert's Road frontage on either side of the Kingscroft Road junction, where some houses show an Arts and Crafts influence. Many houses in both roads were seriously damaged during WWII, but none beyond repair.

In 1944, Solomon Cassoria, the owner of **No.1** (on the east side) was in court. He was accused of fraudulently obtaining money from the government after pretending his house had been demolished by a high-explosive bomb in late 1940.

In June 1959, the writer Hunter Davies OBE came to London to work for the *Sunday Graphic*. He didn't know London at all and after a ten-day search, he rented the top floor flat at **No.6a**. His future wife, fellow author Margaret Forster (d.2016), took an instant dislike to the property. She condemned it as, 'nasty and suburban, the furnishings dreadful, including the fitted carpet'. They were married in June 1960 and lived, as Margaret said, 'not in the ugly semi-detached house in a dreary road off Kilburn High Road', but in a flat in the Vale of Health, Hampstead. Margaret wrote biographies and novels, the best known of which was *Georgy Girl*, made into a 1966 film starring Lynn Redgrave. Hunter Davies is a journalist and broadcaster, who wrote a biography of the Beatles.

The writer Doris Lessing lived across at **No.11** until around 1980, when she moved to Gondar Gardens (p 69). The road curves round to join Shoot-up Hill. The recently built Nos.1-6 **Zen Villas**, on the right, have simply taken their seemingly exotic name from that of the property company that built them.

East of Shoot-up Hill is **FORDWYCH ROAD**. Most of the 3- or 4-storey houses in the stretch of road approved in 1880 from Maygrove Road as far as Mill Lane, were built by Joshua Parnell (p 24) or William Rogers.

In 1996, on the even-numbered west side at No.10 (just south of the junction with Garlinge Road), an official blue plaque was unveiled, celebrating the artist David Bomberg (b.1890), who was here from 1928-34. He was born in Birmingham, one of eleven children of Abraham Bomberg, a Polish immigrant leather worker. A loan from the Jewish Education Aid Society allowed David to attend the Slade

2 Henry Perry Cotton
(Copyright The Powell-Cotton Trust)

School of Art from 1911-13, where his fellow students included Paul Nash and Stanley Spencer. In December 1913 he exhibited with the Camden Town Group and a year later, he was a founder member of the London Group. He married Lilian Holt and his 1932 portrait of her is now at Tate Britain. Bomberg lived at several other Camden addresses but it was in Fordwych Road, that he embarked on the dramatic landscapes, inspired by Ronda, in southern Spain, that were a turning point in his career. Bomberg was virtually ignored during his lifetime, and was to die almost penniless in 1957, but today his work is highly regarded.

One October morning in 1891, astonished witnesses saw a woman throw two young children out of a top-floor back window at **No.18**, and then jump out herself. They fell about 40 feet, smashing the glass as they broke through the roof of the conservatory. Amazingly, they all survived, although badly cut and injured. The actions of Mrs Hewetson were ascribed to 'hysterial mania'.

No.24 was home to a very brave soldier who was awarded the Victoria Cross. Born in Edinburgh, Allan Ebenezer Ker [3] studied law at University. He was sent to the Western Front in 1917 and fought in the major battles of Passchendaele, Arras, Ypres and Cambrai. In March 1918, when attached to the 61st

3 Allan Ebenezer Ker

Battalion Machine Gun Corps, Lt Ker helped to delay the progress of a large enemy force near St Quentin. After their Vickers gun had been destroyed, Ker and his comrades used

revolver fire against the enemy, helped by a single rifle they had captured from a German soldier. Exhausted and suffering from gas poisoning, they were forced to surrender when the ammunition ran out, having managed to hold off 500 German troops for three hours. The citation for the VC described Ker's behaviour on the day as 'absolutely cool and fearless'. Ker was resident at No.24 when he died in 1958 at New End Hospital. He is buried in Hampstead Cemetery, where his decoration is noted on his simple gravestone. In June 1991 his medals were put up for auction, with a guide price of between £16,000 and £18,000. They are currently on display at the Imperial War Museum, Lambeth, in the Lord Paddy Ashcroft gallery.

Professor Lobely, who lived at **No.44,** contributed a chapter on local geology to Thomas Barratt's famous 3-volume work, *The Annals of Hampstead* (1912); he is buried in Hampstead Cemetery. In 1965 the house was adapted by the Kilburn Housing Trust as accommodation for the elderly.

Gilbert Lane lived opposite at **No.45** Fordwych Road. In 1874 members of the Abbey Road Baptist church formed a building society, which later became the well-known Abbey National. Lane was its Secretary and for a while his house was the Society's main office. He stayed in post until his death in 1921.

St Cuthbert's Church [4] was once a dominant presence in Fordwych Road, perched high above the railway cutting and facing down St Cuthbert's Road towards Shoot-up Hill. It was built beside a brick mission church (1882), which itself replaced an earlier iron church on the site. Designed by William Charles Street for 700 worshippers, St Cuthbert's was consecrated in November 1887. A planned tower was never built, presumably because of a lack of funds. The mission church became a hall, until it was bought and demolished in 1902 by the Midland Railway, who needed more siding space and who the following year provided the site for a replacement hall, in Maygrove Road (p 29). In 1988, St Cuthbert's Church was demolished and replaced by a smaller, low-profile building, designed by Jeremy Allen and tucked away alongside a pedestrian link to the West End Sidings Estate (p 30). Some features were salvaged from the old church, including the bell that now stands outside its successor's entrance. The main church site was used for the sheltered housing of red-brick **Davina House**.

The singer-songwriter Roy Harper was living at **No.58** when he recorded *The Sophisticated Beggar* album in 1966. He has been acknowledged as a major influence by many musicians including, Robert Plant of Led Zeppelin, Pete Townsend of The Who, Kate Bush and Pink Floyd. Having released over 30 albums, Harper now lives in Ireland.

Edward Jarvis Cave was the founder member of an extended family of developers who worked in West Hampstead, specialising in blocks of flats (pp 00 & 00). Following his wife's death in 1909, Cave married his mistress Pauline and they set up home at **No.75** soon after.

John Allan Hyatt Box was born at **No.80** in 1920. John became a film designer and worked at Denham Studios with Alan Ladd on *The Black Knight* (1955). He was the designer on *Lawrence of Arabia* (1962), and he and director David Lean continued to work together for 30 years. Box was nicknamed 'The Magician' when he created snowy Russia scenes in midsummer Spain for *Dr Zhivago*

4 St Cuthbert's Church

(1965), but he was most proud of *A Man for All Seasons*, with his 1966 creation of Hampton Court in Shepperton Studios. Box won four Oscars for his film designs.

Nos.85&87 have a long history as care homes of various kinds. In the 1920s, the Caerthillian Nursing Home opened in No.87, later expanding into the premises next door. Jackie Collins was born there in 1937, and singer Dusty Springfield (real name Mary O'Brien) in 1939. The O'Briens had lived locally in Sumatra Road (p 59) before moving to Lauderdale Mansions in the Maida Vale area. The nursing home closed about 1948 and became became the Hotel Shem-Tov for Jewish refugees, run by Isaac Lenkiewicz and his wife, who fled Nazi Germany at the end of the 1930s. Their son Robert Lenkiewicz (1941-2002) grew up in West Hampstead. He was a gifted art student who left London in the 1960s for the West Country. He became an outstanding figurative painter, and often used disadvantaged people as models: vagrants, the handicapped and prostitutes. Said to have had twelve 'wives' and fathered numerous children, Robert died penniless in 2002. Nos.85&87 served as The Treehouse, a centre for vulnerable children, supported by the band Coldplay and part of Kids Company until the collapse of the charity in August 2015. Another charity, now known as UP (for

5 Kilburn Mill, 1860

Unlocking Potential), took over the centre, renaming it The Corner House.

An overall ¾ mile in length, Fordwych Road continues northwards to the borough boundary. By 1890, its southern end had been completed and work on its middle section as far as Minster Road (p 23) was imminent. Inevitable confusion arose when the extension beyond Mill Lane was dubbed Fordwych Road North, although another street of that name already existed (p 22). The problem was eventually resolved by renumbering as Fordwych Road throughout.

The proximity of this locality to the Midland railway line meant that several nearby properties suffered bomb damage during WWII. Fordwych Road was hit by a high-explosive bomb on 2 October 1940. It destroyed Nos.100-110, six houses on the west side just beyond Mill Lane and damaged every property orth to Minster Road. Eleven people were killed. Actor Joss Ackland's family had a lucky escape as they had been living at No.110 in 1938. He visited the road after the war, 'to be greeted only by an empty space'. The gap was later filled by blocks of flats, disparately named **Penn Court, Milford House** and **Canberra Court.**

Renting a room in 1944, along on the east side at **No.125**, was Louis Christopher Walsh, a 37-year- old Irish electrician convicted that year for the manslaughter of a prostitute in Kilburn (*see Streets and Characters of Kilburn & South Hampstead*).

Construction of the most northerly stretch of Fordwych Road, past Minster Road, was sanctioned in 1895/96. By 1939, near the top end, two rooms at **No.241** were home to the Sutch family. David Edward Sutch, better known as Screaming Lord Sutch, was born at New End Hospital (Hampstead) in 1940. His father, a chauffeur and a war reserve police constable, crashed his motorbike and died in September 1941 when David was only ten months old. When his band, The Savages, was formed in 1960, he called himself Screaming Lord Sutch after the American singer Screaming Jay Hawkins. His outrageous appearance and performances gained publicity. From 1963 he stood in parliamentary elections for the National Teenage Party and founded

the Official Monster Raving Loony Party in 1983. He contested over 40 elections with little hope of winning. Depressed after the death of his mother the year before, David committed suicide at his Harrow home in 1999.

The main road, beyond the brow of the hill, continues northwest as **SHOOT-UP HILL** for another 300 metres. Once standing on the Willesden side, and opposite Mill Lane, was the Shoot-up Hill windmill [5]. Built in 1798 to grind corn from local farms, it was owned for many years by Isaac Ennos. In 1829 the mill passed to his son-in-law, William Hale. A year later Edward Walden, dubbed a 'modern Quixote' by one reporter, attacked the building: 'After duly priming and loading a fowling-piece, he marched gallantly up the hill on which the windmill was situated, and fired in the direction of the mill'. In court, Walden couldn't explain his actions other than to say 'he owed the windmill no ill-will or spite', and he was let off with a 5s fine (worth about £23 today). Business seemed to thrive and by 1851 Hale was employing five men. In 1859 he decided to modernise and built a new steam mill alongside the old windmill, which on 3 December 1863 caught fire in a gale. The wind blew the sails around so fast that the friction caused a fire and the windmill burnt like a giant Catherine wheel. The fire also spread to Hale's house. The glare of the flames attracted

thousands of spectators and many helped to carry furniture and personal possessions to safety. The nearest fire engine was called from Paddington but arrived too late to help, and the old mill was wrecked. As a result of this incident the Willesden Vestry agreed to establish the Kilburn Volunteer Fire Brigade in December 1863. Charles Hale continued to use the steam mill to grind corn, but by 1871 had sold out to the Bates Brothers. The mill ceased to operate in 1891 and was pulled down in 1898. Surprisingly, the burnt remains of the century-old windmill outlasted its more modern counterpart, until it finally collapsed in 1903. The high-rise block of flats aptly named Windmill Court and completed in 1967 for Brent Council, now stands on the site.

North of Mill Lane, on the Camden side of Shoot-up Hill, Hampstead Council raised no objection to the demolition of the houses at Nos.56-60 to build flats, and in 1937 the London County Council (LCC) approved the final plans for **Warwick Lodge**. The architect/builder was W H Hayward. In Flat No.17 lived Victoria Modupe 'Chief' Smith (1937-84). Her headstone in Hampstead Cemetery has an attractive bas relief and a Yoruba inscription which translates as 'Market woman of Ago Oko and Egba-Okeona, Chief of Ikija and successful business woman of Ido Ekiti.'

In 1936, **Kendal Court** was being built on

6 Learie Constantine, 1930

the sites of Nos.62-64. A blue plaque records that Lord Learie Constantine [6], cricketer, barrister and politician, lived at Flat No.11 from 1960 until his death in 1971. He was born in Trinidad in 1901 and was a member of the West Indies cricket team that toured England in the 1920s. He obtained a contract to play for a Lancashire team in 1928. In 1954

he qualified as a barrister as well as establishing himself as a journalist and broadcaster. That year he returned to Trinidad and was elected to the government as a minister. In 1961 he came back to England as Trinidad's High Commissioner. He subsequently held important positions on the Race Relations Board and as a BBC governor.

The famous bandleader Joe Loss occupied Flat No.16 in the late 1930s. His record of *Begin the Beguine* sold over a million records in 1939. Astonishingly, he was awarded a 50-year contract with EMI and played several times for the King and Queen at Buckingham Palace.

Between Minster and Manstone Roads, a run of detached Victorian houses has survived on the Camden side. During WWI the corner property at No.70 Shoot-up Hill was a home for European refugees. Newlands (now **No.88**), was the final home of Thomas Bowman (d.1905). In 1864, brothers Thomas and Robert Bowman had opened an upholstery business in Camden Town. The firm rapidly expanded to occupy Nos.112-138 Camden High Street. The shop offered an extensive range of furniture and household goods and eventually closed in the 1980s.

Herbert and Mena Rubin lived at **No.98.** Herbert was a property developer. Their daughter, better known as Lynsey De Paul, was born as Lynsey Monckton Rubin in 1948. After leaving the Hornsey Art School, she

designed album covers and then began writing songs. In 1972 she performed her own song *Sugar Me* which reached the UK top 10. Lynsey wrote many other successful songs and regularly appeared on TV. She died in October 2014.

Opposite, No.71 was once a hostel for children from the Kindertransport. Modern Slade Court flats cover the sites of Nos.75 &77. Lodene, on the corner of Walm Lane, was a large detached house, later renumbered as No.77. The first occupant was Daniel Jay, who moved there after his marriage in 1889. He was a money lender who opened his business about 1883 in Jermyn Street in the West End. In January 1898 Daniel Jay sued Sir Tatton Sykes for £15,872 (about £1.5M today) owed on promissory notes given by his wife. The well-publicised court case gave the public an insight into the excessive habits of Lady Jessie Sykes, and demonstrated she had no control over her spending. Free spirited Jessie was known as 'Lady Silk Tights' and was 30 years younger than her husband, who by then lived in Yorkshire as a recluse. Despite the jury's decision that Sir Tatton had not signed the notes, it appears he paid Jessie's debt to Daniel Jay after the case was over.

Past the junction with Manstone Road the main road becomes **CRICKLEWOOD BROADWAY.** Dating from the 1880s, the Broadway developed into a prime shopping

...strict, with well patronised shops lining both ...des. On the Camden frontage, the commercial ...remises at Nos.2-28, initially known as ...mperial Parade', were set back from the highway ...nd the wide pavement in front allowed the ...ter construction of one-storey extensions. ...pposite was Anson Parade. The shops beyond ...ondu Road (p 23) were numbered as part of ...he Parade'. In 1906 the several groups of shops ...ere combined and renumbered as Cricklewood ...roadway. The **Windmill Bar**, across at No.57, ...s a late-Victorian rebuild of the earlier ...ayside Windmill Inn. At No.22 The Parade ...now **No.68**) was the Welford Dairy, a branch of ...ne of London's most important dairy companies. ...y 1882 they were farming over 300 acres in ...illesden, with a model dairy farm at Kensal ...reen. The firm was absorbed into United ...airies in 1920 but the Welford Dairy ...ontinued trading under its old name for ...nother seven years.

In July 1912, a large crowd gathered outside **No.90** completely blocking the Broadway. They were there for the unveiling of the Coronation Clock [7] at the end of Anson Road. A gift from Joseph Acworth of Shoot-up Hill (p 12), it was made of steel and wrought iron and had four illuminated faces. Subsequently neglected, it became rusty and dangerous and was removed for salvage in 1943.

Some 340 metres northwest of here is the

7 Unveiling the Coronation Clock, 1912

junction with Cricklewood Lane, where the original hamlet of Cricklewood was located (see p 00). The last Broadway property in Camden is the Mediterranean restaurant at **Nos.108-110**. This is the meeting-point of three borough boundaries, beyond which the east side of the main road was in Hendon until 1965 and is now in the London Borough of Barnet. Once ending at the boundary were the rails of the electric trams that from 1904 ran

north to Edgware and on to Canons Park in 1907. An anticipated extension of the tramway south to Marble Arch never materialised, not least because of objections from the Hampstead authorities, who were perennially opposed to such 'working-class' transport running into their area. Public transport from Cricklewood to central London was always by bus, horse-drawn until 1902 when motorbuses first made their appearance. A major

Cricklewood landmark, **The Crown** public house [8] at No.152, was a coaching inn before it became the terminus for LGOC omnibuses in the early 1880s. Today the pub is owned by the Irish company Moran Hotels who built the Clayton Crown Hotel next door. There has been an inn on this site since the 18th century, described in 1751 as 'an ivy-clad house with pretty tea-gardens'. Just as at Kilburn Wells (see *Streets and Characters of Kilburn and South Hampstead*), bare knuckle fights were held here and the pub was home to

sporting clubs and cross country runners. It realised £86,000 at auction in 1898 (worth about £9M today) with permission to redevelop. Clearly the new owners felt this enormous sum was justified by the fact it was in a rapidly expanding suburb and the only public house with an alcohol licence in Cricklewood. The present building was erected in 1899 and 1900 from the plans of Shoebridge and Rising, the main architects for the Cannon Brewery chain. Through much of the 20th century the Crown was a centre for the

large Irish community. In the early morning labourers waited on the forecourt for the 'call on' to be picked up for a day's work. In 1920, Fred Smith began making Smith's Crisps in garages at the back of the pub moving his rapidly growing business the following year to a factory on nearby Somerton Road.

South of the borough boundary is a residential neighbourhood mostly of two-storey semi-detached houses dating from the 1890s and comprising short streets connecting the Broadway with Fordwych Road. Of these the northernmost, and the earliest to be developed, was **RICHBOROUGH ROAD**. The Camden-Barnet boundary runs along the ends of the back gardens of the houses on its north side. Originally called Fordwych Road North, the street was renamed in 1892. House building here was carried out by brothers Richard and Robert Mackley. In 1891, when the road was almost complete, they were living in neighbouring villas, **Nos.14&15**, while a decade later they were at **Nos.17&18**. James Mugliston, owner of the *Paddington Times*, was at **No.22** until the mid-1890s. The street ends abruptly at the embankment of the Midland Railway (opened in 1868). Perhaps the hope was to create a crossing over the rails at this point.

The next street southward is **EBBSFLEET ROAD**, whose name was approved in 1892. At 10pm on 19 September 1961, Detective

8 Crown Cricklewood, c.1904

hief Inspector Rees arrived at No.13 to rrest Kazimierz Spryszynski, a civil engineer uspected of causing grievous bodily harm o one of his employers, Duncan Tucker. pryszynski confronted the police with a ouble-barrelled sawn-off shotgun, but after a truggle they disarmed him. He was charged ith shooting and blinding Tucker. It emerged e was convinced his employers were party to campaign to victimise him and he was eclared mentally unfit to stand trial. Detective Chief Inspector Rees was awarded he British Empire Medal for gallantry.

All the houses in **SKARDU ROAD** were built y Messrs Bridge and Neal. Harold Mills and ohn Dalzell, the proprietors of the Paradise Holiday Camp at Fremington in Devon, were iving at **No.1** Skardu Road in 1933, when hey advertised for business partners. Having ailed to raise sufficient capital and attract enough campers, they went bankrupt the ollowing year. **No.17**, on the left, was home or over 30 years, until his death in 1940, of Loftus Patton Perkins, a member of a well-known family of steam engineers. When in 1893 the prestigious family firm, Perkins & Co., merged with a German company, Loftus was sidelined and offered only a clerkship at £1 a week. Instead, he made a living as a commercial artist, publishing his sketches, particularly of ships, from a studio at Quex

Lodge in West End Lane.

Bridge and Neal also built the houses in **RONDU ROAD**. In 1898 a site for a Presbyterian Church was acquired on the north side at the Broadway end of the road. This was one of many missionary operations supported by Rev. Dr Monro Gibson, minister of the church in Marlborough Place, St John's Wood. He opened the Cricklewood church in June 1900. Four years later the congregation numbered just over 180 both morning and evening, attendances that were the largest in Hampstead. In 1956, permission was given to demolish the church and replace it with a block of 17 flats, and **Rondu House** stands on the site today. In 1974, three men accused of being involved in the Guildford pub bombing lived in the Rondu Road. They were released the following year after all charges were dropped.

Dating from 1895, the southernmost street is **MANSTONE ROAD**, whose houses were built by the Mackley Brothers.

MINSTER ROAD runs eastward from Shoot-up Hill, connecting the parts of the Powell-Cotton estate on either side of the Midland railway line. Even numbers are on the north side, with odd numbering opposite. Development of the earliest, western part of the road was agreed in 1887, but as late as April 1890 no building had taken place. The eventual builders were the Mackley Brothers

and Joshua Parnell (p 24).

At different times from the 1930s to the mid-1950s, **No.1** and **No.6** each served as a Shtiebel or 'little house', typically providing a single room for worship. The congregants were generally ultra-orthodox Jews and frequently the followers of a particular rabbi.

In 1989 permission was sought to convert the empty **No 7** into a day nursery, Mulberry House School, which later expanded to take older children and occupy a vacant nursery at the corner of the road, No.68 Shoot Up Hill. In 1937, a developer was refused permission to demolish Nos.**2-12 Minster Road** and replace them with three blocks of flats.

At the junction with Fordwych Road, a blue plaque commemorates Dame Ida Mann, who from 1902-34 lived on the southeast corner at **No.13.** She was a leading ophthalmologist and, in 1945, the first woman to have the title of Professor at Oxford University. John Edward Thornton was at No.14 (opposite) from 1918 to 1926. He founded Thornton-Pickard to manufacture cameras with his friend Edward Pickard in 1888. Picard died suddenly and Thornton left the company after disagreements with George Pickard, who took over from his brother Edward. Thornton emigrated to the States in 1913 where he worked on cinema projection equipment. On his return to the UK he continued to invent and patent, earning a comfortable income from Kodak, who licensed some of his products. No.14 was demolished and after 1983 its site was redeveloped as purpose-built flats.

Between No.21 and the railway is the entrance to the **Jane Evans Nature Reserve**. Formerly known as the Minster Road Nature Reserve, and cared for by a local group of Friends, it was renamed in January 2018 after a member instrumental in its creation and who had died the previous year.

After 1898, Minster Road was extended from the railway bridge to run east as far as the Hampstead Cemetery boundary.

Westbere Road intersects. In December 1900, when the neighbourhood was still very rural, an encampment of gypsies took up temporary residence close to this crossroads.

By 1902 Fordwych House, **No.28** Minster Road, a detached house on a large plot on the northeast corner, was home to builder Joshua Parnell. Born in Totnes in 1840, Joshua was living in London by 1863 when he married a West Country girl, Rachel Mears from Torquay. Joshua became a major developer on the Powell-Cotton estate, and he lived in several of the houses he built. He died in 1915 and is buried in Hampstead Cemetery. A 1974 permission to demolish No.28 and build a block of 11 flats on the site was never invoked.

After his wife Rachel died in November 1905, Joshua Parnell moved along and across Minster Road, from No.28 to the much smaller **No.57**, where he was living with his daughter Rosa in 1911. She described herself as a self-employed decorator; it seems likely that Rosa was running her father's business by 1908, when she was summonsed for failing to deposit plans before undertaking work. Further east, by the junction with Somali Road (p 27), **Nos.64&66** were hit by a bomb in 1940, necessitating the rebuilding of No.66.

Leonard Upcott Gill (1846-1919) was living at **No.65**, on the corner with Sarre Road, at the time of his death. He created an extensive printing and publishing company. He developed the *Bazaar, Exchange and Mart*, better known as the Exchange and Mart, which offered goods for sale and items wanted, and included articles on many subjects from beekeeping to mechanics.

Lined with 2-storey houses, **SARRE ROAD** has a slight uphill gradient before descending to Mill Lane. There is a pedestrian link to Gondar Gardens (p 69). **No.36** was the home from 1979-81 of musician and club owner Ronnie Scott and his partner François Venet. They were there when Ronnie was awarded an OBE, and before moving back to Chelsea. Fran, who was an artist and photographer, returned to France. Sadly, Ronnie died in December 1996, but the jazz club he founded with Pete King is still in Soho, under different management.

WESTBERE ROAD runs north from a forked junction with Sarre Road, in the angle of which stood West Hampstead's first public library. The land was acquired after many sites had been abandoned as unsuitable for various reasons. But to get their library, the Hampstead Vestry had to agree to a deal over a public footpath to Child's Hill, in the way of Powell-Cotton road plans. Part of the path had already disappeared under Fordwych Road. The estate agreed to donate money towards the purchase of the library site on condition the local authority did not object to their closing the remainder of the path. £360 was paid for the land and a tender of £2,700 was accepted to build the library, which opened on 21 February 1901. The library building was gutted by an incendiary bomb in 1940 and the site later redeveloped for housing, today's **Nos.2-6** Westbere Road.

North of Mill Lane, the building of the Midland Railway cut the Powell-Cotton property in half and road building had to adapt to the line of the tracks. The 1895 OS map shows a few hundred yards of Westbere Road projecting into the fields, and a handful of houses. Further stretches were approved in 1896 (to Minster Road) and in 1897 as far as the parish boundary.

Demolished in 2015, the single-storey nos.12&12A on the east side provided a home and studio space for many artists. The painter and engraver John Moody (1884-1962) exhibited at the RA from No.12 between 1911 and 1914. Resident at the same address from at least 1925 to 1964 was the artist and potter Helen Wickham. She had earlier been a friend of Ellen Ternan, the secret mistress of Charles Dickens.

From the late 1960s No.12 was the home of artist Jo Brocklehurst until her death there in 2006. Born in Hampstead, she had entered Central St Martin's School of Art on a scholarship in 1949 when she was only 14 years old. She is best known for her paintings of punks, though other subjects included clubbers, fetishists, actors and dancers. In the 1980s, members of the anarcho-punk group, Puppy Collective, lived in a West Hampstead Housing Association house at No.39. They called it 'Puppy Mansions' after a communal magazine they published. 'Jo saw them passing by with wild hair and customised clothes, and thought they looked wonderful'; she invited them to her studio to pose for her. They included Tony Drayton, the magazine editor, and his sister Val. Some of Jo Brocklehurst's distinctive work is in the V&A.

Beyond Westbere Road's junction with Minster Road, the undeveloped, one-acre wooded site on the west side is **Westbere Copse**. In the early 1970s the local people took it over as a playspace for children. Today it is part of a Grade 1 Local Nature Reserve and Site of Borough Importance for Nature Conservation. On land owned by Network Rail and leased to Camden Council, it is maintained by the Westbere Copse Association. The southern half of the site is named the Jenny Wood Nature Reserve, after a founder member who died in 1988. There is free public access to the northern half.

Opposite, **No.54** was the home of Dr William Lovell at the time of his death in 1929. His father was an eminent physician and William also became a doctor. Local residents remembered him in pre-WWI days, before the National Health provided free treatment and practising from No.62 Holmdale Road (p 54). As a local recalled, 'he was a wonderful doctor. He used to have a page-boy who wore yellow stockings and a blue suit and had to collect the debts.' The 1911 census does indeed show a page boy in the doctor's household. Locals also remember that Dr Lovell was often to be found in the Alliance pub (p 62), rather the worse for wear. In 1924 he was struck off the Medical Register for unprofessional conduct. The Medical Council was told he had been convicted of drunkenness on several occasions, and during WWI his insobriety had

caused him to be court marshalled and dismissed from the Royal Medical Corps. Lovell was reinstated on the Medical Register in June 1929 but died a few months later.

The jeweller Alfred Abraham Cobden was resident at **No.68** in 1954 when he was chloroformed and robbed at his shop in Hatton Garden. He had taken Hubert Edward Clark and a young woman, into an office to show them some jewellery. Clark stood behind Cobden and suddenly put a pad over his face. Cobden lost consciousness for a while but as he came to, he saw the couple emptying the contents of the safe into a brown holdall. He managed to stagger into the street and yelled 'Police!' as the couple ran upstairs. When the police arrived, they talked to a young woman who said she knew nothing about any incident and calmly walked away down the street. Clark was discovered in the roof space with goods valued at around £4,500 in his bag. He said he only knew his female accomplice as Maria but she had directed the robbery. Maria was never found and may have got away with some of the stolen goods as Cobden estimated his losses at around £8,000 to £9,000. Clark was sentenced to three years in prison.

Sir Geoffrey Finsberg MBE (1926-96) who lived at **No.80** on the corner with Menelik Road (p 27), was a life-long Tory supporter. His parents were living at No.18 Cumberland

9 Haberdashers' School

Mansions West End Lane when he was born. Finsberg served as MP for Hampstead (1970-83), then for Hampstead and Highgate (1983-92). He did not contest the 1992 election and was succeeded by Glenda Jackson. He was also a local councillor (1949-74), and supported many charities, including the Maccabi Association of Great Britain. No.80 was a Montessori Nursery School from 1993 but has since reverted to a private home.

North of Menelik Road is **Hampstead School,** still showing the coat of arms of the Haberdashers' Company with its motto, 'Serve and Obey'. In 1897 the governors of Haberdashers' Askes's School (founded in 1690) announced they were leaving Hoxton. The boys' destination was a school yet to be built on a greenfield site in Westbere Road. In 1899 they moved into two houses on Cricklewood Broadway before the school [9] opened in January 1903. 'Habs' proved popular from the start: by 1906 there were 412 pupils in accommodation intended for a maximum of 300 boys, and numbers had risen to 503 by 1911.

The school was partly evacuated at the start of WWII, but after a couple of years the boys returned to Westbere Road. The school had been hit by a high-explosive bomb early in the war. By 1961, Haberdashers' needed more room to expand and the boys moved to Elstree. Famous old Haberdashers include: controversial art critic Brian Sewell; historian Simon Schama; journalist and broadcaster Alan Whicker; Sir Nicholas Serota, director of the Tate Galleries until 2017; Richard Wright, keyboardist, vocalist and songwriter for Pink Floyd; and Chris Squire bass player with the band Yes. The Westbere Road building was taken over by the LCC in 1961 and, renamed Hampstead School which was first a Secondary Modern and later a Comprehensive. Pupils there have included the actress Sadie Frost and the author Zadie Smith.

Opposite is an area of modern low-rise housing. At the outbreak of WWII this long strip of land between the railway and Westbere Road was cultivated as allotments. A 1947 report noted that the site was now occupied by 80 prefabs facing **WESTCROFT CLOSE**. These were single-storey houses made of prefabricated panels and widely used to house the homeless. They were meant to be temporary, but the prefabs were still there in 1979, when Camden was negotiating to buy the site from British Rail for around £1 million. It was felt the prefabs had long since passed their prime and the plan was to replace them with 120

...ouses and flats. The prefabs were duly demolished in the 1980s but many of their long-term tenants mourned their passing and would have been happier if the Council had simply renovated them.

As late as 1933, a car driving along Westbere Road would have come to a grinding halt outside the school, unable to continue through to Cricklewood Lane. The road ended at a barrier that remained in place until December 1936, erected on a strip of land still owned by the Powell-Cottons. Beyond this was a field belonging to Westcroft Farm, for many years the Home of Rest for Horses. Run by a charity formed in 1908 to help poor people unable to care for their working animals, it was briefly famous in the 1920s, when Tom Mix, the American cowboy film star, kept his horses there. With accommodation for about sixty horses, the place was popular with West Hampstead children. As one said: 'If no one was watching, we'd jump over the fence and have a ride.'

In 1933 Hampstead Council decided the Westcroft fields were ideal for public housing. There were no suitable sites within the borough boundary, so instead, they decided to purchase the 18½ acres across the border in Hendon (now Barnet) and use them to provide some 290 mixed-size dwellings. The Powell-Cotton estate opposed the scheme, as did the Trustees of the Rest Home, but Hampstead Council invoked compulsory purchase powers. The plans for the housing estate went ahead and Hampstead Council agreed to extend **Lichfield Road** to meet Westbere Road.

The streets on the **Westcroft Estate** are called **Westcroft Way**, **Besant Road**, **Galsworthy Road**, **Howard Close**, **Horton Avenue** and **Marnham Avenue**, after various Hampstead worthies. On 29 October 1935, the partly occupied Estate was officially opened by the Duke of Kent. His secretary later wrote to Hampstead Council, forwarding the gold key presented to the Duke when he opened the Estate, intimating that 'His Royal Highness would like the present and any future tenants of No.11, Howard Close to keep the key as a memento of his visit'.

South of Hampstead School is **MENELIK ROAD**, part of an enclave of roads for which permission was given in 1901. But building progress was extremely slow, and the 1915 OS map shows only some houses completed in Somali Road. Much of the remaining area was under allotment gardens, presumably part of the war effort to encourage home-grown produce. Building was only completed at the end of the 1920s. The later-built, typically bow-windowed houses in interwar style give the locality a distinctly suburban feel.

Hampstead Council unsuccessfully petitioned for Menelik Road to be renamed Beckford Road. Though it originally ran only in a straight line east to the Hampstead Cemetery boundary, it was agreed in 1927 that the road could be extended south to meet Minster Road, running parallel to the cemetery wall. All the properties in that stretch of the road were built by Lepley & Toovey, of Cricklewood.

Alan Coren who lived in the Barnet stretch of Ranulf Road (p 91) often wrote humorously about Cricklewood in his column for *The Times*; 'It has often occurred to me that, if one were ever called up to defend Cricklewood to the death, Menelik Road would be the place to take one's stand.'

Running north out of Menelik Road's northern arm is a public right of way known as **Blackberry Path**, providing pedestrians with a short cut to Farm Avenue and Cricklewood Lane.

Striking south opposite the path's entrance is **SOMALI ROAD**. It would have been called Boydell Road if Hampstead Council had had its way.

Living in 1911 at the south end of Somali Road, at **No.2**, was one of Cricklewood's leading shopkeepers: William Hull, who opened his large draper's shop on the corner of Cricklewood Lane and the Broadway in 1903 and traded there for three decades. In

October 1940, **Nos.5-9** were badly damaged by a bomb that caused blast damage to many neighbouring properties. Five people were killed at No.9, four of them members of the Prins family, who are buried in adjacent plots in Willesden Jewish Cemetery.

In 1965 at **No.30**, Bert Jansch and fellow guitarist John Renbourn were sharing the upstairs flat, along with singer Anne Briggs. An *a capella* trio called Young Tradition, of Peter Bellamy, Royston Wood and Heather Wood (no relation), were on the ground floor. Jansch and Renbourn left Somali Road in spring 1966 for St John's Wood. In 1968 they formed Pentangle, the very successful folk-rock group. Jansch left the band to work solo in 1973. Pentangle reformed in 1982 and with various musicians continued to 1995. Their combination of folk, rock and jazz influenced later musicians. Bert Jansch died in Christchurch Avenue (Kilburn) in 2011.

On its northeast corner, journalist Andrew Roth (1919-2010) was at **No.34** in 1955, when he won a libel action and was awarded substantial costs against publishers Odhams Press and the author Geoffrey Hudson. He called the house 'The Gripes of Roth'. Roth was political correspondent for the *Manchester Evening News* (1972-84), a contributor to the *New Statesman* and *The Guardian* from 1996. His sketches of MPs were renowned for their funny characterisations.

Resident in Somali Road at the time of his death in 2015 was David Cesarani OBE, an English historian who specialised in Jewish history. He took a leading role in Holocaust education both in the UK and abroad but could also be critical of specific Israeli policies, especially settlements on the West Bank. Cesarani was able to present lucid arguments on very difficult topics and frequently appeared on television.

ASMARA ROAD runs parallel to Somali Road. Mrs Bertha Lazarus was away on holiday when her home at **No.4** was ransacked and burgled in 1938. Amazingly no one called the police when the door of her safe was blown off. Jewellery and clothing valued at £1,000 was stolen. A maid in a nearby property later said she had seen a couple enter the house through the front door: 'I assumed they were staying there. As I got into bed I heard a loud bang. Then there was silence.' Two weeks later the safe in the manager's office at the Swiss Cottage Odeon cinema was blown open and cash stolen. The police believed these robberies were linked to the activities of a London dynamite gang they had been hunting for months.

No.5, opposite, was home in the 1980s to the grandparents of Tula Contostavlos, better known as the singer Tulisa, a member of the defunct hip-hop group N-Dubz and a judge on *The X-Factor*. Tulisa's parents were sharing the Asmara Road house when she was born on 13 July 1988, moving to a flat in Lawn Road when Tulisa was a few years old.

Nuclear physicist and peace campaigner Sir Joseph Rotblat (b.1908) lived in **No.8** from at least 1950 to his death in 2005. He was awarded the Nobel Peace prize in 1995 and was knighted in 1998. Born into a Jewish family in Warsaw, he studied physics and came to England two days before Hitler invaded in 1939, taking up a fellowship at Liverpool University. Sadly his wife was too ill to accompany him and she died during the War. Rotblat worked on nuclear fission and joined the Manhattan Project at Los Alamos, New Mexico, but had strong reservations about using atomic energy to develop a bomb. In 1955 he was one of a group of eminent scientists who urged an end to nuclear arms and helped organise and participate in the Pugwash conferences on arms control (named after Pugwash in Nova Scotia where the first conference was held). Rotblat went on to explore the medical uses of radiation and became Professor of Physics at St Bartholomew's Hospital. Continuing to campaign ceaselessly against nuclear weapons and to write and lecture well into his nineties, Rotblat is buried in Hampstead Cemetery.

Between the tracks

Maygrove, Loveridge and Iverson Roads, and the area
between the Thameslink and Overground railway lines

At the foot of Shoot-up Hill is **Kilburn Underground** Station, opened in November 1879 as 'Kilburn & Brondesbury' on the Metropolitan Railway's extension to Willesden Green. Adjacent to the station three railway bridges span the north end of Kilburn High Road (see the companion book, *Streets and Characters of Kilburn & South Hampstead*). The middle bridge carrying the original Metropolitan line is flanked on its south side by today's Chiltern line into Marylebone, opened in 1899 as part of the Great Central Railway. The northernmost bridge dates from 1914, when two additional lines of track were added. The tracks each side of the platform have been part of the Bakerloo line since 1939, renamed as the Jubilee line forty years later. In 1977 the oldest bridgework was replaced.

East of the High Road the parallel lines are carried towards West End Lane on a viaduct, diagonally crossing the intervening roads. Displaying some amazing bricklaying skills, the arches of the progressively widened viaduct were enclosed and adapted for commercial use and numbered. Businesses associated with the building industry or with the motor trade have long been the main occupants, and **'The Arches'** forms part of their postal address.

Almost opposite Kilburn Station is **MAYGROVE ROAD**. Together with Loveridge and Ariel Roads and the greater part of Iverson Road (pp 32-36), this was built on land owned by the British Land Company (BLC). In 1869 it bought 24 acres owned by the Ripley family (p 48), including a valuable commercial frontage to the High Road. Building on its estate progressed slowly until the mid-1870s and was far from complete when the Metropolitan Railway intruded. Most of the BLC houses were soon in multiple occupation, with very few professionals and most tenants in manual or unskilled jobs.

Some houses in Maygrove Road were at first assigned individual names, or numbered in terraces, including Maygrove Terrace and Bankside. The Kilburn end is lined by bay-windowed Victorian houses on both sides, many of them with steep steps leading up to their first-floor front doors. This locality would have been partly obliterated and definitely blighted, had the 1960s proposal for the North Cross section of the Motorway Box (alias Ringway One) been approved. The plans for this six-lane highway had included a major interchange at the bottom of intersecting Fordwych Road (p 15). Beyond this point the building styles on either side of Maygrove Road are in marked contrast: modern on the north side, with a mix of 3-and 2-storey Victorian terraces opposite, evidently originally built in groups.

In 1983 actor and singer Jimmy Nail lived at **No.50**. He was one of the stars of the TV series *Auf Wiedersehen Pet*, playing the character Oz. After the programme was first shown Jimmy said: 'I walked along to the end of the street and on to the Kilburn High Road to get a newspaper and read a review of the show, if there was one. All of a sudden all these car horns were honking. I wondered what all the fuss was about, until I saw people hanging out of their cars pointing, waving and shouting – at me. People in the street were coming my way, lots of them. I ran home with a mob on my tail, got in and locked the door. People were climbing up the railings and peering through the windows. I hid behind the settee and wondered what had happened. Fame had happened, and I was woefully ill-prepared for it. I didn't know what to do. Everywhere I went there was madness. It was more than fame, it was hysteria. People believed Oz was me and I was him. I tried to explain he wasn't real, but they didn't want to know.'

Built opposite, in 1894, was an iron Mission Hall for St Cuthbert's Church (p 17); later becoming No.55, it was still used in 1970 by local Boy Scouts. Its site now lies under **Lauriston Lodge**, a block of sheltered housing.

This stands on the corner of Barlow Road, the entry to the 1970s **West End Sidings Estate**, which occupies part of the site of the Midland Railway's extensive sidings of the same name. Camden Council bought the 14 acres from British Rail in 1973. The proximity of the new council housing explains why the neighbouring industrial premises were progressively vacated and demolished or converted into residential and office space. The roads on the Sidings Estate are named **BARLOW ROAD, BRASSEY ROAD** and **HALL OAK WALK**. **The Sidings Community Centre** is in Brassey Road on the edge of the Maygrove Peace Park. Funded by Camden and opened in May 1983, the centre provides a wide range of services for early-years children and young people, and adult education classes.

The Sidings Estate gained notoriety in 1988 with the conviction of John Duffy, known as the 'Railway Rapist' and responsible for a series of violent rapes and murders around London's rail network. Some of them were perpetrated within a few miles of his home on the Estate. In 1985 Duffy's case involved the first use in Britain of geographic profiling, developed by David Canter at the University of Surrey. Canter plotted and analysed the series of more than 20 attacks and produced a very accurate profile which allowed the police to focus their search for the offender. Duffy was arrested in

1988, tried at the Old Bailey and goaled for 30 years. After years in prison, he named David Mulcahy, an old school friend, as his accomplice in the rapes and murders, and in 2001 Mulcahy also received a 30 years sentence.

Wayne Kirkum Way leads down beside the railway to the West End Sidings Estate. Originally the Estate was cut off from Mill Lane, which meant a long walk for children to attend Beckford Primary in Broomsleigh Street and Hampstead Comprehensive in Westbere Road. Plans for links across or under the railway line were ruled out on engineering or financial grounds. The cost of building one or more bridges escalated following the installation of new electric overhead cables for the trains, which meant any bridge needed to be even higher above the tracks. Then, in 1984, 13-year-old Wayne Kirkum was killed, possibly while trying to cross the lines. The Council agreed to create the footpath to provide access to Mill Lane and named after the young boy. He lived in Mitcham and had been visiting his grandmother.

Beyond Barlow Road the north side of **MAYGROVE ROAD** has undergone a dramatic transformation in recent years. Originally there was no building here: an embankment separated the roadway from the West End railway sidings behind. Subsequently, light industrial and commercial premises were

established along the embankment frontage. Redevelopment of their sites, and the acquisition of railway land, has allowed massive regeneration, with Council and private builders providing residential and commercial premises, along with a public open space.

In 1894, on the site of the modern flats at **No.59**, the Midland Railway was building a large warehouse to house tanks for the storage of petroleum by the Anglo-American Oil Company. Despite reassurances that it was 'the highest grade of American lamp oil and not flammable', residents were concerned about the proximity of the tanks and complained that this could cause property values to drop. The London County Council had no power to interfere with the storage of petroleum oil at the time. The General (later British) Petroleum Company also had a depot here by 1904. Both firms had left No.59 by 1933, and the site was later occupied by the garage of Maygrove Motors, opened in 1936 and closed by 2007. Permission was granted in 2010 to develop the present flats.

In 2013, permission was given to demolish Nos.65&67 and replace them with the 91 flats of **Beaufort Court.** In 1922, Francis J Lewis started his wooden handrail business at No.3 Blackburn Road (p 118). In 1936 he built a factory at No.65 Maygrove Road, naming it Handrail House. In 1959 there were 84 employees; by 1986 the number had fallen

36. In 1977, the family firm, by then occupying only the ground floor, applied for a 'change of use' to convert part of the first floor into a licensed restaurant seating 116 people; the proposal was rejected by Camden Council.

No.65 had been shared with other businesses. Established in 1937 by Demetrius Comino, an Australian-born engineer and printer, Dexion Ltd, who made quick-assembly metal racking, occupied space here from the 1950s to at least 1970, before moving to Wembley. In 1953, in response to an earthquake in Greece, the company designed a house that could be erected in hours. 'Operation Ulysses' attracted worldwide attention, and Pathé Films has a short clip filmed at the Maygrove Road site, demonstrating how easily the house could be built.

On the north side of the road, the building line is broken by the entrance to the **Maygrove Peace Park**. First suggested in 1983, its creation was opposed by Conservative Camden councillors, who regarded it as left-wing inspired and a waste of money. But the scheme went ahead and the Park was opened on 9 August 1984, Nagasaki Day, to coincide with the 39th anniversary of the dropping of the atomic bomb. Accompanied by the release of a thousand white balloons, the Mayor of Camden read out a telegram from her counterpart in Nagasaki, who said: 'We hope your Peace Park will be remembered long as a symbol of peace'.

The Council agreed to commission a statue for the Park, stipulating it had to be, 'large and ... of a size to make an impact. It must also be robust, vandal-proof and be able to withstand the weather.' An estimated £12,000 was earmarked as a fee to Sir Antony Gormley for his bronze sculpture known as *The Listening Man* [10], which sits on a granite boulder at the top of the Park. Despite the Council's stipulation, it had to be restored following vandalism, and in early 2016 was the first Gormley statue to be granted Listed status. The Park has been revitalised to include play areas and an outdoor gym.

Just beyond the park entrance, residential **Maygrove House** (No.73) and commercial **Interlink House** (No.73a, at the rear) cover the site of a factory. In 1956 Bernard Rand, who lived in Ranulf Road (p 91), built his Ariel Works here. His company Brandoid Products, later British Button Industries Ltd, manufactured plastic buttons and was the main supplier to Marks & Spencer. The unpleasant smell of melting plastic pervaded the neighbourhood and was a cause of concern when the West End Sidings Estate was being planned. Rand moved the factory to York, commuting there from West Hampstead every day. In 1982, Arnold R Horwell, supplier of laboratory and clinical equipment, moved into No.73.

10 Gormley's The Listening Man (photo: Caroline Sharp)

Opposite the modern offices of Metgroup at Nos.**77-79**, and through an arched entrance at **No.128A**, is the long established Done Our Bit, or DOB, Club for servicemen, working men and veterans. It was first set up at No.357 Kilburn High Road in 1920 as the Discharged Sailors and Soldiers Federation Club. Soon becoming the DOB Club Ltd, it moved to Maygrove Road in 1925. Well patronised during WWII, a drop-in centre helped over 1,600 people affected by the V2 bomb in Iverson Road (p 34). A visitor in 1965 called it 'a friendly club with a stewardess who is Hungarian and can speak seven languages, is a contortionist, and it is rumoured, was once a member of the Hungarian State Circus'. A 2005 proposal to redevelop the site to include new club premises and 15 flats was withdrawn.

Eastward, off the north side of the road, Camden Council used some of the railway land they purchased to build the 33 low-rise units of Liddell Road industrial estate in 1984. After long discussion, much of it critical of the Council's proposals, the businesses left in spring 2015 and the buildings were bulldozed. Renamed as **LIDDELL PLACE**, the site now contains an extension to **Kingsgate Primary School**, opened in September 2017. Also planned are an open space, and new workspace and housing, including a tower block of 11 storeys (reduced from the original 14). Public

concern has centred on the very low number of affordable housing units to be provided. No work had been started by March 2021.

ARIEL ROAD runs south off Maygrove Road, linking it with Iverson Road (p00). Known as Ariel Street until 1885, when all the residents signed a petition requesting the suffix be changed to 'Road', the even number houses were all built by Spencer Green and initially named as Spencer Terrace. Doreen Massey (1944-2016) lived at **No.2**, the southernmost house on the east side. She was a left-wing social geographer who in 2013 – with Michael Rustin and Stuart Hall (her colleague at the Open University) – wrote the *Kilburn Manifesto*.

In July 1961, Rose Nash and Marjorie Davis were chatting on their doorsteps, when a mail van stopped to make the 6pm collection from the pillar box (then) outside **No.12**. Suddenly a car pulled up alongside, three men jumped out and threw a hammer through the van's windscreen. The robbers tried to pull out mail bags but when Rose and Marjorie yelled at them, they drove off with only one bag of letters. At the time, such robberies were quite common, as cash and other valuables were often transported by road. In 1970 two vans delivering staff wages were ambushed in nearby Iverson Road. Three postmen were shot and wounded by six masked robbers. The

thieves got away with nearly £12,000, worth about £187,000 today.

Meeting Ariel Road at a T-junction, and running west, parallel to Maygrove Road, is **LOVERIDGE ROAD**. Here, William Rogers was the builder of most of the 3-storey houses. Near its west end it is spanned diagonally by the railway bridges carrying the Jubilee, Metropolitan and Chiltern (formerly Great Central) lines. When, in 1894, the GCR's proposed route into Marylebone was announced, the *London Daily News* commented: 'Although some undistinguished modern thoroughfares will be cut up more or less – Maygrove-road, Loveridge-road, Iverson-road – there will be no especial cause for regret'.

Off the south side of Loveridge Road, near its junction with Kilburn High Road, is **LOVERIDGE MEWS**. This short cul-de-sac, mostly built by William Rogers and once known as Loveridge Yard, originally provided stables with living space above. Here were some of the several local premises of the Kilburn jobmasters Crook & Sons (see below).

To the south, **IVERSON ROAD** runs east from Kilburn High Road through to West End Lane. Its construction began at either end under different owners, the more westerly stretch being a further part of the British Land Co. development. Original terrace names included Beaconsfield Terrace, Derbyshire ottages and Gilbert Terrace.

From the mid-1880s to at least 1911, **No.1** was home to Charles William Crook. His father Charles had come to Kilburn in the early 1850s and developed a successful family business – advertised in 1899 as hiring out 'fashionable Broughams, Clarences and Open Carriages' and 'Superior Omnibuses for Picnics or Beanfeasts'. In 1982, permission was refused to convert living accommodation at the rear of the house into a reception room and library for the British Olympic Association.

Standing for a century on the corner of the High Road, until its closure in 1980, was the Brondesbury Baptist Chapel [11]. It was a local landmark and its 'sugar-loaf spire' is described by Hampstead author Ernest Raymond in *A Kilburn Tale*, referring to the way sugar was often sold as a tall cone until the late 19th century. **Spring Court**, a block of sheltered housing at No.1B Iverson Road, occupies the site today. At Nos.9&11 was the Brondesbury Hall, housing the Baptists' church hall and Sunday school. In 1984 permission was given to redevelop the hall to provide residential space and a new, smaller place of worship now known as **Brondesbury Christian Church**.

Nos.21&23 are linked by the inscription 'Residential Chambers', a genteel way of saying 'rooms to rent'.

On the morning of Sunday 28 July 1889, in what was called 'The Kilburn Tragedy', Leonard Handford shot his mother-in-law and his estranged wife Sarah Elizabeth. Sarah was living with her parents at **No.42**, Kent Lodge. By the time of the assault the couple had been separated for several months and Sarah had begun divorce proceedings. Leonard had moved out of Kent Lodge but he didn't go far, renting a couple of rooms at No.26. Both families were Baptists and worshipped at the nearby Brondesbury chapel. Sarah and her mother, Elizabeth Deveson, had been to a Sunday morning service and were walking home. Leonard approached the two women, shooting them both in rapid succession. He then turned the gun on himself, firing a single shot to his temple. Possibly because the revolver had a small bore, neither woman fell unconscious. Leonard was taken to hospital, while Sarah and her mother were helped into Kent Lodge and attended at home by local doctor Alfred Tilly (p 14). Leonard survived, and was tried with intent to murder and attempted suicide at the Old Bailey on 16 September 1889. He accused his in-laws of demeaning him and interfering in his marriage. He also said Sarah had changed from 'a splendid woman into a bad-tempered wife who was impossible to deal with'. Leonard was found guilty, but the jury recommended

11 Brondesbury Baptist Chapel, seen from across the High Road

mercy on the grounds of his health, and he was sentenced to 14 years in prison on the Isle of Portland. Both mother and daughter recovered from their wounds.

In the late 1880s, a young Alfred Harmsworth, the future newspaper publisher Lord Northcliffe, was lodging at **No.77** with his friend

Herbert Ward. Ward travelled considerably and joined Stanley's expedition to the Congo. He became a sculptor, illustrator, writer and an explorer. Harmsworth was at No.77 when he married his long-time sweetheart Mary Elizabeth Milner, known as Molly, in 1888. His landlady's son, Bertram Young, became Alfred's office boy and rose to become the company secretary. After their marriage Alfred and Molly rented rooms in Pandora Road (p 55).

At around 4.30 on the 8 January 1945, a bitterly cold snowy afternoon, the first of four V2 rockets that affected Hampstead fell on the elevated (North London) railway embankment behind the houses on the south side of Iverson Road. Amazingly, only four people were killed in the huge explosion, but many more were hurt, of whom 64 were hospitalised. Two of the fatalities, Margaret Edwards and 11-year-old Dennis Wall, died at **No.108**. The driver of the first light rescue vehicle to arrive at the incident had the tragic experience of finding the first casualty to be his own daughter Margaret, aged 21, killed by falling masonry. Ethel Thomas of No.**114** died of her injuries a day later. After the search of the bombed houses had been completed and rescue teams stood down, reports came in that two residents were still unaccounted for. Both were found alive: one was a child who had been taken to hospital, while a search found

the second, a woman jammed under the scullery sink outside her kitchen, buried beneath debris. The V2 demolished 14 houses, seriously damaged 152 and owing to its landing high up on the embankment, a further 1,678 on both sides of the North London line suffered some blast damage. Many residents were made homeless; some were given temporary accommodation, but most were forced to remain in their damaged and freezing homes. Eventually 110 families were re-housed. By the mid-1950s, the bombsite had been used to create a children's playground, now known as the **Iverson Road Open Space**. A large mural (since painted over) was designed for the side wall of surviving **No.128** by architects Tim Bruce-Dick Associates, who were working on a local council project, and students from the Architectural Association did the painting.

Two professional cricketers lived in Iverson Road. Charles Boot came from Sutton-in-Ashfield in Nottinghamshire, and in 1877 joined Hampstead Cricket Club (p 114). In 1880 he hired his friend Tom Gregory, who came from the same small town, and the two men shared rooms locally for a while. Boot was at **No.117** in 1891 and ten years later at **No.127**. He and Gregory spent a great deal of their time working as groundsmen, caretakers and umpires. The 1915 Christmas card sent

to club members on the Western Front shows Tom doffing his cap to 'Father Cricket'.

MEDLEY ROAD, off the south side of Iverson Road, was a late addition. All the houses were built by John Fordham. William Chaffers (1811-92), an author and expert on hallmarks and potters' marks, died at No.3. He was also a skilled organiser of art exhibitions. The yard belonging to partners Boddy and Chapman, who built a large number of houses locally, was behind **No.8**. In September 1897 the buildings were destroyed by fire. Beyond and left of the end of the cul-de-sac is the **Medley Orchard**, where a few fruit trees survive. It forms part of a Borough Site of Importance for Nature Conservation (SINC), that includes rail side vegetation running through to Westbere Road.

Passing a forked junction with Maygrove Road (p 29), **IVERSON ROAD** continues east to meet West End Lane. On the south side the building firm of C Tavener & Sons has had its offices and works at **No.188** since around 1935. This part of the road, east of the BLC property, was built on part of the estate of Old West End House. Its approximate site is marked by **Nos.202-220**, a renovated row of former railwaymen's cottages erected in 1897 and named Heysham Terrace.

Old West End House was probably built by the mid-17th century. In 1775 it passed into he hands of solicitor Thomas Wildman (1740-95), who had West End Lane diverted away from the front of the mansion to the line : follows today. Throughout the years Wildman owned the property he did not live here, and the house was occupied by his employer and eventual inheritor of his estate, Mrs Maria Beckford. The grand-daughter of the Earl of Abercorn and Hamilton, Maria was a widow with a young daughter when she married William Beckford in 1756. His enormous wealth came from sugar plantations in Jamaica where the family were major slave owners. This relationship has given rise to many legends, most of them incorrect, concerning the Beckford family ties with West End. Chief among these is that Maria's husband, William Beckford and twice Lord Mayor of London, was a village resident. But he was dead long before the mansion was bought by Wildman.

William Thomas Beckford (b.1760) was the only child of the marriage, heir to an enormous West Indian sugar fortune and believed to be the wealthiest man in the country. He married Lady Margaret Gordon in 1783 and she was expecting their first child, when Beckford was accused of a homosexual act with the young son of Lord Courtenay. Although he protested his innocence, the fact that William (Kitty) Courtenay was only 17

years old meant that Beckford was rejected by society. He retired with his wife to their country home, Fonthill in Wiltshire, where their daughter Margaret Maria Elizabeth was born. Scandal still pursued William and the couple left England. Beckford's wife died soon after their second daughter Susan Euphemia was born in Switzerland. After his wife's death, Beckford's letters show he was gay. The two daughters lived with their grandmother Maria at West End from at least 1786 to 1796.

Maria Beckford died in 1798 at home in West End, and her estate was held in trust. In 1801 and despite her youth, the census recorded Beckford's 17-year-old daughter Margaret as head of the household at Old West End House. Against her father's wishes, she eloped with General James Orde a month later. They married and had two daughters.

William Thomas Beckford was a book collector and novelist. His best known work, *Vathek*, an Arabian fantasy, was highly praised by Byron. William demolished the old house on the Wiltshire estate and replaced it with a new mansion called Fonthill Abbey crowned by a massive tower. Beckford had few visitors but crowds turned out to see the visit of Lord Nelson and his mistress Emma Hamilton in 1800. Plagued by financial problems, Beckford sold the property in 1822 to John Farquhar, an eccentric Scotsman, for

over £¼ million. This enabled William to clear his debts and have enough money to buy two adjoining houses in Bath where he lived comfortably until his death in 1844. Into old age he would visit London for the Season and ride up to West End to 'gaze upon the old family habitation'.

After his mother Maria's death, Old West End House was rented to a series of tenants. In 1851 Admiral Sartorious was living there. He had fought at Trafalgar and was present when Napoleon surrendered to Captain Maitland of HMS Bellerophon. In 1855 the occupant was Daniel Whittle Harvey. It is said he acquired a fortune of £30,000 through his marriage in 1809. He went on to own the *Sunday Times* and as its proprietor, was fined and sentenced to three months in prison in 1823, charged with libel of King George IV. Harvey became a radical MP but gave this up when he was appointed to the prestigious post of Commissioner of Police in 1839.

During the closing years of the 1850s Margaret Juliana Orde, Maria's great-grand-daughter, sold off her remaining land and the house. They were bought by a consortium, who laid down the, as yet unnamed, Iverson Road, while the mansion found a new, commercial tenant. Robert Hanbury (1823-67) was an extremely wealthy partner in the large brewing firm of Truman, Hanbury & Buxton.

In 1856 he helped set up the Reformatory and Refuge Union, which the following year decided to create a Girls' Laundry & Training Institution for Young Servants. This took possession of the old house and the first three trainees were admitted in July 1858. Three years later there were reportedly 40 girls there, but the enterprise proved unprofitable and by September 1862, Old West End House stood empty.

The consortium who purchased the Old West End House estate had planned to develop the frontage opposite the mansion with large detached villas: three were completed by 1863. Unfortunately, further house building was halted by the Act authorising the Midland Railway's extension to St Pancras, which was passed that same year. Its deep cutting absorbed some of the rear gardens of the newly completed villas, so that the houses were left perched on a greatly reduced plot of land above the tracks. The railway company bought the properties and named them Nos.1-3 Midland Villas. It also bought the old mansion. The 1871 census shows two of the Villas occupied by railway staff and their families: 38 people in all, the men working as platelayers, signalmen and porters. The third, most westerly, house had become the railway's local station, opened as 'West End for Kilburn & Hampstead' on 1 March 1871. The house doubled as the home of stationmaster Thomas Beswick and his

wife. By 1881 the post was held by George Tombs. That year his 8-year-old son Harry was killed in an accident, crushed by the wheels of a cart delivering beer to the Old Black Lion pub near West End Green. The railway company soon moved its employees out of the other two Villas, renamed them as Chesterfield House and Cumberland House and let them to private tenants.

In 1891, Joseph Randall Tussaud was at Chesterfield House. Joseph was the grandson of Marie Tussaud, founder of the famous waxworks, where he worked as the chief wax sculptor. Joseph had financial problems and filed for bankruptcy in 1888. He moved from Iverson Road and died in debt in 1892, having sold the Tussaud Exhibition to a consortium. The artist Alfred Slocombe had moved to Cumberland House in 1891, from West End Green (p 100). The two houses were pulled down around the turn of the 20th century, and the old station was demolished after its relocation in 1905 to West End Lane (p 37).

The frontage on the north side of Iverson Road has undergone radical changes in recent years, as redevelopment has eradicated open space and a handful of small businesses. In 2013 plans were submitted for flats with some commercial space: **The Ivery** (Nos.159-161) on the site of Iverson Tyres, where part of the cobbled entrance to the original Midland

station had still been in daily use. The flats and houses of **The Central** (No.163), on the Hampstead Garden Centre (formerly Maygrove Nurseries) site, were authorised in 2012. The adjoining glassy new entrance to **West Hampstead Thameslink** station was opened in December 2011. The wide pavement approaching it from West End Lane provides the site for a farmers' market at weekends.

Although Old West End House disappeared from the rate books after 1873, it was over 25 years before part of its site was redeveloped as Heysham Terrace (see above). The land on either side of, and behind, the Terrace was used for commercial purposes. The Iverson Works of Beck & Pollitzer was located here from 1926 to the late 1980s. The company is named after its founders, John Beck and Sigismund Pollitzer, who in 1863 established a warehousing and distribution business in the City. In 1907 the firm expanded into exhibition contracting and stand manufacturing, and the West Hampstead site was acquired. The company remained in family hands until 1961. Today, as a 'global provider of machinery installation and equipment relocation services', it is based in Kent.

In 1988 the Beck & Pollitzer site was developed as **Hampstead West**, a group of nine commercial units at No.224, and, behind the railway cottages, residential **ROWNTREE CLOSE**.

Up West End Lane, west side

The west side of West End Lane from Heritage Lane to West End Green. (For the Lane's more southerly section, see *Streets and Characters of Kilburn & South Hampstead*.)

Here we describe one side of the section of **WEST END LANE** to the north of the Jubilee line. The other side of the road is in Area 7. There are three railway stations within some 200 metres. Planners euphemistically call it 'West Hampstead Interchange', although changing between lines will involve crossing a busy road.

The Underground station (p 93) is on the east side of the Lane. Across the road, and a little to the north, is **West Hampstead Overground Station**. This part of the Overground (long known as the North London Line) originally opened as the Hampstead Junction Railway in 1860, with stations on the Edgware and Finchley Roads. Lack of local traffic meant the company did not open a station on West End Lane until 1 March 1888. In common with most of the stations on the line, this one had a red-brick exterior with wooden canopies over the platforms to protect passengers from the elements. A major rebuild of the Overground station began in August 2016, relocating the station entrance south

of its original site, and this has now been completed (March 2021).

South of the station was a terrace of small, single-storey premises. Over the years they were home to a variety of businesses, including coal merchants, a betting shop and builders, and immediately before demolition, a health shop and a café. James Gibb was at Nos.189&191 from the mid-1890s and a firm of that name still traded from here until the 1960s. Gibb came to London from his native Scotland with his wife and son; in 1881 they were sharing a house in Fleet Road Hampstead and James was working as a joiner. He became a major builder in West Hampstead, a surveyor able to lay out estates and responsible for houses in Dennington Park, Pandora and Narcissus Roads (to name but a few), and shops on West End Lane. In 1900 it was noted his business employed a staff of between 50 and 100 people. In 1901 James was living next door to Ernest Owers, at No.280 Finchley Road. Owers was a pioneer developer in Golders Green, and Gibb also worked there alongside his son James junior, who developed an estate agent's business in the neighbourhood. James senior died at his Finchley Road home in October 1930 and is buried in Hampstead Cemetery. His son died in 1936 and is buried in the same grave. Between them they left more than the equivalent of £22 million at today's prices.

An access road led to a tract of land sandwiched between the Underground and Overground tracks. It was home to various industrial premises until March 2014, when work began on a development originally called 'West Hampstead Square', but renamed two years later as **HERITAGE LANE**. Its seven tall blocks provide flats, office space and shops. Among other concerns, residents objected to the height of one of the blocks, which at 12 storeys is much higher than anything else locally. The developers held a competition to name the blocks and the winner suggested local authors. The first five blocks were named **Beckford, Hardy, Lessing, Orwell** and **Milne Buildings** and opened in 2017; the other two have been christened **Charlotte** and **Lily**.

The **WEST END LANE** frontage north of the Overground station was redeveloped in the 1980s. Previously here was another terrace of small, one-storey commercial premises. The first tenants in the 1890s were further coal merchants, one of whom was still there in 1940. When coal was the main fuel used for heating, it was transported by rail and offloaded in nearby sidings.

On the corner of Iverson Road, Nos.205&207 were originally coal offices, and survived until the recent rebuild of the Thameslink station (p 95). Beyond, a third railway bridge carries West End Lane over today's Midland Mainline and **Thameslink** tracks, which opened in 1868 as the extension into St Pancras of the Midland Railway (MR). Engineering work on the line caused immense disruption to the neighbourhood. Though it's almost impossible to visualise today, the fields on either side of West End Lane, from West End Green south to Iverson Road, were more or less on a level until the Midland line was built in a deep cutting, from which hundreds of tons of earth were shifted by hand. The railway workers, called navvies, were tough, hardworking men who travelled the country, sometimes accompanied by their families. They also had a well deserved reputation for drinking and fighting. Near West End, the main concerns were the health and sanitation problems experienced by the navvies and their families, including large numbers of children. The contractor for this stretch of the line, James Firbank, built a number of two-room wooden huts in the fields between Finchley Road and Mill Lane. They quickly became squalid and insanitary. In January 1866 it was reported that some of the hut dwellers operated a hot bed system: where relays of men occupied the beds by day that had been occupied by other men at night. Inevitably there were accidents. That same month an inquest returned a verdict of accidental death on Charles Austin, aged 52. He fell into an unprotected pit at the railway works near West End Lane. There were four shafts, each 30ft deep, but only two were covered. Charles had worked all night and when he wanted to go home at 5am, found his way blocked by three railway trucks that needed moving. He wouldn't wait, took another path and fell into the pit. It was flooded and Charles drowned before he could be rescued.

The MR's West End Station, opened in 1871 on Iverson Road (p 32), was moved in 1905 to the north end of the bridge on West End Lane. Renamed as West Hampstead Midland in 1950 and West Hampstead Thameslink in 1988, it remained there until 2011, when the main entrance was relocated back to Iverson Road.

In 1907 the LCC gave the MR permission to build a row of red-brick commercial premises, aptly named Midland Parade, along the west side of its bridge, partly suspended over the tracks. Although these were described as coal office buildings, some were occupied by general traders. From the late 1950s, No.11 Midland Parade was rented by Myra Allen, a specialist corsetière. Many local teenagers were taken by their mothers to be fitted for their first bra at this tiny shop. She sold the most amazing items of underwear to her older customers, at a time when it was still common for a woman to wear a corset. Myra had left by 1978, when all the shops were occupied and for the most part described as 'thriving;' they included a tailor, bookshop, a school of motoring and an au pair agency. The Parade was demolished soon after this when the height of the bridge was raised as part of the electrification of the main line to St Pancras.

At the far end of the bridge, the 'Black Path' unofficially named as such by locals, leads off towards Broomsleigh Street (p 69), also giving alternative access to the Thameslink station.

The next stretch of West End Lane as far as Sandwell Crescent (p 60) formed part of the boundary of Sandwell House. The house itself stood where Victoria Mansions in Sumatra Road (p 60) are today. It was one of the last big houses to be built in the village of West End, along with its neighbour across the Lane, Canterbury House (p 96). They dated from 1862 and were built for their first occupants, business associates and close friends John Marrian and William Greenwood. The house name reflected the fact that Sandwell borders Birmingham where Mrs Marrian was born and the family lived before coming to London. Marrian and Greenwood stayed only a few years, selling up to the MR, which was about to construct a line at the bottom of their gardens. The railway company disposed of Sandwell House to the Burgess family (p 89). Captain Henry William Burgess died in 1869 and his widow Mary Louisa Burgess remained at Sandwell House until her death in 1890.

George Dunn remembered how, as a small boy, he climbed over the garden fence to feast on wild strawberries that grew in the grounds. One day he met Mrs Burgess. When he confessed that he had been raiding her garden, 'she only smiled and told me that I might jump over again next summer and take as many as I liked'.

In 1891 Sandwell House and its grounds were purchased by Charles Cleverly Paine. The valuable West End Lane frontage was developed with a mix of commercial and residential properties. South of Sumatra Road, the shops with flats above at Nos.217-229, were originally known as Nos.1-7 Cheapside.

At **No.217**, now a bookmaker's, the first tenant was Stephen Hussey, who opened West Hampstead's first ironmonger's in 1893, with his brother as manager, a large double-fronted shop with a sweeping staircase to the first floor. On Hussey's death in 1902, Robert Persey took over and by 1907 J W Carpenters Ltd, who had a shop on Kilburn High Road, had bought the business. They offered an extensive range of services from plumbers, electricians and locksmiths, to grinding cutlery. The shop closed in the 1970s.

At **No.223** (now an estate agent's) were the premises of Epton Perfect. Here from 1914 until about 1972, this was a traditional butcher's shop with sawdust on the floor, a cut above others in the neighbourhood. Towards the end, there was very little meat on display: it was kept in a large cold room at the rear of the premises and brought out on request.

Beyond Sumatra Road are **Sandwell Mansions**, built by David Dakers and completed by 1895, when the annual rent for one of the flats was £90. Scottish born, Dakers worked his way up from joiner to builder's foreman, and lastly independent builder. For many years there was an enamel sign on the nearby Black Path advertising his 'healthy homes' in Muswell Hill.

Film director and part of the Monty Python team, Terry Gilliam [12] lived in Flat No.10. He married the costume designer Maggie Weston and they moved into Sandwell Mansions in 1973. His films include *Time Bandits* (1981), *Brazil* (1985), and *Twelve Monkeys* (1995).

Henry MacNaughton-Jones was in Flat No.12 from 1899-1903. A medical man, he was born and raised in Cork, where he founded two hospitals, before moving to London in 1883, where he continued a successful career. He wrote verse as a hobby, and his poem *The Race of Life* is reproduced on his headstone in Hampstead Cemetery.

Henry and Eleanor Dulley lived in Flat No.12a from 1919 to 1922. Their daughter Clarice May married James William Tate in 1912, and the couple occasionally stayed there. Clarice Mayne, as she was known professionally,

12 Terry Gilliam

was a singer and panto principal boy. On stage she always referred to herself as 'This' and to her husband James as 'That'. James' first unhappy marriage was to the music hall star Lottie Collins (of *Ta-ra-ra-boom-de-ay fame*).

He was an accomplished musician and song writer who accompanied Clarice on the piano, later diversifying into musical revue.

In 1949, the police were hunting for a gang of forgers, who were selling fake US dollars to travellers. That August, 61-year-old Friedrich Óberndorfer, who lived in Flat No.18 Sandwell Mansions, was arrested and questioned by the authorities when he was staying in Vienna. He handed over a number of forged $50 dollar bills, saying he had brought them in London. Two days later he jumped to his death from his fourth-floor hotel window. Friedrich's London neighbours said he was 'a man of mystery' who travelled regularly to the continent.

Across Sandwell Crescent, at 1970s Nos.**237-241**, the Banana Tree restaurant and the adjoining hairdressers trade on the site of one of the oldest buildings on West End Lane. It became the entrance lodge to Sandwell House but pre-dated the House by many years. A surprising survivor, the Lodge was subdivided into three shops by 1895. On the corner at the then No.235, Helga's Record Shop [13] opened in 1958. Throughout the 1960s it drew youngsters like a magnet to buy the latest hit single. Only a couple of customers could fit in the shop at any one time. Helga Nicholls sat behind her narrow counter guarding one or two racks of records.

Alongside were an old-fashioned jeweller's and a sweetshop, both run by the Clarke family. These were the days of farthing sweets – four a penny or 48 for a shilling. Fizzy drinks were limited to Tizer or White's products such as

cream soda and lemonade, and you paid a refundable deposit for the glass bottle. They had all closed by 1970 and the site was redeveloped.

Nos.243-255 line what was originally the

13 Helga's Record Shop

ain road frontage to Lauriston Lodge. This was not a purpose-built mansion; rather a short terrace of smaller properties which were bought by Germaine Lavie and converted into a single house between 1797 and 1812. Lavie was a lawyer and a member of the syndicate involved in the purchase and resale of the Belsize estate for development. He was also the leader of the campaign to abolish the West End Fair. Like many of its counterparts, what began as providing simple, largely local entertainment had, by the close of the 18th century, become a regular annual event held over full three days in July. It spread along road verges, and in 1818 into a field on Mill Lane. The rising numbers of visitors was a source of increasing annoyance to the more affluent West Enders. In 1819 the Fair was targeted on two successive days by a gang of organised thieves who violently assaulted and robbed a number of innocent fair-goers. The Hampstead Magistrates, Lavie among them, met and agreed to ban the Fair and it was never held again. Meanwhile some of the ringleaders of the gang were caught and tried. A number were sentenced to be publicly executed, others to be transported to Australia.

In 1876 Eugenius Birch, a very successful civil engineer, moved into Lauriston Lodge. He specialised in that very Victorian phenomenon – the building of seaside piers. At least twelve were by him, including the famous (but now damaged and derelict) West Pier at Brighton, where he also constructed a sea water aquarium. He died at West End in January 1884.

By the late 1880s, the large Jewish community in Kilburn and West Hampstead was under increasing pressure to establish a local place of worship. In May 1891 the local paper reported: 'a site has been secured whereon now stands the old ivy covered Lauriston Lodge. The total cost amounts to £2,300. The entire cost of the building, with the class buildings which it is proposed to erect in connection with it, including the cost of the site, is estimated at nearly £13,000.' The original plan was to front West End Lane, but the Synagogue was turned round to face Dennington Park Road (p 41), with a small back entrance to the main road. This freed the West End Lane frontage for commercial development, Nos.243-255, with living space above. They were built by George Neal and called Dennington Promenade. Until recently you could still make out the hand-painted name above No.255.

At **No.243**, Alban Atkin the Chemist took over from another homeopathic chemist in 1904. A local councillor, he is buried in Hampstead Cemetery and was succeeded in the business by his son of the same name. The shop closed around 1990 and was a time capsule to the very end, with large glass-fronted wooden cabinets and beautiful glass apothecary jars. The dispensary was at the far end of the shop, under a huge clock. The window display was a low-key one, and for many years its centre piece was a red neon sign, advertising Yardley cosmetics. The shop fittings were sold and have been reassembled in the Nakatomi Memorial Medicine Museum in Tashiro, Tosu City, Japan.

No.245 is a now a restaurant, but in 1906 housed Croizier's, French Court hairdressers and wigmakers. The high quality of the wigs supplied was, 'entirely due to the best quality of Natural Wavy and Curly European Hair, at very moderate prices'. Two of the other shops were among the longest established in West Hampstead.

Samuel's Stores, at **No.255**, was a grocer's and delicatessen. A family business, it was started by Samuel Gelbfarb, who took over an existing provisions shop in 1922. The shop offered a regular delivery service until it closed, many of their clients living in the St John's Wood area. Mrs Samuel would stand in the window, thinly slicing some of the best smoked salmon in London. The shop shut around 1981. There is a curious relief of a devil on the side of No.255 in Dennington Park Road, above '1892', the date the parade began building.

Across the junction, West Hampstead Library

(p 48) stands on the site of an old property called Gothic Lodge. An erroneous belief that the Victorian writer Sarah Doudney once lived there, probably arose from the fact that the last occupant's name was Dewdney. The West End Lane frontage here was developed by James Gibb, as Dennington Parade, and the premises were numbered in 1898 as Nos.257-279. The ten residential flats of **Dennington Park Mansions**, over the shops, became No.271, as they were reached up the still extant flight of steps between Nos.269&273. In 1891, they were described by Gibb as, 'handsome convenient and commodious flats, consisting of four bedrooms, two reception rooms, bath room, kitchen, scullery and lavatory, with rents ranging from £80 to £100 per annum'.

In 1931, Mrs Tom took over a confectioner's shop on the library site at No.259 selling Dorlon Chocolates, the name based on her and her husband's forenames: Dora and Leon. The chocolates were originally made on site and later at premises in Rosemont Road (p 116). By 1967, they were sold at most West End theatres and over 1,000 Rank cinemas, with an annual turnover estimated at over £500,000. But the company went bankrupt in 1970.

No.263 opened as a butcher's shop about 1891. John Cross took over the business two years later. His son George remembers life in the embryonic West Hampstead as hard for the traders, many of whom struggled to make a living. 'Father had bought the lease of our new home, 263 West End Lane, (carrying an option to purchase the freehold) and goodwill of the butcher's business which had only been established for a short time, for £500 – far too much, but he thought it had possibilities. Few multiple firms came in the early stages, and most of the shopkeepers were poor, struggling helpless fellows, with little or no capital, who would have been better off earning forty shillings a week as assistants.' Family members all pulled their weight by helping in the business, which was saved when Cross acted on a suggestion to cook and deliver, complete with china and cutlery, a hot dinner to every new resident who promised to buy his meat. After that, takings rose substantially.

A terrible family tragedy occurred on 19 February 1941 when a party was being held at No.3 Dennington Park Mansions, the flat over No.263. Thomas Elcome's son was a soldier who was going to be married later that day. At ten past one in the morning a high explosive bomb demolished the upper part of the building and fire broke out. Rescue services tried to work their way up from the basement but were constantly beaten back by the flames and falling debris. Tragically, the only survivor of the family party of eleven men, women and young children, was painter and decorator Thomas Elcome. Two of the children who died were aged just four months and nine months. Considerable damage was caused to adjacent properties and the resulting bombsite was an unofficial playground much used by the neighbourhood children. In the mid-1950s, the site of Nos.257-265 was cleared and used for the new library (p 48) and the local council flats named **Dennington House**.

In 1917 Sidney Venning bought out his partner in their ironmonger's business at **No.273**. Marianne Colloms can remember the shop from the 1950s until it closed in 1986. For some of the time, the second and third generations of the family lived in the flat above and she spent many happy hours in their front room, listening to pop music. The shop [14] was bursting at the seams with stock, and a variety of items ranging from watering cans to brooms were suspended from the ceiling. Customers queued single file between the high counter on one side and shelves of goods on the other, and often one had to leave the shop before another could enter. There was a large storage tank under the premises and paraffin for domestic heaters was dispensed using a pump at ground floor level. Sidney senior died in 1982; apparently, he was once mistaken for Dr Crippen and arrested at Margate. He always maintained he looked a lot like the doctor!

14 Venning, 273 West End Lane

Father and son specialised in locks with their key grinding machine at the back of the shop. No.273 became La Brocca, run by David Locke for 24 years until he retired in 2015. David loved jazz and held regular jazz nights at the restaurant. It became Bobby Fitzpatrick, a Seventies themed bar and pizza restaurant.

In 1978 Errol Drew set up Beta Bikes at **No.275**. In 1983 he created Ridgeback, the UK's first mountain bike. Drew later emigrated to America, where he set up a chain of bike shops. In 1999 the shop in West End Lane became Cycle Surgery which lasted until 2020. DropGym announced they would open there in January 2021, but this was delayed by the Covid-19 restrictions. **No.277** was a family run dairy for many years until it became a United Dairies branch in 1928. Today it houses the vibrant West End Lane Books which opened in 1994.

Immediately behind the shops of Dennington Parade, Gibb also built Dennington Park Mews to provide stabling for local businesses. Later renamed Inglewood Mews (not to be confused with a modern-day namesake, (p 53), it is now only a car park off Inglewood Road (p 50).

West End Lane, from here to the Green, formed the heart of the old village of West End. Redevelopment in the 1890s swept away almost all the original buildings. **Inglewood Mansions** cover the site of the home of Hannah Bowstead, who ran the original dame school in the village for many years, catering for about twenty children. Aged 73, she still gave her occupation as that of infant school teacher in the 1861 census. Back in the 1840s and 1850s, an earlier building at No.291 was probably home to the Black Horse beershop. Like the Prince of Wales up the road at Fortune Green (p 84), the Black Horse also sold coal, potatoes, bacon and drinking water at ½d a pail. The tenant stopped selling beer in the 1860s. Post-1950, it was a hardware business run by father and son, Herbert and Brian Archibald. It shut in July 2000 with closure largely blamed on the large DIY superstores nearby. No.291 and No. 293, survived demolition until 2003.

Next door, the **Black Lion** at No.295 has also variously been called The Black Lyon and Ye or The Old Black Lion [15]. The name first appears in the licensing records of 1751, but the property was probably here before that date. The tenant was a co-signatory to a petition addressed to the Magistrates in 1820, to try to persuade them to reverse their decision banning West End Fair: 'This Fair is to your Petitioners like a good harvest to a Farmer, namely the means of greatly assisting him towards paying his rent and taxes'. But the eloquent plea had no effect. In 1900, Edward Jarvis Cave bought the freehold and wanted to redevelop the pub and adjoining cottages. It was then described as 'very dilapidated, in a tumble-down condition and an eyesore'. Before obtaining a full licence in the late 1920s, the rebuilt Black Lion was only a beerhouse. It has since expanded into No.297 and, after a brief spell as the Rat & Carrot, has reverted to its original name.

For a brief period in 1812/13 a neighbouring property was rented to the poet and essayist Leigh Hunt. Then recovering from a debilitating illness, he wrote to his friend, the radical

15 The Old Black Lion, 1885

lawyer Henry Brougham. 'I am only now gaining strength by slow degrees and small portions of exercise. I shall get, however, into the country, though scarcely out of town – being about to move, as I believe I told you, to a cottage at West-end Hampstead, where I do not despair of seeing you sit down with me to a plain joint and pudding. The cottage is really and bona fide a cottage, with most humble ceilings and unsophisticated staircases; but there is green about it, and a little garden with laurel: and I can put you into a room where there will be a little library of poets, and an original portrait of Milton to overlook us as we sit drinking our glass of wine - so that you shall not help enjoying yourself in some measure. The lane to West-end runs out of Kilburn a little beyond the turnpike. My cottage stands in the heart of the place and on the gate is my name in a fair plate of brass.' But in 1813 Leigh Hunt was imprisoned for libelling the Prince of Wales. During his two years in goal he was visited by Lord Byron, Charles Lamb and other sympathetic writers. He was also a close friend of John Keats.

Providence Place was a group of eight cottages built on three sides of a little square, open to the Lane. These were replaced by five hops, with **West End Mansions** above, all originally Nos.301-317 and completed by 895. But closer examination of the shop onts today will show some numbers are issing. They disappeared around 1900, emoved when the local authority sought to istinguish the residential accommodation om the shops below. In September 1900, o.315 was Thomas Medcalfe's newly opened airy on the corner with West Cottages. 'The rge window, gaily bedecked with ferns, resents a clean and attractive appearance. oultry, new laid eggs and fresh butter may ways be relied upon, for they are received irect from Saffron Walden. Mr Medcalfe upplies his customers with pure milk twice aily; while for the special benefit of invalids nd children the milk of particular cows ay be regularly procured.' Despite Thomas' tention to detail and the fact his customers cluded several of the district's leading milies, the dairy had closed by 1904.

The singer Billy Idol lived in a flat above a hinese restaurant at No.315. He and his rlfriend Perri Lister, who was an actress and ancer in Hot Gossip, were together from 1980 to 989. They were a very distinctive couple when ney lived in West End Lane. Billy Idol in eneration X was playing on the pub scene nd they were one of the first punk bands to ppear on *Top of the Pops*. In 1981 he moved

to New York and the following year he had a major success with *White Wedding* when the video was shown on MTV. He is still performing today.

Opposite West End Green, on the site of a Little Waitrose, there was a terrace of houses numbered 1, 2 & 3 The Green, and later **Nos.319-323**. In 1896, a family tragedy occurred at No.1. Mrs Emily Hughes killed her son, aged eight months, and then committed suicide. A newspaper reported: 'The bodies, which were both enclosed in one coffin, the child lying on its mother's arm were taken in a covered hearse to No.1 The Green, West Hampstead. There was pitiless rain at the time, but a crowd, chiefly composed of women, many of whom carried infants in their arms, assembled outside the house, and a much larger crowd, similarly constituted, awaited the arrival of the cortege at the Hampstead Cemetery.'

From 1795 to about 1828, No.2 The Green was home to Cantelo (Charles) Bestland, engraver, print publisher and miniaturist who exhibited at the Royal Academy and the British Institution. He was another member of the local committee set up to abolish West End Fair. Alfred Slocombe was at No.2 in the 1870s and '80s. A flower painter, etcher and watercolourist, he likewise exhibited at the RA on several occasions. Alfred got involved in the fight to save West End Green as an open space

before moving to Cumberland House in Iverson Road (p 36) in 1891, where he stayed until his death in 1899. He is buried at Hampstead Cemetery.

The three houses were demolished and replaced by Carlton Garage in 1930-31. The building over the garage was called Carlton House and divided into flats. From November 1935 to the end of October 1936, the composer Benjamin Britten (1913-1976) (16) lived at Flat No.2 with his sister Beth, moving from there to No.559 Finchley Road. Beth wrote, 'The only

16 Benjamin Britten

snag we found out later was the cold. It was over the entrance to a garage, and consequently had concrete floors and nothing but air all around. It was fun furnishing it and setting up our first home.' Britten entered the Royal College of Music in 1930. While living in West Hampstead he was composing music for documentary films produced by the General Post Office. There he worked with W H Auden on *Coal Face* and *Night Mail*. Britten's later works include the opera *Peter Grimes* (1945), *The Young Person's Guide to the Orchestra* (1946), *The Turn of the Screw* (1954) and *War Requiem* (1961). The leading English composer of his time, he was made a life peer the year he died. The garage was trading as Cavendish Motors when it closed in the early 1990s. It was replaced first by a pizza restaurant and then the Little Waitrose supermarket, with **Carlton Mews**, a housing development, at the rear.

The land north of West Cottages belonged to a mansion, West End Lodge, near the corner with Mill Lane, and was acquired by the Potter family during the 1860s and '70s. The entrance to the Priory Lawn Tennis Club was next door to Nos.1- 3 The Green. Amongst its members was Alfred Harmsworth , later Lord Northcliffe (p 56). Referred to as 'Adonis' by lady members because of his good looks, Harmsworth caused great consternation when he brought his fiancée to the club. Taking his first steps towards fame and fortune, 'he was heard to say that he had had no luck so far as a publisher and that if "Answers to Correspondents" failed he would be in a bad way'. Harmsworth need not have worried; inside of four years, it was selling over a million copies a week.

The seven tennis courts, much used by residents from 1886, were sold off around 1899, to be developed as a bus yard off Mill Lane (p 61) and as **West Hampstead Fire Station**, No.325 West End Lane. The foundation stone was laid on 24 June 1901; the year is recorded on the front of the building [17], which is Grade-II listed. Its site cost around £1,800 and it was built by the LCC's Works Department at a cost of £11,373. Designed by the LCC Architect's staff, after Voysey, this was the first fire station where doors opening outwards were fitted. Four terraced cottages at the rear were provided as additional firemen's accommodation. In 1911, 60 people were living at the Station: 10 firemen, 3 coachmen (the engines were pulled by horses) and their families. In 2018, Camden certified the cottages for use as residential occupation by firefighters or other employees of the London Fire Commissioner.

From 1780 to 1801, West End Lodge was rented to Samuel Brawne, father of Fanny Brawne. Fanny was later to gain fame by her association with John Keats. She was born at West End and the Parish Church register for 1800 records the event: 'Frances daughter of Samuel and Frances Brawn born 6th August, baptised November 1st.' Once they acquired it in 1872, the Potters renamed the Lodge as The Cedars, after a pair of trees that stood in front of the house. However, within five years, it had been replaced – not with streets and terrace houses – but by two new detached mansion-style properties set in their own grounds. The first, again called The Cedars, later No.333, used part of the original carriage drive leading off West End Lane. The second and smaller house near Mill Lane was The Elms, later No.335. Clearly the Potters felt there were enough wealthy tenants to ensure the houses would let, as indeed they did, for most of their brief 25-year lifespan, but their market appeal was increasingly limited. Rev. Davys, the vicar of Emmanuel Church, rented The Elms as his parsonage. But the Church wanted to buy a freehold, which the Potters were unwilling to sell, and the vicar moved on to Dennington Park Road. The Cedars was last occupied in the 1890s as a 'High-class School for the Daughters of Gentlemen', run by the Sisters of the Church. Both houses were up for sale in 1902 and were demolished, making way for Cavendish Mansions (p 67) on Mill Lane, and

hops originally named Cavendish Parade,
ter **Nos.327** to **No.341** with West End Lane
ontage and wrapping around the Mill Lane
orner. In October 1993, an IRA bomb
xploded under a car parked outside the
hops. No-one was hurt and, aside from
hattered shop fronts and windows, little
amage was done.

In 1997 **No.335** was the Transilvania (sic)
orror Bar. It was part of a chain of themed
estaurants owned by the Italian horror film
irector Dario Argento and his business partner
mberto Ferri. There were also branches in
ome, New York and Tokyo. You could have
rac Burgers and Dead Body, with drinks like
osferatu and Blue Blood. These were served
t coffin-shaped tables by Goth waitresses
ressed in black from head to toe with a white
ace and fangs. But it didn't prove popular and
losed suddenly in 1998.

No.341 bears the Parade building date
f 1903. It was another longstanding local
usiness, run from at least 1907 until his
eath in 1959 by Edward Albert Dickins, a
onfectioner and tobacconist. This had been
career change for Dickins, who had trained
s a surgical instrument maker. The shop
emained a confectioner's, The Corner Shop,
ntil the 1990s. Today it is David's Deli.

17 West Hampstead Fire Station

West of West End Lane

Roads in the area bordered by Sumatra Road, Mill Lane and West End Lane

The land here was mainly owned by two families: the northern portion by the Potters, and the southern part by the Ripleys.

Charles Cleverly Paine, who bought Sandwell House (p 38), also acquired the Ripley property, which originally extended from West End Lane across to the Edgware Road. In 1814, it was divided between two brothers, Thomas and Jeremy Ripley. Jeremy got the West End fields and in the 1830s built himself a home in the village: Little Dene, which is incorrectly identified as 'Lauristone Lodge' on the 1860s OS map. Paine bought the house and its grounds in January 1881. In May 1881 plans for roads on the prestigious sounding Denington Park Estate were submitted. These were Denington Road (the Park and double 'n' came later), Kingdon Road, Pandora Road and Sumatra Road. Paine sold the freehold of the property to the Prudential Assurance Company for £12,682 in October 1884, the sale including 48 houses and the Little Dene mansion.

Running west off West End Lane, and curving south to meet Sumatra Road, **DENNINGTON PARK ROAD** partly followed the line of Sweetbriar Alley, a field path that led to Kilburn before railways severed its route.

Its north corner with the Lane has been occupied since the mid-1950s by the local authority flats of **Dennington House**, and **West Hampstead Library**. The plaque by the latter's main entrance shows that Cllr Geoffrey Finsberg, the future Hampstead MP (p 25), was present at the laying of the foundation stone in 1954. The branch library was officially opened by the Mayor, Emanuel Snowman on 17 July that year.

Hampstead Synagogue, across the road, was the work of architect Delissa Joseph and is Listed Grade II*. The foundation stone was laid on 13 March 1892 and the building was consecrated that September. It was extended in 1901. The main stained-glass window, by Maurice Sochachewsky and depicting Mount Zion, is beautiful when illuminated by the internal lighting.

Actress Dorothea Forster Baird was the sixth daughter of barrister John Forster Baird. Sometime after John's death in 1882, the family moved from Fitzjohn's Avenue to St Aidan's, No.3 Dennington Park Road, leaving before the 1891 census. Dorothea's great break came when she was personally chosen by George du Maurier to play the title role in the stage version of his novel, *Trilby*, about a young girl who falls under the influence of Svengali. She is tone deaf, but after he hypnotises her she can sing beautifully. Svengali dies, and without him Trilby loses her voice, following him to the grave. The play opened to rapturous reviews at the Haymarket Theatre in October 1895, and overnight Dorothea became a star. She married Henry Brodribb Irving, Sir Henry Irving's son, the following year. They are both buried in Hampstead Cemetery.

The Synagogue bought and demolished Nos.1&3, to build a Community Centre designed by Richard Seifert, which opened in 1964 on the corner of Kingdon Road (see below). There are plans to demolish and replace with a state of the art building, to serve the Synagogue and the wider community.

Little Dene (see above) survived until 1903, by which time it was known only by number, not name, as No.5. After the land sale to Paine, the house was rented to a series of tenants including the wine merchant Arthur Bethune Woodd. Arthur's grandfather was Basil George Woodd, known as the father of the London wine trade, with a shop in New Bond Street. Three blocks of flats, **Dene Mansions**, were built by Alfred Bretzfelder n the site of Little Dene. In 1911, Wyndham Albery, the son of playwright James Albery and actress Mary Moore, was living there in flat **No.4**. He had chosen a rather safer profession than his parents, that of a chartered accountant. He stood for Parliament in 1923 but was not elected.

The artist and teacher Leonard Rosoman was born in **No.15** Dene Mansions in 1913. At the outbreak of War, he joined the London Auxiliary Fire Service with other writers and artists such as the poet Stephen Spender and the novelist William Sansom. He was an official war artist in the Far East and his work is now in the Imperial War Museum. Rosoman taught at the Royal College of Art from 1957 until his retirement in 1978. His most famous pupils were Peter Blake and David Hockney. He died in London in 2012.

The singer and actress Olivia Newton John [18] bought the top floor flat at **No.9** Dennington Park Road. Born in Cambridge in 1948, Olivia went to Australia when she was five. She appeared on Australian radio and TV shows, and about 1965 she returned to England and lived in West Hampstead for a couple of years. Her first single was, *Till You Say You'll Be Mine*, (1966). Towards the end of the summer 1966 she met Bruce Welch, guitarist with The Shadows. He was 24 and married at the time, she was 17. They dated

from September 1966 and lived together; he often visited Dennington Park Road. In 1969 they moved from a flat overlooking Lords to Totteridge. She became well known for her role in the film *Grease* in 1978 with John Travolta. From then on, her singing career blossomed and she still tours today.

Actor George Layton rented rooms in **No.28** and **No.34**, before moving to Achilles Road (p 73).

No.32 was used as the base for a day's shoot in 1961, filming *The Rebel*. Tony Hancock played a clerk turned sculptor. His masterpiece, a huge female statue called *Aphrodite at the Waterfall*, was left on the back of a lorry in the road. The scene had Hancock ringing front door bells to rent a room, but the footage never appeared in the final version. Tony Hooper lived in the basement flat for a short while in the 1960s. He was a founder member of the Strawberry Hill Boys, later renamed the Strawbs, a folk rock group.

The first vicar of Emmanuel Church, Rev. Edmund Davys, lived at **No.34** from about 1885 to the mid-1890s, when No.1 Parsifal Road (p 85) was purchased as a vicarage. During refurbishment in the 1970s, No.34 lost its capstone, dated '1882', which was taken and erected on **No.30** instead, thus providing a source of confusion for local historians.

18 Olivia Newton John

49

Olivia Newton John wasn't the only singer of note to live in the road: Robert Palmer rented a basement bedsit in **No.35** in the early 1970s. He left after the flat was flooded in 1975, destroying most of his belongings. After working with several bands Palmer and Elkie Brooks joined Vinegar Joe and released their first album in 1972. His first solo album, *Sneakin' Sally Through the Alley*, was recorded in New Orleans in 1974. Palmer had a successful career and a number of major hits. His iconic music videos for *Addicted to Love* (1985) and *Simply Irresistible* (1988) featured identically dressed women with pale faces, dark eye makeup and bright red lipstick. Robert died in France in September 2003.

Actor Michael Elphick (d.2002) lived in the basement flat of **No.37** from about 1975 to 1982. He is best known for his gruff cockney voice in TV shows such as *Boon* and *East Enders*. In the 1970s and 80s he appeared on stage and in many films, including *The Elephant Man, Quadrophenia,* and *Withnail & I*. His daughter Kate wrote about her happy memories of Dennington Park Road.

The name originally proposed for **KINGDON ROAD** was Lauriston Road. In the 1990's a hall at the back of Hampstead Synagogue housed 'The Garage' (funded by the Jewish Spiro Institute), used for a variety of activities, including talks and meetings. In 2005, the junior Synagogue immediately adjacent to the Seifert community hall, was demolished and replaced by **Claddagh Court**, offering affordable housing. The funds released were used to help restore the main Synagogue.

In 1896, a local reporter visited **Nos.14&16**. It was a home for up to 48 Armenian refugees, 'who have fled to this country to escape the cruel massacres perpetrated in Asiatic Turkey'. Men lived in one house and women and children in the other. The former occupations of the residents ranged from wealthy merchant, author and professor, to clerk, student, mechanic and porter. The home's resident superintendent was a refugee, while his English wife acted as matron. There was no staff, so the residents had to do all the domestic work themselves. It was intended merely as a short-stay facility; the refugees moved on after a fortnight or so, some emigrating to America. The home had closed by 1898.

Later, No.14 was a squat, providing a short-term home for several Australian musicians until they were evicted. In 1979 Robert Forester and Lindy Morrison, members of the Go-Betweens, moved in, and another Australian musician, Rowland Howard (of the Immortal Souls and The Birthday Party) lived on the top floor. Dave Graney and Clare Moore were there briefly in 1983. They have been in many bands including the Moodists and the Coral Snakes and are still playing in Australia today.

Peregrine Platt lived across at **No.15** from at least 1885 till his death in 1909. He was the Secretary of the Field Lane Institution which owned the nearby Industrial School in Hillfield Road (p 73), a post he held for 36 years. An active member of Emmanuel Church, he created strong links between the School and the Church. Platt is buried in Hampstead Cemetery.

John Clement Bell was at **No.27** for part of the 1890s. He was the son of one of the founders of Clayton & Bell, stained glass artists, and in 1881 along with Clayton's son, was made a junior partner. At its peak, the firm was the largest and most celebrated of its kind in the UK, if not the entire world, employing over 300 people. They did much work locally, including windows in Hampstead Parish Church.

INGLEWOOD ROAD links West End Lane with Holmdale Road (p 53). The site of ***Poplar House*** lies under the roadway, a short distance from the Lane. The publisher and engraver Josiah Boydell lived there from 1783 to around 1810. Josiah moved in society and court circles and included many eminent ampstead residents among his friends. He ook an active part in local affairs, helping to uy a new organ for the Parish Church and orking to alleviate conditions of the poor. In 798 he was largely responsible for creating a cal defence force, the Loyal Hampstead ssociation, with an eye to a possible French vasion. His ambitious project to produce an lition of Shakespeare, illustrated by aintings commissioned from celebrated rtists, ran out of money, and he was forced to se Poplar House as security to obtain loans. is business was saved when the King granted im permission to hold a lottery to dispose of e paintings.

Boydell was succeeded at West End by oseph Lescher, a leading figure in establishing t Mary's Catholic Chapel in Holly Place, ampstead. After his death in March 1827, oplar House was up for sale, described as convenient distance from London, and a neerful ride through the Regent's-park to the ity'. In 1848, Fr Dominic Barberi attempted establish a religious community there. The assionists were a Roman Catholic order itroduced to England by Dr (later Cardinal) 'iseman, and the first since the Reformation lead a strict community life and wear their abit in public. They must have made a triking addition to village life. One of the four riests was Fr Ignatius Spencer, the great-

great-great uncle of the late Diana, Princess of Wales, and the great uncle of Sir Winston Churchill, whom he closely resembled. From the beginning, the Passionists had to cope with a lack of funds. Dr Wiseman allocated care of all the Catholics who lived 'below' Finchley Road to the Passionists. This gave them an enormous parish, extending as far as Watford in one direction. Fr Dominic regarded this as unjust and said: 'to us there remain all the poor people scattered over an immense extent of country; to (the chapel in Holly Hill) belong the few rich people of Hampstead. We had the bones left to us to gnaw.' Eventually, because of problems with the title to the property and its poor condition, the Passionists moved to The Hyde, Hendon in September 1849. The Roman Catholic Church has taken the first steps towards elevating Fr Spencer to sainthood. A decree recognising his 'heroic virtues' means he now has the title 'Venerable'.

Thomas Potter arrived in West End the following year. Born in Sussex, he was one of the new 'aristocrats' of commerce, and by the time he moved into Poplar House, had a thriving business based in South Molton Street, off Oxford Street. The letterhead describes the range of services on offer: 'Statue, iron and brass founders, engineers, smiths and medieval metal workers; manufac-

turers of wrought iron, fireproof flooring, girders, joists, strong room doors and safes, kitchen ranges and stoves, hot water apparatus and gas works erected'. The firm won the contract to carry out and manage extensive renovation works at Welbeck Abbey, the stately home of the Duke of Portland in Nottinghamshire. Potter was paid upwards of £130,000 between 1869 and 1877 (worth about £12.5M today), and the work was still ongoing two years later. In London, they did much, if not all, of the delicate grille work on the front of St Pancras Station, and the railings at the Royal Courts of Justice. Thomas kept South Molton Street as his business address, but after a decade of living at West End he decided to build an iron foundry there, possibly because of the work required for the Welbeck contract. No objections seem to have been raised, despite the unpleasant pollution it produced. Completed late in 1860 or early 1861, Potter's foundry stood where Welbeck Mansions (p 52) is today.

Poplar House was demolished around 1890-91. The following year Inglewood Road – originally intended to be called Poplar Avenue – was laid down across what remained of the grounds. Along the side wall of No.2 is a group of run down garages built on a section of the road that once led to Potter's foundry.

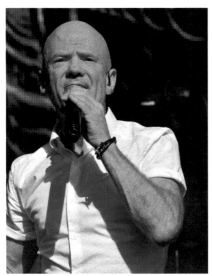

19 Jimmy Somerville

In the 1980s, singer Jimmy Somerville [19] was at **No.12A**. In 1983 he co-founded Bronski Beat with the other members of the band. They had a hit with their first record, *Smalltown Boy* (1984). In 1985 Jimmy and Richard Coles formed The Communards. Their record *Don't Leave Me This Way* stayed at number 1 for four weeks in 1986. Later, Jimmy went on to a successful solo career.

Born in 1883, Charles Maurice (known as Maurice) and Edward Julius Detmold were twin brothers with outstanding artistic ability. Their parents Edward and Mary were living with her uncle, Dr Shuldham when it seems their marriage failed and Edward left. Mary and her three children stayed with Dr Shuldham and his family. They all moved to Hampstead and from 1906 to 1910, their home was **No.13** Inglewood Road. As child prodigies, at the age of 13, Edward and Maurice Detmold were the youngest people to exhibit water colours at the Royal Academy. In 1903 they created a portfolio of sixteen superb illustrations for Kipling's *The Jungle Book*. But their productive partnership ended in April 1908 when Maurice Detmold committed suicide. He was found in his room in Inglewood Road by his brother, in the bedroom they shared. Maurice was lying on the bed with a bag over his head and a cotton wad soaked in chloroform. There were three bottles of chloroform nearby and two dead cats in a box. He had left a suicide note which read: 'This is not the end of a life. I have expressed through my physical means all that they are capable of expressing, and I am about to lay them aside – Maurice'. The verdict of the inquest jury was: 'suicide whilst of an unsound mind'. Edward was stunned by his brother's death, but he continued to work into the 1920s and 1930s, creating etchings, drawings and paintings, and coloured block prints. Then he largely withdrew from public life and moved to Wales. On the morning of Monday 1 July 1957, like his brother Maurice almost fifty years before, Edward committed suicide. He shot himself in the chest and died of a haemorrhage. His sister said that in the past year Edward had become very depressed, having lost the sight in one eye and the other eye deteriorating rapidly. The coroner's verdict was, 'death by self-inflicted gunshot wound while the balance of the mind was disturbed'.

The graphic designer Storm Thorgerson died at **No.27** on 18 April 2013. Of Norwegian descent, he was born in Potters Bar in 1944. He went to school with Syd Barrett and Roger Waters, and was a teenage friend of Dave Gilmour, who were later members of Pink Floyd. He formed Hipgnosis in 1968 with Aubrey Powell, designing hundreds of famous record covers, including 'The Dark Side of the Moon' (1973) for Pink Floyd. In the early 90s Thorgerson set up StormStudios at his flat above 205-207 Haverstock Hill, before moving to West Hampstead where he stayed for over 20 years.

Late in 1896 Potter's foundry, bordering on the north side of Inglewood Road, was in the process of being replaced by a large block of flats, aptly christened **Welbeck Mansions** after Potter's largest commission. The

Mansions and the foundry appear side by side in the rate books until the turn of the century, indicating that demolition of the latter was progressive.

In 1921 the actor Robert Marsden was born in **Flat No.14** as Robert Henry Marsden Levy. He had a very successful career working on the stage and then in radio, films and TV. He played many Shakespearian roles and worked with Laurence Olivier and John Gielgud. In a 1965 Dr Who series he played Abraham Lincoln. Marsden later became a theatre director as well as a teacher at RADA and Central School. He died in Elstree in 2007.

Adjoining Welbeck Mansions at their eastern end is Inglewood Mews, a residential redevelopment of old garages with living space above.

Leading off West End Lane north of Inglewood Road is the cul-de-sac named **WEST COTTAGES**. Beyond a narrow entrance, and off the south side, is **Salmon Mews**. Previously here were Salmon's Garages, originally built as stables for retail tobacconists Salmon & Gluckstein. Family members were co-founders of J Lyons & Company, which opened teashops up and down the country. When redevelopment plans were submitted in 1992, the building still had a rare horse ramp, leading to what had been first-floor stables.

Despite hard local campaigning, permission was given for conversion into flats and the ramp was removed.

On opening his foundry at West End in the 1860s, Thomas Potter had needed trained ironworkers, but the villagers were hostile to the idea of renting rooms to his employees. This problem was simply resolved by building 13 cottages facing the foundry. Though initially called Potter's Cottages or Potter's Buildings, by 1867 they had become known as West Cottages.

The attractive 2-storey properties, with small front gardens, are the oldest buildings still standing in the neighbourhood, and some retain pleasing period details. Behind a wall at the end of the cul-de-sac is Holmdale Road. In 1975, the great storm that burst over Hampstead caused substantial damage to parts of West Hampstead. One of the amazing spectacles was the roadway of West Cottages, which turned into a raging torrent several feet deep. This was strong enough to break through Holmdale Mansions on the other side of the wall, where the water poured out of the front door in a 4ft-high stream. It had happened before, if not quite so spectacularly. In 1927, the owner of No.13 Holmdale Road complained that 'whenever a storm of rain occurs his house is flooded by torrents of water rushing down from the cottages'.

Developed on Potter land, and one of four parallel roads running north to meet Mill Lane, is **HOLMDALE ROAD**. In 1895, this came close to providing a site for the first West Hampstead Library. The Vestry had agreed a 3-year lease and to erect a corrugated iron building, when the deal fell through.

Ambassador Court, a block of flats on the corner with Inglewood Road, was completed in the early 1970s. It replaced three rows of lock up garages built in 1928, and in doing so removed a popular play space used by local children. Residents first appear in the electoral roll of 1972 and one of the first occupants of Flat 7 was Martin Bell OBE, a British UNICEF Ambassador, former broadcaster, war reporter and independent politician. He served as the MP for Tatton from 1997 to 2001, and is sometimes referred to as 'the man in the white suit' which he frequently wore.

Next door, **Holmdale Mansions** were built in the early 1900s by Alfred Bretzfelder, also the builder of Dene Mansions (p 53). In 1908, Flat No.7 was rented to the actor Richard Abraham Greene while he worked in London. He was the father of Richard Greene who (literally) sprang to fame playing Robin Hood in the popular 1950s TV series. The theme tune, *Robin Hood, Robin Hood, Riding Through the Glen* was familiar to hundreds of children at the time.

All of Holmdale Road's houses north of Inglewood and Pandora Roads were built by Jabez Reynolds. No.13 was the home of Harold Allen and his family from 1895 to the mid 1930s. He was a local land agent and surveyor. Permission to demolish and replace with flats and garages was granted in 1936. The contractors were C Tavener & Son (p 54) and the name chosen, **Westcott Court**, obviously derived from West Cottages immediately behind the site.

The 1929 local directory carried an advertisement for 'The Home for Maids' at No.18. The Home's charges were 1s per night, or 6s a week, including use of bath. This accommodation was linked to a business in Kilburn High Road, where householders could hire domestic servants, and described as being 'run by a man for women'. It was owned by the flamboyant Captain (retired) Fred Russell, who was goaled for four years at the Old Bailey for fraud in 1939. The house was converted into flats called **Holmdale Court** in the early 1930s.

In 1932, Mrs Florence May Perriman, a spiritualist medium, who lived in **No.30** Holmdale Road, was awarded £106 damages for injuries when the cab she was in collided with a car. She told the court she earned around £10 a week but had been unable to hold séances since the accident. Mrs Perriman was asked if she could predict the future, to which she replied that if this were the case, she would have predicted the accident and not ridden in the cab. Florence was a society clairvoyant, using the professional name 'Madame Faustina'. She was consulted by stars of stage and screen, including Gladys Cooper and Ivor Novello. He wrote the foreword to her autobiography, *Secrets of a Famous Clairvoyante*. Florence died at No.30 in 1936.

A stick of bombs that fell across the neighbourhood in September 1940 killed three people in Holmdale Road, at Nos.33&35. In the early 1950s **Nos.33-39** were rebuilt as a block of four flats, rented to Metropolitan Police personnel.

Robert Washington Hart was at **No.50** from at least 1898 to 1904. He started the family business responsible for building many houses in Hampstead.

In 1914, the death of Frances Maria Voysey at **No.56** appeared in *The Times*. She was the mother of architect C F A Voysey and widow of Rev. Charles Voysey. Charles had been condemned for his unorthodox teaching, and in 1871 was finally deprived of his living near Tadcaster. He moved to London, where he founded the Theistic Church in Swallow Street, off Regent Street. He died in 1912, at Annesley Lodge, Platts Lane, the house designed for him by his son.

No.62, on the corner of Mill Lane, was occupied by medical men for many years. These included, by 1911, Sir Francis Lovell and his son William (p 25). Sir Francis was the Chief Medical Officer of Mauritius and a member of the Legislative Council from 1878 to 1893; Surgeon-General in Trinidad and Tobago (1893-1901), and later the Dean of the London School of Tropical Medicine. Dr Gunasekara was next: he came to England from Sri Lanka in 1904 and studied medicine. Qualifying in 1916, he entered general practice two years later at No.62, where he stayed until his death in 1971. Locals remember Dr Gunasekera with affection: 'He was a gentleman. He always wore morning coat and pinstripe trousers.' His obituary called him 'a sincere, gentle and kind man'. In the days before the NHS, he used a sliding scale of charges, reflecting what a patient could afford to pay.

Harold Lough White was a debonair playboy by day with a private plane and a yacht, but a safecracker by night, nicknamed Peter the Plotter. In 1954 he was sentenced to seven years in jail and his accomplice Gordon Simpson who lived in Holmdale Road, got six years. Simpson had used his job as a broker to pass on detailed information about properties worth raiding, drawn from the annual insurance survey privately supplied to nderwriters by Lloyds.

The Potter family had begun developing their property before Poplar House was demolished, marketing their 'West End Estate' in the late 1870s and starting with an area off Mill Lane. In 1877 Potter applied to lay down Glenbrook, Narcissus and Solent Roads, and part of Sumatra Road. Potter's son Arthur was a solicitor and responsible for conveyancing most if not all of the house or plot sales, with family members acting as directors of their West Hampstead Land Development Company. Progress was slow. By the time of the 1881 census, only fourteen houses had been completed, including Nos.1-15, on the west side of an embryonic **NARCISSUS ROAD**, jutting out into the fields south of Mill Lane. In 1882, when John Greer, an author of Irish tales and dramas was living at **No.1**, one of his sons received a severe reprimand from the staff of Hampstead Cemetery at Fortune Green. He had been caught in the act of 'plucking a rose from the Cemetery Chapels'.

By 1963, writer David Nobbs (1935-2015) was sharing a flat at **No.15** with Peter Tinniswood (1936-2003), when they were writing scripts for *That Was The Week That Was*. They lived here for a few years. Nobbs wrote material for many leading comedians including Kenneth Williams, Frankie Howerd, Les Dawson and the two Ronnies. He adapted his novels to create the 1970s series *The Fall and Rise of Reginald Perrin*, starring Leonard Rossiter. Peter Tinniswood also wrote for TV and radio. His best known series was *I Didn't Know You Cared*, featuring the Brandon family which ran on TV from 1975 to 1979. For radio he wrote the *Uncle Mort* series based on his novels.

From 1950 to 1970 at least, Eric Shirley was at **No.41**. In 1963 he ran after and caught a man who he had surprised in the act of breaking into his house. The magistrate commented: 'Perhaps you have some special knowledge about gaining speed. You certainly used it.' It seems he wasn't aware that Shirley had represented his country in athletics. He took part in the 3,000 meters steeplechase final at the 1956 Melbourne Olympics, and the 1960 Olympics in Rome. Still running, he holds British records for the over-80-year-olds.

84-year-old Raymond Leopold, Baron de Berenger de Beaufain, died in 1903 at **No.52**. He was sharing the house with his sister Matilda. Their father was Charles Random, a colourful character who had assumed the baronial title when he married the Baroness. He was convicted, with others, for perpetrating an early example of Stock Market manipulation. England was embroiled in the Napoleonic Wars when, in 1814, de Berenger posed as a staff officer and with others, announced that Bonaparte was dead and that the monarchy had been restored in France. For a few hours, the erroneous belief that the war with France was over allowed huge profits to be made by selling shares. De Berenger was prosecuted and sentenced to 12 months in prison, where he wrote *The Noble Stockjobber*, giving his version of the scam. In the 1830s, he was running The Stadium in the grounds of Cremorne House, Chelsea, an outdoor training facility for all types of sports, including archery, shooting and horse riding. The business failed and the site was used for the popular Cremorne Pleasure Gardens.

PANDORA ROAD straightened out the boundary between the Ripley and Potter properties. Local builder James Gibb (p 42) built most, if not all, of the houses.

At the eastern end on the south side, Monsieur Maurice Gally was living in 1887 at **No.5**. An eminent French actor, he trained at the Paris Conservatoire and toured with Sarah Bernhardt for nearly seven years. He died suddenly aged 34, in 1891, while living in Battersea.

Philip Arthur Layman, herbalist and distiller, lived at **No.7** from at least 1933 until his death in 1963. He was the great grandson of Charles Random, Baron de Berenger. In 1934 Layman was fined £10 and 5 guineas

20 Alfred Harmsworth, by Spy (from Vanity Fair, May 1895)

costs, for 'possessing an illicit still and depositing spirits at his address with intent to defraud his Majesty of duty'. He used banana skins and an old oil can to make a sort of gin, described by the magistrate as, 'a foul and filthy mixture, a lethal type of cocktail'. In 1947 he was again summoned, this time for selling medicines, including an 'elixir of life', without disclosing the ingredients; he was fined £30. In the 1950s he was a familiar sight, riding in a stately, upright manner around the local streets on his bicycle. The rear ground-floor rooms in his house were gloomy and dark owing to a jungle of foliage in the garden. The tools of his trade – species of herbs – were much in evidence.

In December 1910, Mrs Jeannette van Raalte formed the West Hampstead Branch of the Women's Freedom League at her home at **No.23**, where she had been living since at least 1901. For a short while, Cricklewood was also covered in the League. The members held open air meetings on West End Green, Fortune Green, West End Lane and Cricklewood Broadway. Founded in 1907, the League was dedicated to using non-violent means to obtain female suffrage. Some members refused to pay taxes or fill in the 1911 census form. This probably explains why Mrs van Raalte's name is absent from the family's return and why a question mark appears besides her husband's description as Head of the family. By 1915 the van Raaltes had moved to Ashbourne Avenue NW11, where Jeannette continued campaigning for the Golders Green branch.

Opposite Solent Road, a blue plaque at **No.31** marks the brief residence there, in 1888-91, of Alfred Harmsworth [20], the future 1st Viscount Northcliffe (see also p 33). On 11 April 1888 at Hampstead Parish Church he married Mary Milner and the house in Pandora Road was their first home. Alfred was just starting to build his publishing empire. In 1890, with his brother Harold (later Lord Rothermere), he set up the Pandora Publishing Company and launched a humorous halfpenny magazine called Comic Cuts. The brothers went on to found both the *Daily Mail* and *Daily Mirror*. Once he became successful, Alfred left West Hampstead, for Broadstairs.

In 1891, Janet King was living with her husband at **No.42**. As a nurse known as Sister Janet, she cared for the sick and wounded in war, and was one of a party of nine women sent to the Balkans in 1877/78. Belatedly, in 1904, she was awarded the Imperial Order of the Red Cross of Russia for her help to the Russian army. The nurses endured considerable hardship: travelling conditions were appalling, the weather was bitterly cold and some fell ill with typhus. Janet was also awarded the South Africa Medal and the decoration of the Royal Red Cross (1883) for 'the special devotion and competency displayed in nursing duties with her Majesty's troops during the Zulu Wars'. The Kilburn photographer Frederick William Muncey took a photograph of Janet in her nurse's uniform, displaying her medals. In 1882, she married George King, later one of the founders of the magazines *Tatler* and *The Sphere*. They left West Hampstead soon after the birth of their second daughter Daisy in 1893.

Initially **SOLENT ROAD** only ran as far as Glenbrook Road. Extended to meet Pandora Road after 1889, the southern portion was named Solent Crescent until the entire street was renumbered as one road in 1893. All but six of the houses in Solent Road were built by John Chapman, who was living at No.1 in 1891.

In 1940 bombs destroyed and damaged houses here. One person living at No.11 was killed. By 1951, the sites of Nos.9-17 had been redeveloped as an LCC Maternity & Child Welfare Centre. In the 1970s local mums would take their babies there for check-ups and immunizations. Post-1989 it was rebuilt as the **West Hampstead Medical Centre**.

What are the chances of two conjurors living in the same West Hampstead street at the same time? During the 1920s and 30s, Bernard Douglas Marks (who worked professionally as Douglas Dexter) was at **No.34**. In 1931, he sued a fellow Magic Circle magician for stealing his blindfold card-stabbing trick, in which he identified a chosen card in a pack by stabbing it with knife. But the jury could not agree on a verdict. Marks left for Hendon

in the late 1930s, but William Ellis Stanyon lived in Solent Road for over half a century. He moved into **No.76**, at the north end, around 1900. In the next year's census he described himself as a jeweller's clerk, but he was also known as Professor Ellis Stanyon of Stanyon's School of Magic, Solent Road. He never appeared on stage but invented many tricks, including some for Houdini. In 1906 he opened a shop at No.182 West End Lane (p 96). His daughter taught at Emmanuel School for over thirty years. When Stanyon died aged 81 in 1951, his obituary noted his secrets were safely locked away in the cellar. His son Cyril – who was a conjuror - had the only key.

In 1911, two builders who started successful local businesses doing renovations and repairs rather than house building were living in the road. Charles Munn whose offices were nearby on Mill Lane, was at **No.40**, and William Leadbetter up at **No.70**. William started in a small way near West End Green, later moving to No.152 West End Lane. His brother Charles became head gardener at Cholmley Lodge (p 77). William was still at No.70 when he died in 1942.

The modern block of flats, **Nos.77-105,** stands on the site of a plot sold by the Potters for £420 and used to build the Ebenezer Primitive Methodist Chapel, which opened in September 1887. In the late 1970s the

Methodists were forced to sell off the building when the congregation could not afford the bill to eradicate dry rot in the roof. The 15 flats (1981) were by architect Peter Tábori who also designed Highgate New Town and Oakshott Court in Somers Town, for Camden Council. Hungarian-born Tábori had worked with Denys Lasdun and Ernö Goldfinger before joining the Council's Architect's Department. Four storeys high on Mill Lane, the block steps down to 2-storeys facing Solent Road, with vivid red brickwork contrasting with bright blue painted metalwork.

GLENBROOK ROAD links Sumatra Road and Narcissus Road. Its 17 sequentially numbered houses were completed by 1890. The stick of bombs that fell in 1940 damaged seven properties here and Nos.16&17 are post-war rebuilds. Killed in the same air raid were seven residents of adjacent Narcissus Road.

SUMATRA ROAD was built across three properties. The Mill Lane end was on Potter land; the middle section ran across Ripley property; and the link to West End Lane was finally created after the sale of Sandwell House in 1891. In 1895 the road was renamed throughout as Sumatra Road, after a request to call it Sandwell Park Road was refused, and renumbered north to south, with even numbers on the east side.

It comes as a surprise to find someone who wanted to give away her properties. In 1950, Mrs Corcoran of **No.10** told a reporter she was tired of being a landlady and had decided to stick to giving music lessons. As the owner of a Paddington flat in poor condition, she had been taken before the rent tribunal but said she couldn't afford the repairs. Having already given a house in Hendon to her builder in lieu of payment for work done she said, 'If I can get anyone else to take them off my hands, I shall give away my other properties'.

Commercial traveller William Arthur Vassar of **No.43** was a victim of the 1915 sinking of the *Lusitania*, surviving several hours in the water before being rescued. He was returning from a business trip and the experience didn't stop him sailing to America the following year.

In Sumatra Road, the September 1940 stick of bombs destroyed six houses; many more sustained severe blast damage and four people died. The sites of Nos.76-86 were cleared to create a playground, known as the **Sumatra Road Open Space** which was opened to the public on 6 April 1957 and is still well used today.

For many years the detached house **No.98** with a large studio, was home to a number of artists. Frank Kelsey was there from 1901 to 1903. He was a marine painter who worked in Cornwall and had 28 exhibits at the RA. From 1910 to 1915 the artist William Ewart Gladstone Solomon lived here with his mother Georgiana and sister Daisy. Georgiana was the widow of Saul Solomon, a renowned South African liberal, newspaper proprietor and MP. Mother and daughter were suffragettes who had joined the Woman's Social & Political Union in 1908. Son William supported the movement, designing a banner for the Kilburn branch. Daisy, later Secretary of the WSPU's Hampstead shop and office (p 121), was involved in the February 1909 'Human Letters' publicity stunt when she and Elspeth McClelland were posted for 3d to 10 Downing Street. A post boy accompanied them to the front door where they were refused entrance to see Prime Minister Asquith [21]. She was subsequently sentenced to a month in prison; in 1912 her mother was jailed for a month for smashing the windows in the office of Black Rod. In the 1911 census like many suffragettes, they refused to provide any information.

In 1922 the house was up for sale and described as suitable for 'artists, musical or dancing academy'. For many years from 1962 it was the home of Dolf Rieser (1898-1983), artist, etcher and engraver. Born in South Africa, Rieser became a painter in the 1920s and in Paris he studied engraving under Joseph Hecht. His work was influenced by the cave paintings of African bushmen which he

21 Daisy Solomon and Elspeth McClelland, 'The Human Letters' at 10 Downing Street, 1909

used with the surrealist movement. A strong critic of Fascism, Rieser fled Paris the day the Nazis entered the city. He came to London and offered his knowledge of French and German to help the Special Operations Executive (SOE). After the War he developed two new techniques of colour printing and printing onto plastic. This fusion of art and science dominated his work for the next 30 years. Rieser had over 20 one man shows and his works are exhibited in many of the world's art galleries. He is buried in Hampstead Cemetery.

George Bennett of **No.99** was a chauffeur working for Taylor & Lown (p 116). In 1910 he was driving along Lymington Road (p 112) and nearing the bend in the road, when an elderly lady started to cross in front of him. George slammed on the brakes and the car skidded, knocking her down. He discovered to his horror that he had hit his own grandmother, who later died from her injuries. This was one of West Hampstead's earliest road fatalities.

In the 1950s, the site of **Nos.105-109** was occupied by two lines of garages. By 1964, it housed Cornwell Motors, a firm that maintained three-wheeler invalid cars for the Ministry of Health. These blue vehicles were a common sight in the surrounding roads, often with an instructor hanging onto the side as he gave a new owner a lesson on how to work the

controls. Before moving to West Hampstead, H G Canning was in business in Canterbury Road Kilburn, repairing invalid chairs. In 1975 the Ministry of Health began phasing out the three-wheelers on safety grounds. The site was redeveloped in 1989 as offices and commercial space which was later modified to include residential accommodation at first floor level.

In February 2018 **No.163**, which had been empty for several years, was being redeveloped when the builders saw cracks appearing in the walls. They managed to get out before part of the front suddenly collapsed from the roof to the ground. Luckily, no-one was hurt.

Cecil Maxwell Cade (b.1918) and his wife Isabel lived at **No.169** from the early 1970s until his death in 1985. Max Cade had a lifelong interest in yoga, Zen Buddhism and Sufi teachings. He became a scientist and worked on the development of radar for the Admiralty during WWII; in the early 1960s, he was the chief research officer at Smith Industries in Cricklewood. He also developed a body heat scanner which was used in the detection of breast cancer. In the 1970s Max used a machine called the Mind Mirror that measured skin resistance and brain waves to enable people to reach greater states of awareness, running courses in Hampstead and central London. His work of combining Eastern philosophy and electronics was

pioneering in the field of biofeedback. Max published over 150 scientific papers and books, including *The Awakening Mind* (1979).

Dusty Springfield (1939-99), considered by many to be the greatest British soul singer, was born Mary Isabel Catherine Bernadette, in the Fordwych Road nursing home (p 18). She was the daughter of Gerard and Catherine O'Brien, who lived at **No.104** from about 1933-38. When her father registered her birth on 5 May 1939, they had already left West Hampstead for Lauderdale Mansions, Maida Vale. Her father, who had grown up in India, was a tax consultant. By 1944 the family had moved to High Wycombe and some years later they moved again to Ealing. After leaving school in 1958 Dusty answered an advert for a female singing trio called the Lana Sisters. Then in 1960 she joined her elder brother Dion (who became Tom Springfield), and Reshad Field, to form The Springfields, a pop-folk trio. In 1963 she began her solo career with *I Only Want to Be with You*, which reached Number 4 in the charts. Her most famous songs were *The Look of Love* which was featured in the Bond film *Casino Royale* (1967) and *Son of a Preacher Man* (1969). In 1998 she was awarded an OBE. Dusty was diagnosed with breast cancer in 1994 and she died in March 1999.

Root Jackson, who also lived in Sumatra

Road, had a hit with his cousin Jenny with *Lean on Me* in 1969. He has been a member of groups such as FBI (1976), The Breakfast Band (1989), and the GB Blues Company. A track on his album *Funkin' With Da Blues* (2011) is called *Kilburn High Road Blues.*

James Moyes is a guitarist and composer who still lives in West Hampstead. He formed Sagram with sitarist Clem Alford and tabla player Keshav Satte, and in 1971, with the addition of singer Alisha Sufit, they became Magic Carpet. Their 1972 album *Magic Carpet* was described as 'one of the finest Indian-influenced psychedelic folk albums of the 1970s'.

In 2002, chef Jamie Oliver [22] and his wife Juliette Norton were living in **No.179B**. He had become famous when the BBC TV programme *The Naked Chef* first aired in 1999. The couple later moved from Sumatra Road to Hampstead.

In 1901, 49-year-old Nancy Melzer of **No.205** was found badly burnt and lying semi-conscious on her bedroom floor. She died at St Mary's Hospital. Daughter Ethel said her mother used to wash her hair using a mixture of paraffin and alcohol. Nancy had tried to light the gas lamp above her basin, causing the inflammable vapour to ignite.

The *Daily Express* published a report of the sad death of a toddler and her mother, killed while crossing West End Lane in December 1954. It described Sumatra Road where they lived as, 'the long, dismal street of grey brick houses they call the Street of Lonely People'. The article commented on the many displaced persons and refugees who had found a home in this and other local streets. It appeared that neighbours were often strangers, and a visit to the road by the reporter seemed to bear this out, so far as many of the newcomers were concerned. However, 12-year-old John Turner, who lived at **No.213,** wrote a letter that robustly contradicted this view. 'I know this is not so. I think Sumatra-road is a road of great activity and a road of many good friends and neighbours.'

The 15 flats of **Victoria Mansions**, on the site of old Sandwell House (p 38), were described as newly built in March 1900. They offered a resident porter, electric lighting throughout and tradesmen's lift, at an annual rent of £65.

Originally called Sandwell Park, this stretch of Sumatra Road was the last to be developed. Charles Cleverly Paine agreed to its extension east from Kingdon Road after his purchase of Sandwell House in 1891. All the new houses were built in 1893 by David Dakers, as in the same year were those of **SANDWELL CRESCENT**. In 1915, No.1 was the Sandwell Nursing Home & Trained Nurses Institute, offering a 'Comfortable Home for Medical, Surgical, Maternity and Chronic Patients'.

Around 1982, when aged only 17, the actress, film producer and fashion designer Sadie Frost bought her first flat in the Crescent, moving here from Gondar Gardens (p 69). It was on the first floor and she paid £39,000. 'I basically painted it all grey. It was small but I loved it. The bathroom was off the kitchen so if your flatmate was cooking, you could chat while you had a bath'. She stayed for only a couple of years, moving to Kentish Town after she met her first husband Gary Kemp.

22 Jamie Olivber

Along and off Mill Lane

Mill Lane, Broomsleigh Street triangle,
Gondar Gardens and the 'Greek roads'

One of the oldest roads wholly in Hampstead, **MILL LANE** may date from the Middle Ages. It's had several names, including Cole Lane, Shutt Up or Shoot Up Hill Lane and Windmill Hill Lane. In 1882, a reporter described how rural it had been until recently: 'Walking between hedgerows of privet and wild flowers, the saunterer found very little to disturb him. The hedge on either side was generally high and thick yet the lane [23] had a charm of its own in its quiet, green restfulness.' But, he noted regretfully, with the building of new roads and houses, 'London is fast coming'. In 1899 the Mill Lane's named terraces and individually named houses were numbered, and the present numbering scheme was officially adopted, for what was then a suburban road with a mix of residential and commercial properties.

Today, east of Fordwych Road, are **The Mill Lane Apartments** at Nos.1-7, a block of mixed private and affordable flats which were approved in 2009. The complex borders the Thameslink/Midland railway line and extends back to Minster Road. Its construction involved the demolition of No.1 Mill Lane, No.3 having

already been pulled down in 1989, and Nos.5&7 back in 1941.

Opposite, the nine houses at **Nos.2-18** form an attractive curve set back from the main road. Dating from 1893 and originally called Fordwych Crescent, they are further examples of builder Joshua Parnell's work (p 24). In 1901, Charles Schlisky, professor of music was living at **No.10**. His second wife was born in Australia and Charles took up a post in Adelaide, where he died in 1931. His son Eric was an artist who lived locally, and another son Trevor became a film and TV actor, using the name Trevor Austin.

A bridge carries Mill Lane across the railway line, here in a deep cutting. In 2000 the artist Charlotte Gerrard and local children painted a mural of 64 colourful panels on the bridge. But now it is sadly faded and defaced by graffiti.

The houses on the north side at **Nos.9-17** began life as Westbere Villas, and **Nos.19-29**, beyond the junction with Westbere Road, as Sandown Villas. **No.19** was once home to Arthur Rathbone, a builder very active locally, who also bought and sold property. He had a penchant for fast driving (and possibly alcohol), which led him into trouble. In November 1890, he was ejected from the North London Hotel in Brondesbury for being the worse for drink and accused of the 'furious driving' of a horse and trap on the Kilburn High Road, at speeds of

23 The road to Hampstead, from Mill Lane (Edward Walford, Old and New London, 1878)

61

between 12 and 13 miles an hour. The following February he was fined £1 for failing to get a licence for his trap. In June 1891 Rathbone was summonsed for another speeding incident on the High Road. The magistrate dismissed his defence: that 'his pony had been standing with his head towards home, and he could not restrain it'. He died in 1894 and his widow Emma died in 1919. In 1923, Ernest Owers (p 93) held an auction of her property empire, which consisted of 141 houses and shops in West Hampstead and Kilburn.

No.19 Mill Lane was later home to the Amor family. On 31 December 1935, an Imperial Airways flying-boat plunged into the sea off Alexandria. 26-year-old Flight Engineer William Amor was one of 12 people who died. His father Albert, who had recently retired from the aircraft industry, told the press that his three sons were all flight engineers, who had earned their job at his factory: 'William had four years flying experience and was a powerful swimmer, so that if he had got clear of the fuselage he could certainly have kept up until rescue came.' He was seen in the water after the crash and despite his father's prediction, sadly he drowned. The inquest came to no firm conclusion as to the cause of the crash.

Over on the south side of the road is No.30, **Ellerton**, a 4 and 12-storey block of flats on land bought by Camden in 1965, from British

Rail. Begun as a project for the Camden Community Housing Association by Gerd Kaufmann, it was taken over by the Council when the Association pulled out. By 1874, the Midland Railway Company had built ten cottages, overlooking the railway cutting, to house its employees. Known variously as Railway Cottages or Midland Cottages, the five that faced Mill Lane were later numbered as Nos.22-30. The toilets and sinks were outside. In 1910, a horse pulling a van down Sarre Road took fright and dashed across the Mill Lane junction, crashing into the front of No.26. Mrs Reedman, the wife of a railway signalman, found to her astonishment a horse standing in the middle of her front room, with one of its hooves planted through the bottom of a chair. In 1962 the cottages were lying derelict, a dangerous playground for local children. They were demolished and replaced by Ellerton in 1972-74.

On the corner of Ravenshaw Street, at Nos.40-42 (originally Nos.6-7), is the **Alliance** pub, which opened in 1886. Samuel Shott Death was a Suffolk farmer turned licensed victualler in Kilburn, and then at the Alliance, which he owned. His son Charles became the business partner of Ernest Owers, West Hampstead's leading estate agent. Samuel also speculated in property, being a member of the consortium that purchased the Woodbine

Cottage estate, (p 79). He had left West Hampstead by 1901. The pub is named after Alliance House, the headquarters of the Land Society who owned the plot. During the WWI Zeppelin raids, locals would shelter in the cellars. The pub was known around 2010 as the Pickled Newt, but subsequently reverted to its original name. In response to the brewery's putting the Alliance up for sale in 2016, Camden Council designated the lower floors as an asset of community value (ACV). Residential units have been added and residents are concerned that a 2020 proposal to convert more space into housing may render it unviable as a pub.

Opposite, and on either side of Gondar Gardens, are the two blocks of **Gondar Mansions** and then, rounding the corner of Hillfield Road, **The Mansions** (No.33), also once called Hillfield Mansions. Una Mason (1905-65), poet, playwright and journalist, was born in Jamaica. In 1928, she became Jamaica's first female editor and publisher of her own magazine, *The Cosmopolitan* featuring articles on feminist topics, local social issues and workers' rights. Una first came to England in 1932 and her subsequent work was influenced by the racism and sexism she encountered. She spent two years in Jamaica before returning to the UK in 1938. She worked during WWII for the BBC, where she produced a radio series with George Orwell.

Una was living at **No.14** The Mansions by 1939 in a very large three- bedroom flat, where she hosted many parties, turning out dishes from her rations and food parcels brought by her guests, many of whom were West Indian servicemen.

Across Hillfield Road, **Sington House** (No.33A) was built for the Camden Community Housing Association about 1967.

Until very recently, there were no houses on the north side of Mill Lane east of the Hillfield Road junction as far as today's No.35B. The frontage was formed by the garden walls and fences of houses on the south side of Hillfield Road (p 73). Some of the garages added later have now been replaced by new houses, **Nos.33B-33G**.

A busy shopping parade [24] developed opposite, extending from No.32 (west of the Alliance) all the way to No.114, just past Sumatra Road. Norman Clifford Bowler (1899-1993) ran The Clock House from **No.54** for over 70 years, living over the shop. For some years, Norman's parents John and Emily toured as the humorous Musical Boldens, 'banjo experts and instrumentalists', but Norman didn't follow them onto the stage. After military service in WWI, he worked in the jewellery trade in Manchester, but when told he would have to take a pay cut, he decided to leave. He bought the Mill Lane premises plus tools,

MILL LANE, WEST HAMPSTEAD.

24 Mill Lane, looking east from near the Alliance

for £100. Norman used to sit in the window to work and had many regular customers. The shop was a jumble of spare parts and dismembered clocks, but he knew where everything was. Bowler was disappointed that his sons did not want to learn the business (Norman junior becoming a well-known actor). Local film-maker Conrad Blakemore made a short film about

Clifford Bowler at work in his shop, which was shown on Channel 4 in 1991. A plaque in the doorway commemorates his many years as a Mill Lane tradesman.

Built in 1888 on the north side of Mill Lane, and now **Nos.41-83**, was a parade of shops named The Pavement. Bass player Steve York lived over the shop premises at **No.55** from

1972-77. He was in the band Vinegar Joe and has recorded with numerous musicians including Marianne Faithful, Ringo Starr, and Joan Armatrading. While he was in America he let the organ player Graham Bond use the flat. The Graham Bond Organisation was a group which included Jack Bruce, Ginger Baker, and Dick Heckstall Smith (see below). Guitarist John McLaughlin was also in the band in 1963. Brilliant as he was, Graham had a major drug problem and he may also have been suffering from schizophrenia. Tragically, he committed suicide by jumping in front of a train at Finsbury Park station in 1974.

From the late 1920s, Express Dairies had two shops at **Nos.60&62**. Talking about the 1930s, a local boy who worked there said: 'We had to be in the yard at 4am to load up the hand-cart and do a round. Then we had breakfast before doing another round. Every day at 5.30 I had to take half a pint of milk to a lady at 65 Shoot-up Hill; she thought it would then be absolutely fresh.' No.62 Mill Lane was home to the West Hampstead Community Centre from 1972 to 2008.

Nos.80&82 were the premises of C P Munn, builders, established in the 1920s. Every summer Munn loaned his lorries to transport children on the Emmanuel Sunday School outing.

The Pavement's name, and its construction date, can still be seen on the front of **No.83**

at the corner of Aldred Road. A local resident told of a proposal to use this shop for a public house. Reverend Davys, the Vicar of Emmanuel Church opposite (see below), strongly resisted the suggestion. Local resident actor Joss Ackland (b.1928) who lived in Hillfield Road, wrote: 'I remember the little row of shops around the corner. The sweet shop with liquorice bootlaces - all different colours; Mickey Mouse toffees – twopence a quarter; packets of Imps - tiny sweets made from liquorice with menthol, with the kick of a mule; penny slabs of chocolate - brown and white; packets of sherbet with liquorice straws; bottles of Tizer and fizzy tablets that exploded in the mouth. There was a chemist that smelt of camphor and a grocer where the salty rashers of bacon blended with the sweet icing smell of biscuit animals, and a hardware store with bundles of wood to light fires and the smell of paraffin lamps, and of course, the newsagent and toy shop with copies of the Buzzer, Magnet, Gem, Champion and Film Fun and many others, sometimes with magnificent free gifts.'

The shops in Mill Lane provided many local jobs. A plaque notes that **No.100** was originally Downshire House, built in 1884. At first a draper's, it became a branch of the Co-op. A local talked about working there as a 14-year-old boy in the 1920s: 'First thing in

the morning I had to wash the windows and sweep out the shop. One horrible job was washing the currants which came loose in those days – the washed ones could be sold at a higher price. Nearly everything had to be weighed out, sugar, soapflakes, soda, tea; I did the deliveries on a box tricycle.'

In 1895, Arthur Watson was running his chemist shop from **No.110** on the corner of Sumatra Road, with a branch in Heath Street, Hampstead. Many chemists made their own patent medicines and Arthur was no exception. His neuralgic mixture was advertised as 'a cure as complete as it is rapid' and his 'balsamic cough elixir was a splendid remedy for all afflictions of the chest'. Smart boys dressed in livery delivered prescriptions all over North West London. Watson's premises were lit by electricity, powered by a dynamo at the back of the shop.

Dispensing to the less well-off, three doors away at **No.116**, The Firs, was the West Hampstead Provident Dispensary, opened in 1888 as a branch of the Hampstead Provident Dispensary founded in 1846 and run by a committee of members. In pre-NHS days, families paid a penny a week per child to receive medical treatment.

On either side of the Narcissus Road junction stood Nos.1-6 Cedar Villas, now **Nos.132-142**. Part of the Potter family's ate-1870s development (p 51), these properties represent the earliest speculative housing built at West End, and replaced the village smithy and forge that had been on Mill Lane since the 1820s.

Across Aldred Road, **Nos.1-12 Cholmley Gardens** (p 78) cover the site of the first Emmanuel Church, opened on 1 January 1875 for 120 worshippers. West End was still very rural but growing, and the church was enlarged in 1884. A period of rapid population growth followed and a new church that seated 400 was built on Lyncroft Gardens (p 80). There was a ready purchaser for the old church building: Captain Notman of Cholmley Lodge (p 77), who paid £1,750 in 1900 and added it to his property. The church was demolished the following year.

Once standing in Mill Lane, on the site of **Nos.134-165 Cholmley Gardens**, were Watts Cottages. In 1893 they were condemned. A year later, a newspaper report described them as 'the last lingering remnant of the old rural lane'. Notman acquired and demolished them too, adding their sites to his grounds.

The site for the original **Emmanuel CE Primary School**, at No.101 Mill Lane, was jointly provided in 1845 by Mr Evans the current owner of Cholmley Lodge and Sir Thomas Maryon-Wilson, Lord of the Manor of Hampstead. It meant the children of West End no longer had to climb the hill to Hampstead to get an education. The one-classroom school with places for 143 children, plus a cottage for the school mistress, were designed by Charles Miles, son of John and Anne Miles who lived nearby in West End House (p 97). The cottage became part of the school in 1874, after the headmistress complained that growing pupil numbers meant she was holding classes in her kitchen. A new home was built for her in the playground, followed by more remodelling and extensions in the 1890s. Children [25] were taught and did activities off the small school premises: cookery at Kingsgate Road School in Kilburn, laundry at Beckford School (p 67) and netball on the Heath. Empire Day, 24 May,

Emmanuel School class, 1936

was always celebrated, with dancing on West End Green. The Green was also used at playtimes. At the start of WWII, 98 children were evacuated to Bedford in 1939 but the school was reopened in 1941, when the hall was converted into an air raid shelter and blast walls were built. The need for a bigger school had been apparent for many years and relocation was the obvious answer. But the pupils and staff had to wait many more years before a new building materialised and the school moved diagonally across the road. The old Victorian premises, now renamed the **Alpha building**, have been refurbished to create an open-plan Early Years' Foundation Stage Unit.

The school's new main **Omega building**, designed by architects Hawkins/Brown and opened in November 2012, has a grey-brick façade at Nos.152-158. Built on this frontage in the late 1880s were a row of eight semi-detached houses, four of which still stand, and a single-storey studio, No.158A. By April 1891, artist John Percival Gülich was living at Mill Lane Cottage, No.158, and using 158A as his studio. Gülich's career advanced by leaps and bounds. He was elected to the Royal Institute of Painters in Water Colours in 1897 and one critic predicted, 'Mr Gulich is apparently a man to watch'. But he never fulfilled his potential, as he died suddenly at Mill Lane on 11 December 1898, of typhoid fever. Arthur John Gough lived at No.158 from 1901-15. He too was an artist, best known for his many illustrations that appeared in books and magazines during the early part of the 20th century. From 1903-12, his pictures were regularly exhibited at the annual show of the RA. Sadly, Gough died in the Bedlam mental hospital in 1918.

Countess Mollie Russell was briefly at No.158 in 1921-22. Born about 1857 in Ireland as Marion Cooke, she married her first husband, James Watson, in 1881. He left to join a spiritualist commune in New Mexico in 1884, but Mollie stayed behind with her son in Aberdeen. They divorced in 1888 and the following year she married her second husband George Somerville, an electrical engineer with whom she had two boys. By the late 1890s she was living in London where she met Frank, the 2nd Earl Russell. Frank was also married, so in 1899 they went to Reno Nevada to get his divorce and as soon as it was granted they married. But neither ceremony was recognised in the UK. On their return to England, George Somerville sued Mollie for divorce which was granted in June 1901. Frank was arrested for bigamy. Tried by his peers in the House of Lords, he was convicted in July 1901 and imprisoned for three months. Frank and Mollie then had an English marriage in Holborn in October 1901. She published two novels in 1911 and 1912. In his memories the philosopher, George Santayana, describes Mollie as, 'a fat, florid, coarse Irishwoman, with black curls, friendly manners and emotional opinions; a political agitator and reformer'. Mollie divorced Frank in January 1916 after he agreed to pay her £400 per year. When he died in 1931, Bertrand Russell, his younger brother, became the 3rd Earl and continued to pay Mollie until she died in August 1942.

The studio at No.158A was demolished around 2014 and replaced with a block of flats. An entry beside it leads into the **Mill Lane Open Space**. After the courts of the Priory Lawn Tennis Club (p 46) were sold off, a number of businesses occupied this site. From 1900 it became a bus yard. Its planned construction was described in the local press: 'the General Omnibus Company intend building extensive stabling for 286 horses, an extraordinary proof of the wonderful development of the neighbourhood'. By 1926 the site was home to a number of garages until 1962, when it became a General Post Office depot. Around 1969, No.160 was chosen as the site of the new Emmanuel School. Work was expected to begin in 1974 but the plan was shelved. The cleared site became the present Open Space, with a play area and also housing plant nursery, now the Mill Lane Garden Centre run by Unity Works, a charity supporting people with mental disabilities; and the Sington (children's) Nursery, since demolished to make way for the new primary school and relocated to Dornfell Street).

Cavendish Mansions were built in 1903. A narrow roadway beyond them leads into **West Heath Yard**, which has commercial premises over garages below. West Heath Studios was opened here in the late 1980s by the composer and conductor Robert Howes to record his music for TV. The studio was taken over by the singer and record producer Edwyn Collins in 1995. Edwin's major success was *A Girl like You* which became a worldwide hit in 1994. After he and his wife Grace moved to Kilburn, Edwyn had a stroke in 2005 which left him paralysed. He has since made a remarkable recovery and started to perform again. Edwyn's friend, guitarist Bernard Butler who lived locally in Fawley Road, recorded Duffy's hit album *Rockferry* (2008) at West Heath Studios. Early in 2015, Grammy award winner, producer Jimmy Hogarth took over the lease and moved here from the studio he had built in Kilburn Lane. Jimmy completely renovated the studio in Mill Lane, renaming it Hoxa HQ. As a producer he has worked with artists such as the late Amy Winehouse, James Bay and KT Tunstall.

Off the south side of Mill Lane, about halfway along, is an self-contained enclave of roads comprising Broomsleigh, Dornfell, Glastonbury and Ravenshaw Streets. Around 1882, a nine-acre triangle of land, sandwiched between the steep embankment of the Midland Railway and the Potter family's property, was sold to the Land Building Investment & Cottage Improvement Company Ltd. The awkward shape of the site imposed limitations on the road layout. Nonetheless, four streets of small terrace houses were crammed in, all approved in March 1881. The land was divided into 250 plots and offered for sale in November, with the first houses listed in the rate books of 1884/85. In the years preceding WWI, and for some time after, many properties housed large families. The 1911 census shows houses shared between as many as four households, some of them taking in lodgers. Twelve or more occupants per house was not uncommon. One family with nine children put boys at the bottom and girls at the top of a single bed. Washing was done in a tin bath in front of the kitchen range and wives took it in turn to use the copper in a downstairs scullery to wash clothes.

One attraction for families to rent in these streets was their proximity to the large Broomsleigh Street Board School, opened in 1886. Actually with a **DORNFELL STREET**

address, it was renamed Beckford School in 1929 after the Beckford family (see p 35). In 1884, the London School Board compulsorily purchased 38 of the building plots. They paid £2,880 and accepted the quote of £10,550 from the Chelsea-based Charles Wall to construct the school. The school opened with a roll of 793 children, boys and girls entering through different gates and playing in segregated playgrounds. The first boys' headmaster was James Walker, appointed in July 1886 at a salary of £200. His wife Louisa was the influential and well-respected headmistress of Fleet Road Infant School in Hampstead. Broomsleigh Street did not provide free education until 1891. Prior to this the cost was 3d per pupil, reduced to 2d for subsequent children from the same family. It was 2d to attend the Infants.

In 1895, Mr Walker was prosecuted by the parents of 12-year-old Willie Tidd, who lived at No.11 Ravenshaw Street. Late for school one day, Willie was told to 'go out' by Walker, so he went home. Next day, Walker punished him for leaving school premises with four strokes of the cane on his back and legs. When Tidd tried to escape, he was given another two strokes and a third when he was back in his classroom. The magistrate agreed that the boy had wilfully misconstrued what his teacher had meant by 'go out'. He concluded three floggings was excessive but also accepted Walker had acted out of character, and so reluctantly fined him 10s with 23s costs. Local sympathy was generally with Walker and he remained in post. In 1915 there were 1,264 children attending the school by which date Walker's salary had doubled. As well as the usual subjects, girls were trained in practical skills such as knitting, cookery and laundry work. Boys walked to and from the Heath Extension to play football and cricket. The school closed during WWII and became a rest centre for bomb victims.

In 1969 Beryl Gilroy was appointed as the second black head teacher in London. She had arrived from Guyana in 1951. She was also a novelist and writer of children's books, and over a 30-year period had more than twenty books published. Her autobiography *Black Teacher* (1976) gives an account of the reality of teaching predominantly white working-class pupils. With her marriage to Patrick Gilroy, a white Englishman in 1959, she encountered considerable racial prejudice. She left the school in 1982 and died in 2001.

In 2020 parents, pupils and staff were asked to re-name the school following the Black Lives Matter protests. The wealthy Beckford family had obtained their income from sugar plantations and thousands of slaves in Jamacia (p 35). After a vote it was decided

on 1 December to re-name the school West Hampstead Primary School, rather than Broomsleigh Street School, or Gilroy Primary School. The plan is to change the name in September 2021.

Famous people who attended the school include the actors Joss Ackland and Emma Thompson, and Bow Wow Wow's singer, Annabella Lwin.

Emmanuel Church bought Nos.8&10 Broomsleigh Street and used their sites for a Mission Hall on the corner with Dornfell Street. Officially opened in October 1905, as well as holding evangelistic services for those who didn't attend the main church, there were many activities and meetings including a Men's Institute, the Band of Hope (which promoted teetotalism), lantern slide lectures, billiards and sewing classes. In the 1920s and '30s, regular attendance at the Sunday School meant a child would qualify for the annual outing, a high spot of the summer. Known as the **Broomsleigh Hall** and numbered No.17 Dornfell Street, the building is now used by the West Hampstead Community Centre with the relocated Sington nursery underneath.

On its south side Beckford School is bordered by **GLASTONBURY STREET**, where all the houses were built by Edward Garrett. He was also the main builder in **RAVENSHAW STREET**. In November 1898, a local Police

Inspector described Ravenshaw as 'almost the poorest street in the division'. David Dakers lived at **No.12** and **No.31**, two of the nine houses in the road built by him. He later built houses in Sumatra Road and Sandwell Crescent. **No.15** carries a heart-shaped plaque to Elizabeth, wife of tailor Karl Hagedorn, who the family described as an exceptional mother But the now blurry dedication, which says 'lived here 1892-1945' is misleading, as the couple occupied at least three houses in the street: No.108 (1891); No.15 (by 1901) and No.24 (1911), returning to No.15 by 1926.

During a severe storm in the late afternoon of 8 July 1891, **No.25** (then named Oakley Villa) was struck by lightning. The newspaper report says: 'A chimney stack at the back of the house surmounted by four pots, was struck with the electric current so severely that the stack was completely cut in half, leaving one part standing. One side of the room below was shattered, and the house was filled with dense smoke. There was a loud explosion and several people declared they saw a ball of fire passing through the air just before the house was struck.'

Professional cricketer James Burns who worked at Lord's Cricket Ground was living at **No.49** in 1911.

In his long career as a carpenter, William Winyard worked on many properties in West

End, including carrying out substantial repairs and alterations to Cholmley Lodge (p 77). In 1861 he and wife Ellen were sharing a cottage on West End Lane near the Old Black Lion. They stayed there for over 30 years before moving to **No.77** Ravenshaw Street. By the time he died in 1912, William was one of very few people who had known the neighbourhood when it was a country village.

In 1901, 34-year-old James Pimm, an Army deserter since 1888, was living at **No.89** when his identity was proved in court and he was handed over to his old company, the Royal Artillery.

At night during WWII, residents remembered hearing the 'pom pom' noise made by an anti-aircraft gun that ran up and down the railway lines in the cutting below their gardens.

In **BROOMSLEIGH STREET** at least 19 of the houses were built by Arthur Rathbone, who lived on Mill Lane (p 61).

When WWI broke out, 31-year-old Private Charles Miles and his wife were living at **No.43**. His father Nelson had moved to West End in the 1870s, perhaps to work at Potter's foundry while his wife ran a general shop, but he soon became a greengrocer and fruiterer. Charles had enlisted in Middlesex Regiment by 1901 but returned to civvy street and re-enlisted when WWI broke out. He was an early casualty of the war, dying of his wounds in a London hospital on 15 December 1914. Charles was buried at Hampstead Cemetery with full military honours. The Broomsleigh Street School Cadet Corps formed a guard of honour as the coffin, draped with a Union Jack, was drawn up the road on a gun carriage.

Before the Mission Hall was built, **No.38** at the forked junction with Ravenshaw Street, served as the Mission House for Emmanuel Church.

At **No.42**, until her death in 1907, was a small shop where Mrs Lambert sold sweets from her front room. A local remembered, 'You could have a ha'penny dip, which meant rummaging about in some sawdust for a piece of rock'.

Edward Wrangles, a coalman, was living opposite at **No.71** in 1937, when it was reported he had raised the magnificent sum of £1,677 over 10 years, all in copper coins, for the funds of Manor House Hospital, opposite Golders Hill Park.

At the bottom of the street, five properties, Nos.89-97, have been demolished to be replaced by **No.97**, a small block of local authority flats.

Broomsleigh Street may be a dead end for cars, but not pedestrians. For the convenience of the residents, the Land Company rented land from the Midland Railway, to create the path that still leads southeast to West End Lane. The railway company refused to allow it to become a public footpath, arguing they might need the land in future. The company closed the path every Good Friday to assert its ownership and put up notices saying 'for use by passengers only' – which were ignored. It was called the **Black Path** by locals. No-one seems to know the origin of the name: perhaps it referred to its rather gloomy nature, or the tarmacked surface, or even a desire on the part of some West Enders to upset the more nervous of their neighbours. The footway was eventually taken over by the local authority.

Almost opposite Ravenshaw Street, off the north side of Mill Lane is **GONDAR GARDENS**. Two arms of the L-shaped road wrap round a disused reservoir. In 1855, the Grand Junction Waterworks Company compulsorily acquired 22 acres of pasture land bordering on the Lane. The purchase was made to anticipate future demand, as water companies had problems supplying the top floors of houses without recourse to a high-level reservoir such as this. The *Shoot Up Hill* (or *Kilburn) Reservoir* was completed by April 1874 with a capacity of six million gallons. In 1894 it was sold to the West Middlesex Waterworks Company. Their supply area covered Hampstead parish west of Haverstock Hill, including the developing area around the Reservoir. Ownership of the reservoir subsequently passed to the Metropolitan Water Board and later Thames Water.

There is very little to be seen above ground, other than a raised, turfed area over the reservoir itself. Internally the construction used brick arches to create a huge vaulted tank. The grassed area above the reservoir provided recreational space. From 1889-90, the aptly named, if short-lived, Acquarius Tennis Club was there, and by 1913 it was the Gondar Gardens Tennis Club; although this flourished, its lease was not renewed after the end of WWII. During the 1970s a small plot was used as a children's playground, but Camden Council's proposals for sports facilities and use as an open space were never implemented. The completion in 2002 of a new ring main for London led to the reservoir being decommissioned and emptied. The site was sold and the decision taken to use it for housing, a move strongly opposed by local residents. In 2015, permission was finally granted for a scheme that involved housing along the Gondar Gardens frontage and demolishing most of the reservoir roof and internal structure, with landscaping to retain most of it as open space. Then, in early 2016 the property was sold on. In 2018, Camden

refused an application to build Persephone Gardens, a complex of retirement flats and a nursing home. The issue remained that the property is a Site of Nature Conservation Importance, in view of its rare slow-worm population. This protection covers all of the land, except for a small strip on the street frontage. In June 2019 the developers lost their appeal against Camden's decision.

As the Shoot Up Hill reservoir only occupied three of the 22 acres acquired by the water company, it disposed of the surplus land. In 1890, William Elsdon bought the land between the reservoir and Hampstead Cemetery. The next year he got permission to build Gondar Gardens, a road partly replacing an existing track from Mill Lane to the reservoir. Elsdon was also the developer behind the 'Greek roads', which probably explains why Gondar Gardens runs east to meet Agamemnon Road (p 72). House building began at that junction in 1893 but progress was slow; by mid-1894, it was described as 'only slightly developed'. Gondar Gardens was eventually lined by a mix of tall terrace houses and 13 blocks of mansion flats. In 1907, a request to change the road name from Gondar to Apollo was refused.

Sloping up from Mill Lane, the west side of Gondar Gardens formed the boundary of back gardens of properties in Sarre Road (p 24).

Near the south end, some of their garages and a few other small buildings have recently been rebuilt to provide a short run of new houses. Farther north there is a pedestrian cut-through to Sarre Road.

One of Gondar Gardens' mansion blocks, **South Mansions**, was erected south of the reservoir. The remaining dozen are clustered around the corner where the road makes a right-angled turn – **Lawn**, **Snowdon**, **Kenmare**, **Clyde**, **Downe**, **Tudor**, **Spring**, **Oliver**, **Eden**, **Pine**, **St Elmo** and **Chase Mansions**.

Dick Heckstall-Smith was an outstanding tenor sax player with Blues Incorporated, John Mayall, the Graham Bond Organization (p 64), John Hiseman's Colosseum and Big Chief. He lived in Flat 5, **Eden Mansions** from 1972 and continued playing, despite ill health, until his death in December 2004.

In 1914, the talented ballerina Helen May who was a pupil of Pavlova, offered training to 'a few gifted girls' at her home in Flat 5, **Snowdon Mansions**. Ken Russell who worked as a photographer before he became a film director, included Helen May in his 1950s series of great British eccentrics. He shows Helen then in her Notting Hill flat surrounded by old posters advertising her performances. A year later she featured in his hip bath series 'dressed to the nines and waving a watering ver his favourite prop. The marriage of ar-old John Ireland to Dorothy Phillips place on 17 December 1926, and caused ter in the musical world'. At the time she ving with the mother of a fellow pupil in , Snowdon Mansions. Only a few friends aware of the couple's intentions. They net at a musical party; he was an lished composer and she was a talented ar-old music student. Dorothy's parents their consent to the match but did not d the ceremony. But it didn't last; they divorced in 1928.

st of the mansion blocks, gabled 3-storey rick houses line the northern arm of lar Gardens. Internationally renowned or Doris Lessing CH OMG (1919-2013) at **No.24** from around 1980, moving from Kingscroft Road (p 15). Born in Iran oris May Tayler, her parents moved to abwe when she was five and she spent hildhood on a remote farm. Her first and was civil servant Frank Wisdom; they two children but their marriage ended in . She became involved with the Commu- Party and her second husband was fellow ber Gottfried Lessing. They parted in , when Doris [26] came to London with son and the manuscript of *The Grass is ing* (1950) in her suitcase. Her first lished novel, it describes the relationship

of a white African farmer's wife and her black servant. It later emerged Doris was under surveillance by MI5 for many years. The file said: 'Her communist sympathies have been fanned almost to the point of fanaticism, owing to her upbringing in Rhodesia which has brought out in her a deep hatred of the colour bar'. She left the party, outraged by the Soviet invasion of Hungary. Doris Lessing wrote fiction and non-fiction, several volumes of memoirs, plays and poems. When she was awarded the Nobel Prize for literature in 2007, she told reporters, 'I've won all the prizes in Europe, every bloody one. I'm delighted to win them all, the whole lot. It's a royal flush'. Her final book *Alfred and Emily* was published a year later. She died at her West Hampstead home, aged 94.

Living in 1911 with his wife and family at **No.50**, and staying there until 1927, was organ builder Frederick Rothwell. With a factory in Willesden, he built or rebuilt all the organs connected with his good friend Henry Walford Davies (p 109).

During the 1970s and '80s, the talented Casely-Hayford family were at **No.51**. Joe was a fashion designer, Gus is a cultural historian, Peter is a company director of TwentyTwenty TV, and sister Margaret is Chair of Action Aid. Joe Casely-Hayford began selling his clothes in a shop in Mill Lane where his customers included locals Doris Lessing, Sadie Frost and

Billy Idol. His clothing became fashionable with musicians and film stars and he was awarded the OBE in 2006. Joe died in January 2019.

In April 1927, the press reported a disturbing incident in this quiet road. Ten-year-old Beryl de Meza, whose family lived at **No.58**, was shot in the back while playing in the street with friends. The police believed

26 Doris Lessing CH OMG

the heavy-calibre bullet was fired from a revolver. It entered Beryl's right side, pierced her lungs and lodged behind her heart. The children said they had seen a man on the opposite side of the road but hadn't heard the shot. When Beryl fell to the ground with blood streaming from her wound, they managed to get her indoors, before summoning help. She was rushed to New End Hospital, Hampstead. Beryl's survival was described as something of a miracle. Fortunately, the wound wasn't fatal and records show she was married in 1933. The man who fired at her was never found.

The parents of actress Sadie Frost (p 60) moved from Manchester to Primrose Hill, where Sadie grew up during the 1960s. She then lived with her mother in a first-floor flat in Gondar Gardens. In her autobiography Sadie says, 'It was a light, sunny flat arranged over two floors and Mum worked hard to make it a home. We had new furniture, including a beige corner sofa that was her pride and joy.'

Gondar Gardens runs east to meet Agamemnon Road. In March 1866, William Elsdon (see above) had applied to the Vestry to form four streets on the Fortune Green Estate: Agamemnon, Achilles, Ulysses and Ajax Roads. These are the so-called 'Greek roads' named after people in the Greek myths (not as some believed, Royal Navy battleships). The Vestry tried but failed to get the names changed, arguing that 'the classical names selected are hardly suitable for the rural district of Hampstead'. Building began in 1887. A great many builders were involved, often working in more than one road. Difficulties arose owing to the proximity of Fortune Green (p 73): allegations were made that Elsdon's roads had illegally encroached on the open space. Many of those who joined the Fortune Green Protection Society came from the 'Greek roads'.

AGAMEMNON ROAD has two arms, running north out of Hillfield Road (p 73) before turning east towards Fortune Green. From a map it seems that one section was initially planned to be called Penelope Road, but the name was not used.

Near the south end today is a row of three modern houses, **Nos.1-5 Norman Terrace**, built in the 1970s in the back gardens of three properties in Hillfield Road (p 73). The actor Burt Kwouk OBE [27], was perhaps best known for his appearances as Inspector Clouseau's servant Cato in the Pink Panther films starring Peter Sellers, and latterly as electrician Entwistle in the BBC's *Last of the Summer Wine*. He lived at **No.6** Agamemnon Road from 1990 until his death in 2016, and a Heritage Foundation blue plaque in his memory was unveiled here in February 2017.

Agamemnon Road was the site of one of the most serious incidents during WWII. On 19 February 1944 (the same night that West End Lane was hit), eight bombs fell here within 100 yards of each other. Only three exploded but 17 people who lived at Nos.21-29 lost their lives. In 1950 work began to build a terrace of eight 3-storey houses with gardens. They were

27 Burt Kwouk (OBE) with kind permission of Caroline Kwouk

ompleted the following year, at an estimated ost of £20,000. The Council noted that most amilies would prefer to live in a house, but to rovide the greatest number of homes, it was usually necessary to build flats. Round the orner, **Nos.49&51** were also rebuilt following wartime bomb damage.

Blacksmith and farrier Joseph Compodonico of **No.53** was on the Committee of West Hampstead Football Club. In 1902 problems arose when Shepherd's Bush FC complained about West Hampstead FC. This was a time when there was considerable disagreement about amateurs and professionals; those gentlemen with sufficient income to play as amateurs and the working-class players who wanted to be paid. The FA held a commission of inquiry in January 1903 which concluded (among other things) that along with fellow committee members, Compodonico should be suspended for a season for bringing in four 'ringers' who were all professional players from Scotland.

Long-serving local councillor, Flick Rea has lived in Agamemnon Road for many years. The actor/writer Edward Petherbridge and his actress wife Emily Richard occupied **No.45** until recently.

In **AJAX ROAD**, which runs along the west side of Fortune Green, there is only one numbered house, **No.3**.

Stuart Hall lived in **ULYSSES ROAD** until his death in February 2014. Born in Kingston Jamaica, his father was the chief accountant of United Fruit. Stuart received a traditional style English education at Jamaica College. In 1951, with a Rhodes scholarship, he studied English at Merton College. Stuart abandoned his PhD on Henry James and came to London, where he worked as a supply teacher in Brixton by day and the editor of the *New Left Review* by night in Soho. Stuart went to Birmingham University as a lecturer in the new field of cultural studies. From 1979-98 he was Professor of Sociology at the Open University. He coined the term Thatcherism in a visionary article in *Marxism Today*. A film about him called *The Stuart Hall Project* was made in 2013. On *Desert Island Discs* he talked about his lifelong passion for the music of Miles Davis. Illness slowed him down, but his house in West Hampstead continued to welcome a constant stream of visitors and friends.

In **ACHILLES ROAD**, at **No.8**, lived Charles Munich, the secretary, treasurer and founder of the Hampstead Antiquarian & Historical Society. He might have been amused to find that in later years locals called the street 'Ackles Road'.

In June 1944 a Swissair Corvair airliner went down in the sea off Folkestone when the fuel ran out. The pilot showed great skill in landing on the water, but passengers and crew had to swim for their lives. Ethel Bexley, who lived at **No.40**, was one of three people who drowned, her body eventually washed up in the Netherlands. At the time the airline carried no lifesaving equipment nor was there any emergency drill for the crew. Swissair told the inquest that life jackets were now carried on all cross Channel flights.

George Layton, actor, director, author and screenwriter lived at **No.51** from 1978 to 1980. In the 1970s he regularly appeared in the 'Doctor' series. He played Bombardier Solly Solomons in the BBC series *It Ain't Half Hot, Mum* and has worked in many other TV series and stage roles. He appeared in *EastEnders* and co-wrote TV sitcoms with Jonathan Lynn.

HILLFIELD ROAD runs mostly from west to east, with a short arm at right angles near its western end, linking it with Mill Lane. The Real Property Company purchased two fields on the north side of the Lane in 1865, but when the estate was sold on three years later to the Land Company of London, no building had taken place. The new owners obtained permission for Hillfield Road and Aldred Street (now Road, p 76) in 1868. They built sewers almost immediately and divided the land into 61 building plots, but take-up was slow. The 1881 census shows only three houses completed in Hillfield Road with another five building, and none in Aldred Street. The estate also included a valuable frontage to Mill Lane.

Hillfield Road is unusual in retaining many glass fanlights over front doors which show the original gold-painted house names. The western end originally stopped dead before a grassy slope that later turned into Gondar Gardens, and when that was developed the great difference in levels between the two roads meant that the only possible link was a flight of steps for pedestrians.

Praise Cottage occupied the westernmost plot on Hillfield Road from around 1882. This was the second of two Mount Hermon Girls' Orphan Homes offering shelter for up to 112 children (the first being in Kilburn). The founder Miss Mary Ann Cole moved to West End from her original Kilburn base. She died in 1887 at the comparatively early age of 49, and like so many other locals she is buried in Hampstead Cemetery. The orphanage survived her death and 19 orphan boarders were recorded by the 1891 census under the watchful eye of Miss Mace, the matron. In 1895 the cottage was up for sale. The plot was used to build **Nos.2&2A** Hillfield Road and also The Mansions fronting Mill Lane (p 61). In the 1970s **No.8** Hillfield Road was home to Mike Brearley, the England cricket captain.

The steeply sloping nature of the natural terrain is reflected in the fact that the front doors of the odd-numbered houses opposite are approached by flights of more than twenty steps. One such house is **No.11**. Arthur and Catherine Waugh moved here from rooms over a dairy in Finchley Road. They were described as: 'a quiet, unpretentious couple, well-to-do but not wealthy. Arthur earned about £600 a year but had no urgent ambition to leave this unfashionable address; it suited their needs and income'. Arthur was the managing director of the publishers Chapman & Hall. Alex Waugh was born at No.11 in July 1898 and his brother Evelyn [28] five years later. Both sons became famous novelists. Evelyn's works include *Decline and Fall* (1928), *A Handful of Dust* (1934), *Brideshead Revisited* (1945) and the Second World War trilogy, *Sword of Honour* (1952–61). When Alec's novel, *The Loom of Youth*, was published in 1917 it caused a sensation for its honest depictions of love among schoolboys. The Waugh family moved to North End Road in 1907.

The founders of the very successful band Hot Chocolate both lived on the south side of Hillfield Road. Tony Wilson was at **No.64** and Errol Brown was at **No.84**. Errol was born in Jamaica and came to England when he was aged 11. From south London the family moved to Hillfield Road. Errol said: 'In 1968, through mutual friends, I met Tony Wilson. Tony and I formed Hot Chocolate'. In 1970 the debut single of the band, *Love is Life*, reaches number 6 in the UK charts. A string of hits followed including, *It Started with a Kiss* and

28 Evelyn Waugh

Everyone's a Winner. In 1981 they performed at Prince Charles and Princess Diana's wedding reception. In 1997 their previous 1975 hit, *You Sexy Thing*, was revived in the film *The Full Monty*. Errol was awarded the MBE in 2003 and died at his home in the Bahamas in May 2015.

There were many private schools in West Hampstead and Kilburn, generally occupying a single house and offering varying standards of education. By 1891 the recently widowed Sarah Spashett had opened her Ladies school at **No.80**. She taught music and her two daughters Mary and Ada were probably the only other members of staff. After Sarah's death in 1924 her daughters carried on the school, which was still functioning in 1939. They are buried in Hampstead Cemetery: Mary died in 1952, Ada in 1955.

Sidney Edmond Jocelyn Ackland, CBE, better known as the actor Joss Ackland (b.1928) was three years old when his family moved into the basement flat at **No.86**. He remembered taking the bus to a cinema near Golders Green for the Saturday morning Mickey Mouse club and the theatre: 'My first theatre visits were to the Golders Green Hippodrome. Open-mouthed I stared as a new world opened up before me. I discovered another great excitement – the public library in Westbere Road [p 25]. Hour after hour I would spend there, trying to decide which two books to take home.' In 1938 the family moved briefly to Fordwych Road (p 15), then to Stoke Newington, to be near his new school. Joss studied drama at the Central School of Speech & Drama and married the actress Rosemary Kirkcaldy. He spent a few years in Africa, where in addition to acting roles he also managed a tea plantation. The couple returned to the UK in 1957 and Joss's career began to take off. He has appeared in hundreds of productions on stage, TV and cinema screen. He was with Alec Guinness in the TV serial *Tinker Tailor Soldier Spy* and he portrayed C S Lewis in *Shadowlands*. Some of the films he has appeared in are *White Mischief* and *The Hunt for Red October*.

In 1891, Robert Washington Hart and his family were at **No.98**. He and his sons built some of the best houses in the district, notably on the nearby Burgess estate and in Parsifal Road. They also built extensively on the Kidderpore estate across the Finchley Road and moved on to streets off Hampstead Lane, Highgate.

Aside from nine houses (**Nos.61-77**) close to the Agamemnon Road corner, all the plots on the north side of Hillfield Road from there as far as Fortune Green Road were purchased by the **Field Lane Refuge**, as the site for a large **Industrial School**. It moved here from smaller premises in Holborn. Opened in October 1878, it could accommodate 100 boys, the number later rising to 140. Some were destitute; others were orphans, while young offenders were also sent to establishments like these, to be detained until they were 16. Of the 105 boys in 1881, the census shows around a dozen were as young as eight or nine. The School did not get off to a good start when an inspection just two months after it opened found the place in a mess. The boys looked dirty and neglected, several had absconded and worst of all, some punishments had been so severe that the Management Committee had intervened. The superintendent Mr Owen was replaced by George Peall. A repeat visit two months after he took over found the school had been transformed. All was neat, clean and in order.

The aim was to rehabilitate the boys by combining academic and practical skills, the latter including gardening, baking, tailoring and shoemaking to craftsman level. This meant a job could be found for a boy when he left, and he was provided with a good suit of clothes. Many local residents had their firewood supplied, bread baked or laundry done and delivered by the boys. The school band regularly played on Fortune Green in the summer months and would give annual concerts. Peregrine Platt (p 50), the Secretary of the Field Lane Refuges, was churchwarden of Emmanuel Church and the two institutions established strong links. The boys attended Sunday morning services and the school grounds were made available to the Church for outdoor events.

The boys don't seem to have caused any problems for their neighbours, but one resident said the locals usually referred to the Hillfield Road establishment as 'the bad boys' school. In 1882, 12-year-old Henry White was charged with setting fire to the school. He had been sent there in 1880 but had already absconded three times. Early one April morning Henry admitted to setting fire to clothes and a sheet in a lavatory, 'because the master gave us a slice of dry bread on Sunday night'. This was a punishment for refusing to sing at Sunday school. At first the magistrates were inclined to recommend a birching, but they changed their minds when it was pointed out the fire could have killed many people. Henry was sent for trial at the Middlesex Sessions and sentenced to three weeks imprisonment and then five years in a reformatory.

The Field Lane Industrial School sold its playground in 1906 and the site was used for Berridge House, (p 82). Admissions dropped after the introduction of the probation service and approved schools. By 1930, there were only 53 boys at Hillfield Road and the school shut the following year. The building was taken over by Berridge House as an accommodation block. It survived until 1988, latterly providing student housing for Westfield College. It was hoped the site would be sold to a Housing Association while other suggestions included a car park, school or nature reserve. In the event it was replaced post-1993 by **BERRIDGE MEWS**, a private development of mews-style houses.

ALDRED ROAD runs down from Hillfield Road to Mill Lane. The name was officially changed from Aldred Street in 1889, as the house deeds had all been issued in that name. Today, Cholmley Gardens blocks line the east side of the road. Today, the mansion flats part of Cholmley Gardens, line the east side of the road.

Modifications to the original plan for Aldred Road resulted in an awkward parcel of land hemmed in by houses and shops, accessed by a narrow road alongside **No.1**. In 1889 the residents were alarmed by unfounded rumours that a sugar boiling works was planned for the site, also one of several later considered but dismissed as unsuitable for West Hampstead's first library. From the mid-1890s it became plant nursery, let for a while to William Grove, a greengrocer on Mill Lane. Permission for 19 lock-up garages was granted in 1924 and by 1939 the premises had expanded to offer garage accommodation for 80 cars. In the 1980s, it became **ORESTES MEWS**, a development of town houses. It was briefly renamed Melaris Mews but has since reverted to the original name.

Area 6

Fortune Green Road and environs

Up and east of Fortune Green Road via Hampstead Cemetery, north to the borough boundary in Burgess Hill

Originally, the road north from the village of West End was a muddy track called Fortune Green Lane. Until Hampstead Cemetery opened in 1876, the only buildings on the Lane itself were a group of nine small isolated cottages near Fortune Green.

Built around 1813 off the west side of the Lane, north of its junction with Mill Lane and set in extensive grounds, was *Cholmley Lodge* [29]. Dr Herbert Evans rented the Lodge in 1844 and later purchased the property, but only lived in West End for a few months. He had been family physician to John Constable and cared for his wife Maria, who died of tuberculosis in 1828, at the family home in Well Walk, Hampstead. Constable painted the doctor's portrait the following year. Barrister Edward Thornton lived at Cholmley Lodge from about 1847 to 1852. He did a great deal to help the West End villagers, who presented him with a written testimonial and silver inkstand as an expression of their gratitude. He must have been a remarkable

man, given the sacrifices involved in raising the money for such an expensive gift.

One of the last owners of Cholmley Lodge, in 1874, was Scottish-born Captain Henry Wilkes Notman, under whom the estate took its final shape. He was a wealthy businessman and the managing director of several railway companies including the South Indian Railway Co. Notman supported the West Enders in their fight to protect Fortune Green from the developers and contributed £100 to the

fighting fund to save West End Green. He also gave £350 towards building the new Emmanuel Church in Lyncroft Gardens. For several years before his death at the Lodge in April 1914, Notman was rarely at home, as he travelled extensively on the Continent. In his will, the property and £106,451 (today worth about £9M) were left to his nephew, Arthur Clyne, a well-known Aberdeen architect. Arthur and his wife Isabel moved into the Lodge in 1914 and left for Surrey in 1919.

29 Cholmley Lodge, from the garden

The estate was then put up for sale, but not before some residents tried to buy it as a park for the neighbourhood, suggesting it would be a fitting memorial to those who had died in the Great War. Hampstead Council declined to act and the sale of the 6 acres and the old house was reported as realising £18,000. Further efforts were made to save the property, until December 1922, when Hampstead Council approved Martin William Harvey's first application to build flats on the site of the Lodge and grounds.

The builders were Domiciles Ltd and the twenty-two **CHOLMLEY GARDENS** blocks were completed in 1928, with frontages to Fortune Green, Hillfield and Aldred Roads, and Mill Lane. They surround a large communal garden area with tennis courts and garages. Originally, a putting green was also provided.

In 1926 Alan Keith changed his name from Alexander Kossoff; he was the uncle of Paul Kossoff, the guitarist with the band Free. Alan won a scholarship to RADA and worked as an actor on the West End and Broadway stage. By 1935 he was an established voice on BBC radio and he also appeared in several British films, playing Americans because of his facility for American accents. In the early 1950s he presented music programmes for the BBC and in 1959 he devised *Your Hundred Best Tunes*, which he originally chose himself but were later voted for by the listeners. Alan ran the programme for an astonishing 44 years and in March 2003, aged 94, he announced his retirement. He fell ill soon after and the final programme was broadcast twelve days after his death.

The family had lived in **No.81** Cholmley Gardens since 1951 to Alan's death in 2003.

Alan's daughter Linda had a far from conventional life. In 1964, aged 17, she became a model and was photographed by David Bailey on numerous fashion shoots. Her best friend was Sheila Klein, who was dating and later married Andrew Loog Oldham, the manager of the Rolling Stones. Linda was encouraged by Sheila to talk to the shy Keith Richards at a party and he fell in love with her. Linda travelled with the Stones on their American tours and met and befriended Jimi Hendrix in May 1966 in New York. She persuaded Chas Chandler to become his manager and bring him to England. The relationship between Linda and Keith Richards ended in the spring of 1966. The following January he and Brian Jones wrote the song *Ruby Tuesday* about Linda. She now lives in New Orleans with her husband, record producer, John Porter.

John Hillaby, reporter, naturalist and writer (d.1966) lived at **No.85** for over forty years. In the 1950s John had worked for the *New York Times* and the *New Scientist*. He was a passionate and eloquent pedestrian who once estimated that he had walked the equivalent of five times round the Equator. He loved Hampstead Heath where he walked every day, and wrote several books describing his walking tours of England and Europe, Africa and the UK. He was a frequent broadcaster on radio and TV. He lived in York for the last four years of his life and suffered from osteoarthritis of the spine which rendered him practically immobile.

Naum Gabo, the world-renowned sculptor and pioneer of kinetic art, was at **No.101** Cholmley Gardens from 1937 until the outbreak of WWII, when he moved to Cornwall to be with Ben Nicholson and Barbara Hepworth. His wife Miriam said that his first sculpture, *Construction in Space: Crystal* was made at No.101 in 1937. Born in Russia, Gabo had studied in Munich and Paris, and in 1928 he had taught at the Bauhaus. He emigrated to America in 1946, where he died in Connecticut in 1977.

When the first West Hampstead Library on the corner of Westbere and Sarre Roads was bombed (p 24), the Council took out a five-year lease for £250 pa on **No.119** Cholmley Gardens facing West End Green. The library moved to its temporary home on 19 November 1945 and relocated to the Dennington Park Road building (p 48) in 1954. No.119 is now called The Old Library and occupied by DMFK architects.

Although old West End village was surrounded by meadow and pasture land, there was only one farmhouse, close to the Green. West End Farm and its yard stood behind the site of the mansion blocks on the southeast corner of Fortune Green Road and Lyncroft Gardens. In December 1882 the tenant farmer, John Lock, was killed in tragic circumstances. The newspaper report says; 'He set off down West End Lane to get supplies one morning but the fog was so thick that he decided to turn back. Unfortunately, he missed the road and instead turned into the railway yard where his cart was destroyed by a train on the Hampstead Junction line'.

Built on the edge of the farmyard around 1810 was **Woodbine Cottage**. It is surprising to find that, in the 1850s, rural West End was the setting for one of the first industrial premises established anywhere in Hampstead parish. William Thomas Eley and his widowed mother Susannah moved from Soho into Woodbine Cottage and the 1853 rate book noted a new factory nearby, for the manufacture of Eley's percussive caps. Charles and William Eley had started the business, and after William's death in 1841 – 'blown to atoms' in a mercury fulminate explosion at his Bond Street factory – it passed into the hands of his three sons, William Thomas, Charles and Henry. Almost certainly, the brothers had

chosen West End because of its remoteness. Then in September 1854, the press noted that the widow of a percussion cap maker at West End had died of cholera. As there were no other deaths in the village, why was Susannah singled out? At the time, there was a serious outbreak of cholera around Broad Street in Soho. Before moving to West End, Susannah had lived close to the pump and liked the taste of the water, so had a bottle delivered daily to her new home. Unfortunately, the supply was contaminated. Her death, and that of a niece who also drank some of the water, helped Dr John Snow prove that cholera was a water-borne disease.

For a short time in the late 1870s, Captain Du Barry (real name Christian Klug) rented the old Eley factory in West End to manufacture his Revelenta Arabia Food. Widely advertised and sold as 'a light delicious breakfast food', the secret recipe was made from ground lentils and claimed to permanently cure indigestion, constipation, morning sickness, nervousness, headaches, asthma and depression, among many other complaints. It gained unwanted notoriety in 1889, at the trial of Florence Maybrick for the murder of her husband James. He felt unwell after eating a meal Florence prepared, using Revelenta Arabia. The remains were analysed and found to contain arsenic, which Florence had extracted from fly paper.

She was found guilty, but the Home Secretary considered there was insufficient evidence to prove murder, and instead of being hanged she spent 15 years in gaol.

By 1884, Woodbine Cottage, its grounds and the old farm buildings had been bought by the very wealthy Augustus Frederick Thistlethwayte. In 1852 he had married Laura Bell, who was exceptionally beautiful, and had been one of the most famous courtesans of the Victorian period. Born in Dublin in 1831, she began work as a shop assistant when she was 14. But Laura soon found more lucrative employment, becoming notorious for her many lovers. These included Dr William Wilde, a well-known Dublin dental surgeon and the father of Oscar and Willie Wilde. In May 1850, after moving to London, Laura met Jung Bahadur, the prime minister of Nepal, and accompanied him on a trip to Paris. During their short affair Laura is said to have been given presents worth £250,000, or an astonishing £27M today. After their marriage, Augustus Thistlethwayte and Laura lived in Grosvenor Square, where they entertained lavishly. In 1856 Laura announced her religious conversion. She began preaching and her talks, at places such as the Regent Street Polytechnic, attracted large crowds. In December 1864 she met the Prime Minister William Gladstone. Their 30-year friendship was very close; Gladstone confided in her and visited her at West End, but there is no evidence of a physical affair. Laura's marriage was not a happy one. Her extravagant spending put her massively in debt and forced Augustus to refuse, legally, to settle any more of her bills. On 7 August 1887 he was found dead in bed at Grosvenor Square from a pistol shot. Strangely, he had kept a pistol on his bedside table and used it to summon the servants; a visitor had remarked on the bullet holes in the ceiling. In the light of this evidence, it was decided that Augustus had stumbled against the table and accidentally shot himself, although rumours circulated widely that he had committed suicide.

After his death, Laura moved to the quiet seclusion of West End, where she became one of the village worthies, contributing generously to local charities, especially those associated with Emmanuel Church. Laura died at West End in 1894. Her will left instructions for Woodbine Cottage to become a 'Retreat for Clergymen of all denominations', but the property was sold to a consortium for about £13,000. Immediate plans to lay down Lyncroft Gardens meant that Woodbine Cottage and the remaining farm buildings were demolished.

Although the Retreat never materialised, in March 1896 a £1,750 plot on the corner of Fortune Green Road and **LYNCROFT GARDENS** was used as the site for **Emmanuel Church** on its relocation from Mill Lane (p 65). In June 1897, a copy of *The Times* was placed under the foundation stone of the church and the consecration service was held the following October, when the building was partly completed. Now Grade-II Listed, it was designed by Whitfield & Thomas and the builders were Messrs Bentley & Sons of Waltham Abbey. The original plan included an imposing tower, but this never materialised.

Two eminent composers began their professional lives as organists at Emmanuel Church: Martin Shaw (1894-1903) and Harold Darke (1906-11). Shaw spoke of his time there: 'the amazing thing is that any respectable body of people could have swallowed me so long. I used to go about with a cloak, sandals and long hair. I was agin everything'. But many praised the music he made.

The basic design of the present Vicarage, adjacent to the church, was the work of the vicar, Rev. Jack Dover Wellman, and it was completed in February 1968. That November, Wellman disturbed an intruder in his new home. He grabbed a sword hanging on the wall and held it to the man's throat, yelling, 'Don't move or I'll run you through'. But the man escaped and brandishing the sword over his head, the vicar and his wife Dorothy gave chase. She told a reporter, 'the vicar was in his pyjamas and a coat. I did not have anything on my feet and was wearing a trench coat over my nightie. About 100 yards along the road I caught hold of the man. He was very surprised.' In 2016, the vicarage interior was refurbished and rooms for community use were created inside the church building.

Lyncroft Mansions, nine blocks of flats lining the east side of Lyncroft Gardens, were built by Edward Jarvis Cave. He was one of a new breed of professional builders like the Harts, who specialised in quality family houses, while the Cave family mainly built mansion flats.

Martin Stellman, the son of a jeweller, who grew up in Flat No.46, is a screenwriter. His first script was for The Who's *Quadrophia* in 1979, and he also wrote the screenplay for *The Interpreter*, the 2005 film starring Nicole Kidman and Sean Penn.

The terrace houses on the opposite side of Lyncroft Gardens include **No.9**, the home from 1899-1914 of William Frederick Allan, who adopted the name Alan Leo when he was the editor of *Modern Astrology*. His work sparked a revival of interest in the subject. He stood trial twice on charges that he 'unlawfully pretended to tell fortunes'. Although he won the first case in 1914, he lost the second in 1917 and was fined £5 and costs. By then he was living in Dollis Hill and he died a few weeks after the verdict while recuperating in Cornwall.

David Day lived at **No.11** from 1906 to

911. He was the managing director of Francis, Day & Hunter Ltd, a very large music publisher in Charing Cross Road.

In 1957, Dudley Pope, naval historian and author, was sharing **No.13** with several other families. Pope's successful series of 18 naval novels featured the fictional Lord Nicholas Ramage.

Major James J Mackay was at **No.25** in 1907. He held the grand title of Chief of the Scottish Clans Association for two years. When WWI began he was in command of the Harrow National Reserve. Mackay was asked by the War Office to organise recruitment and within a month he had enlisted 1,700 men. He was next asked to form a regiment of public school men and recruited 3,000 from the Harrow area alone.

Richard Wilson, best known for playing the curmudgeonly Victor Meldrew in *One Foot in the Grave*, was renting a room at No.25 in 1959. He was working as a laboratory technician at Paddington Hospital and took the 28 bus to work every day. He wrote that his bedsit was: 'Up two flights, on the side of the house, it was a dark room, with a single bed in one corner, and a washbasin in the other, a gas fire with a chair on either side, a Baby Belling gas ring for boiling a kettle, and a gas meter which had constantly to be fed with coins, or so it seemed.' Richard shared the bathroom, toilet and pay phone with the other tenants.

FORTUNE GREEN ROAD was renamed as such in 1896 and renumbered three years later. In the late 1890s, six double-fronted blocks of mansion flats were built near its southeast corner. Of these **Holly Mansions** still stand, as do Lyncroft Mansions, renamed **Rosemary Court**. Here **Flat No.1** was home in the early 1900s to Dr F Harcourt Gervis. Every Christmas he gave a doll and chocolate to the children of local widows, and in the days before the NHS, he worked at the West Hampstead Provident Dispensary in Mill Lane (p 65).

John Hargrave (1894-1982) lived in Flat **No.3**, Rosemary Court. In a working life of 70 years he was an artist, illustrator, cartoonist, copywriter, Boy Scout commissioner, inventor and author. He joined the Scout movement and published a series of articles about the values of scouting and open-air life under the name of 'White Fox'. His experiences in the Royal Army Medical Corps during WWI were used to write *The Great War Brings it Home* (1919), in which he argued that civilisation had failed and that a programme of outdoor education was needed for regeneration. In 1920, Hargrave founded the Kibbo Kift to put his views into action and was promptly expelled from the Scouts. In 1923 he met C H Douglas, who believed the root of all economic and social problems was a lack of purchasing power. The solution was to give a living income to everybody, called Social Credit. Hargrave formed the Social Credit Party, whose followers adopted a green shirt as a uniform. Green-painted bricks were thrown through the windows of 11 Downing Street. The movement was attacked by the media and, although few in number, it became quite well known as the Advisory Committee included Havelock Ellis, H G Wells and Julian Huxley. In 1937 Hargrave invented a moving-map automatic navigation system for aircraft. Thirty years later he was surprised to discover that a version had been installed in Concorde. Hargrave battled for nine years to get recognition of his original idea. He succeeded in forcing the Government into a Public Enquiry in 1976, but while this conceded that his invention had been copied and developed to produce the modern instrument, it disallowed any financial award on a point of technical procedure. It was a crushing blow from which Hargrave never fully recovered. He died in 1982 and is buried in Hampstead Cemetery.

In September 1940, the stick of bombs that fell across West Hampstead badly damaged properties along Fortune Green Road, killing an air raid warden in Beech Mansions. At the end of July 1944 further damage was done by a V1 flying-bomb. Fortunately, there were no fatalities, but ten people were hospitalised and

30 Berridge House

twelve more needed first aid treatment. A fallen ceiling trapped a couple in their bed and it took rescuers three hours to free them. Laurel, Beech, Oak and Willow Mansions were demolished and replaced in the late 1950s by the flats of **Walter Northcott House**, named after a long-serving local Councillor, (p 90).

The terrace houses on the east side of Fortune Green Road north of Parsifal Road include **No.38**, into which Lymington House School for Girls (and Kindergarten) moved in 1929, from a site on West End Lane near Lymington Road. It later became co-educational and closed in the early 1960s. From about 1945 and into the early 1950s, **No.44** was home to the playwright Philip King, who was born in Beverley (Yorks.) as Percival King

in 1904. He wrote numerous farces over three decades from 1939, the best known of which was *See How They Run* (1944). The artist Isaac Snowman (p 92) occupied **Nos.46&48** around 1900-05, using No.48 as his studio.

Opposite, north of Hillfield Road, the Police Station stands on a corner occupied until 1966 by **Berridge House** [30]. The neighbouring Field Lane Institution (p 75) sold the site in 1906, suggesting it was suitable for flats and houses; instead it was bought by the National Society, who built Berridge House as a training college for teachers of domestic science. Opened in 1909, it took its name from Richard Berridge, who left a large sum of money in his will for technical education. There were 150 non-resident and 30 resident students, who paid 15s a week for full board. As well as obvious subjects such as cookery and laundry, the curriculum included instruction on how to choose a home, and manage rents, rates and taxes, savings and investments. During WWI, the college was occupied by the WRAF for training purposes, and in WWII it was used as a first aid post and mortuary. In the 1950s, it was a common sight to see students carrying covered and steaming dishes of hot food out of the main entrance in Fortune Green Road, the product of a day's labour being taken back to their digs for supper. In 1964 the College amalgamated

with St Katherine's College in Tottenham and Berridge House was sold.

It was demolished in 1966 to provide the site for the relocated **West Hampstead Police Station**, which included stabling for horses. It cost £180,000 and opened in April 1972. Given its rather stark exterior, it may come as a surprise to find it was specially designed by J Innes Elliott, the chief architect and surveyor of New Scotland Yard, to 'blend in' with the surrounding streets and houses. In 1982, it was reported that composer Wilfred Josephs (1927-97) had been sent to the stables at the Police Station by his wife Valerie, to help him conquer his fear of horses. This was essential, because Josephs had been commissioned to write the music for the ballet *Equus*, based on Peter Schaffer's play. Time spent with the well-disciplined police horses gave him an insight into their behaviour and the sounds they made. Josephs went on to complete the music and the ballet premiered in New York, in 1982. Until recently, the front office at the Police Station was manned by volunteers for a few hours a week.

The short parade of shops rounding the corner into Achilles Road includes a long-lived retail outlet. By 1901, a fishmonger had opened at No.1 Monro Terrace, later renumbered **No.27** Fortune Green Road. It continued trading under different owners, until declining sales suggested conversion into a fish and chip shop. Opened by 1962, it later expanded into **No.29**, adding seating, and is still trading as the well-known Nautilus.

In 1888, **Fortune Green** was sold at auction to the Kent, Sussex & General Land Company. Angry locals pressured Hampstead Vestry to try to get the land back for the public, and the Land Company dropped out of the sale when no title could be established. Questions were raised in Parliament and a Fortune Green Protection Society was formed in July 1891. Matters came to a head in December 1893 when a gypsy caravan and tent were pitched at the northern end of the Green [31]. Gypsies had been coming to the Green for years, but feelings were running high, and it seems they were being used as pawns by the land owners to establish their rights over the Green. On 23 December a huge crowd assembled and their leader George Saxby, who lived nearby at No.36 Achilles Road, used a chisel to cut through the chain which attached the caravan to a tree and the crowds pulled it away through the mud. After the crowd wished them a Happy Christmas, the gypsies left. The case to determine the status of the land was heard in the High Court in July 1895. The Vestry pleaded the right to play lawful games on the Green or 'the right of recreation'. They produced elderly people who said for many years they had played games such as rounders, quoits, trapball and cricket there. The judge said he was sympathetic to the Vestry but he concluded that there was insufficient evidence to show that Fortune Green had a reputation as a village green. But the locals went on fighting and eventually Hampstead Council bought the land. A final problem was that three of the original nine cottages stood on what was now the Green and had to be demolished. During January and February 1898, the Green was turfed, paths were laid out and the people of West End finally had their open space. In 1903, the granite drinking fountain was placed at the entrance, later joined by two decommissioned WWI guns. During WWII much of the west side was turned into underground shelters. The community Jester Festival which started in 1972, is held on the Green every summer.

On the east side of Fortune Green Road, the stretch north of Burrard Road (p 86)

31 Gypsies on Fortune Green

developed into another important local shopping parade. In 1904, the traders included the usual butcher, dairyman, baker and grocer, as well as a watchmaker, dressmaker, ironmonger and stationer; there was also a laundry. A narrow roadway between **No.94** and **No.98** led to No.96, a property behind used as the Woodbine Nursery from about 1895, when George Chambers moved his greenhouses here from a site opposite West End Green. The business closed in the late 1920s and became a car park for several garage businesses. Nearing completion on the site in December 2006 was **ROSE JOAN MEWS**, a secluded development of ten mews houses in a triangular formation, designed by architect Piers Gough for Sager Group Ltd. with curved copper roofs and terraces; the bedrooms are at ground-floor level and the living rooms above.

Across **FORTUNE GREEN ROAD** is **Alfred Court**, also by Gough for Sager. The development was opposed by many residents: 'the building will appear to be moored off the Fortune Green frontage like an ocean liner at a quay side'. Completed in February 2010, the long, grey complex provides a mix of residential and commercial space. It replaced all the premises from the former Prince of Wales pub at No.37, immediately north of the open space, to No.65, a petrol filling station.

Originally No.4 Fortune Green, the Prince of Wales [32] was part of the row of nine cottages built in the 1840s. It became a beerhouse in the 1870s and probably doubled as a local store, selling basic groceries such as flour and even drinking water. It was only granted its first licence to sell spirits in 1941. Remodelled in the 1960s, 'the unspectacular exterior of this modern pub conceals an unusual interior layout – bars at three levels, the higher ones overlooking the lower. The setting is vaguely barnlike with pitched roof and oak beams with some way-out lights and fantasy décor.' A restaurant was added, and in the language

32 The Prince of Wales pub

the mid-1970s, the patrons were mainly 'young and hip'. Successively renamed as The ... on the Green and Finnegan's Wake, the ... b was known finally as the Dog & Six ...ories until 2006.

After standing derelict for some years, the ...st of the nine cottages (Nos.45&47) were ...molished in the late 1980s/early 1990s and ...eir sites added to that of the adjacent Honda ...r dealership.

The five fields of West End Farm (p 41) ...ached north and west beyond what is now ...e Fortune Green open space, with valuable ...ontages to Finchley Road and Fortune Green ...ad. In 1876, twenty acres were sold to the ...ampstead Burial Board as the site of ...ampstead Cemetery (p 88). The farm's last ...wner, estate agent and surveyor Charles ...apman, took possession of the land in about ...881 and two years later began selling off the ...emaining farmland. Sold in 1884, to Mr F R ...loyd, was an 8-acre field adjoining Fortune ...reen, which later provided the site for the ...reek roads' (p 72). The previous year, 7 acres ...orth of Woodbine Cottage, described as 'ripe ...r immediate development', had been bought ...y the National Liberal Land Company.

PARSIFAL ROAD was the only street ...uilt on the land they acquired. Unlike ...ther developments in West Hampstead and ...ilburn, where land companies created streets lined with tight terrace housing, the aim here was to attract a better class of resident by building 'first-class villas'.

No.1 was bought for £2,325 in 1894, as the vicarage for Emmanuel Church. Before urgent repairs were carried out in 1956, it was suggested the property should be replaced by a smaller house. Further deterioration decided the matter and the new vicarage was built in Lyncroft Gardens. No.1 was sold to the GLC in 1970. Two years before, there had been a proposal to demolish **Nos.1**-9, and use their sites for a new Emmanuel School. This was strenuously opposed by the residents and the plan was abandoned the following year. Permission to build the terrace of four properties, **Nos.1A-1D** was given in 1977 and two more houses, **Nos.1E&1F** behind, the next year.

No.5 was home to the sculptor Phillip King, who had moved from Acol Road in the mid-1960s. A student of Anthony Caro, he worked as Henry Moore's assistant at St Martin's School of Art in 1959. Exhibitions of his work have included one at the Hayward Gallery in 1981. King was President of the RA from 1999 to 2004. He worked at a studio in NW6 until his death in July 2021.

George Douglas Howard Cole and his wife Margaret lived at **No.7** from 1925-33. He joined the Fabian Society but had a disagreement with Beatrice and Sidney Webb, who he thought were too elitist. He wrote more than 25 books about political theory, history, and political figures from William Cobbett to Robert Owen. He averaged one book every other year all his life. And he also had the energy to write, with Margaret, over thirty detective novels. In 1935 one of Cole's students at Oxford was Harold Wilson who said, 'It was G.D.H. Cole as much as any man who finally pointed me in the direction of the Labour Party'. Having served from 1952-57 as president of the Fabian Society, Cole died in 1959.

More recently, Mark Carney, the Governor of the Bank of England lived in **No.8** from 2013-15. As a Canadian, he was the first non-Englishman to hold the post.

Sir Herbert Jackson was living at **No.9** by 1924. Born in Hampstead in 1863, he became professor of chemistry at King's College, London. He did pioneering research on the production of phosphorescent and fluorescent materials. He also worked on the problems of storing gun cotton and the chemicals needed for wet plate photography. Jackson was awarded the KBE in 1917 for his work on scientific committees during WWI. The Royal Society produced a long obituary when he died at No.9 in 1936. He was buried in the churchyard of St John's Hampstead and he left £29,464 to his widow Amy.

Count Casimir Ignace Mankowski lived

opposite at **No.10** in the early years of the 20th century. In 1879 he had married American heiress Grace Sterling Bixby and the couple moved to England. They had two sons, Casimir Sterling and Robert. In 1901 Grace was declared insane and confined in a private asylum. She later went to live at Parsifal Road with her husband before the couple returned to the USA in 1906. Her son Casimir Sterling became a renowned motorboat pilot who won many prizes. The Count died in 1911 in Switzerland. His body was returned for burial in Hampstead Cemetery. Grace died in New York in 1929.

For a short period immediately after WWI, **No.13** was a hospital for RAF personnel. The actress Lilli Palmer (1914-86) lived at Rosemount, **No.17**. The road name's Wagnerian connection had decided her to rent the house with her mother and sisters in 1938. Born in Poznan (now in Poland), as Lillie Marie Peiser, she had trained as an actress in Berlin before coming to England in 1933. She had a few small parts before appearing in Hitchcock's film *Secret Agent* (1936) with John Gielgud and Peter Lorre. She was married to Rex Harrison from 1943-57 and for much of the time they lived and worked in Hollywood and on Broadway. Lilli appeared in over 70 films, including *Moll Flanders* (1965), *Murders in The Rue Morgue* (1971) and *The Boys from Brazil* (1978). She appeared with actors such

as Fred Astaire, Gary Cooper, Clark Gable and Lawrence Olivier. Her last film was *The Holcroft Covenant* (1985) with Michael Caine. Lilli wrote five novels and a very candid autobiography which received high acclaim from critics, but not from Rex Harrison. Some confusion is caused by the fact Lilli is remembered on her mother's gravestone in Hampstead Cemetery, though she is buried in Forest Lawn Los Angeles. During WWII, Rosemount was a Jewish children's home run by Rose Peiser, Lilli's mother, and the Children's Movement responsible for the Kindertransport. By 1956 it was a Jewish retirement home.

In 1884 seven more acres of West End Farm land were sold by Charles Tupman (p 85,) to the National Standard Land Mortgage & Investment Co., as the site for Burrard and Ingham Roads. Building progressed more rapidly than in Parsifal Road, the smaller, 2-storey terrace houses here being in great demand. The main builder was Arthur Rathbone (also trading as Rathbone Brothers), who was involved in many other local developments (p 61). The land company went into voluntary liquidation in 1888. Ten years later there was a rumour that the houses might be demolished to make way for high-class flats.

Near the southwest end, **No.8 BURRARD**

ROAD was home in 1894 to Neocles Mussabini a diplomat, journalist and war correspondent. His son Scipio was known as Sam. Sam Mussabini established a reputation as a coach who used scientific principles to train athletes and professional cyclists. He is memorably portrayed by Ian Holm in the film *Chariots of Fire* as the coach of the English sprinter Harold Abrahams in the Paris Olympics in 1924. Sam told Abrahams, 'Only think of two things, the report of the pistol and the tape. When you hear one, just run like hell until you break the other.' Following this advice, Abrahams won the gold medal, equalling the Olympic record time of 10.6 seconds. For his brilliant portrayal of Sam Mussabini, Holm received an Oscar nomination. Sam is buried in the family grave at Hampstead Cemetery.

The Massey family lived at **No.15**. In December 1940, 35-year-old Sergeant Louis George Massey and two colleagues escaped from the prisoner-of-war camp Stalag XXA in Winduga Poland. They trekked an astonishing 1,600 miles through five countries, travelling by night to arrive in Russia. People shared food with the soldiers and hid them from the Nazis. Otherwise, they lived on grass and anything else they could find in the fields. They were held by the Russians in state prison suspected of being German spies. Eventually, they were handed over to the British Embassy where

Massey stayed on to work. He was awarded the DCM in 1941 and presented with it at Buckingham Palace by King George in May 1944. After the War Massey moved next door to **No.17**, where he died in December 1982 aged 75.

From about 1890 to 1910, the organ builder Frederick Rothwell (p 71) was resident at **No.54**.

Artist and engraver William Caxton Keene, of **No.56**, was one of the illustrators for the popular book *Picturesque London* (1890). He suffered a strange fate: on his death in 1910, the Hampstead coroner ruled that he had died from 'the effect of shouting at an election meeting'.

Jon Moss was a drummer with several bands in the 1970s and 80s, including Culture Club and Adam and the Ants. He said he lived in a terrible flat with no heating in Burrard Road, where his landlady, dressed in black like a Goth, turned up to collect the rent in a hearse.

The blacksmith and footballer Joseph Compodonico lived at **No.4 INGHAM ROAD** (in 1891) and at No.26 from 1893-1901, before moving to Agamemnon Road (p 72).

The first eight houses in **WEECH ROAD** were under construction in April 1881, on land owned by the Burgess family (p 89). On the south side, composer and ethnomusicologist Peter Crossley-Holland (1916-2001) lived

at **No.6** in the late 1950s and early '60s. Inglis Sheldon-Williams was at **No.11** from 1934 until his death in 1940. Born in the UK, he first went to Canada in 1887 as a homesteader. He returned to England to study art and went on to become one of Saskatchewan's major artists, his landscapes capturing the space and loneliness of the prairies. His wife Ina was also an accomplished painter.

Brian Jones [33], the guitarist and founder of the Rolling Stones lived briefly in Weech Road.

Born in Cheltenham, he came to London at the beginning of 1962 and met Mick Jagger and Keith Richards at Alexis Korner's blues club in Ealing. Brian's young girlfriend Pat Andrews from Cheltenham arrived in April with their baby son Julian who was born in October 1961 and named after Julian 'Cannonball' Adderley, the great American sax player. They had a short stay in a flat in Weech Road but were asked to leave because of the baby. In September 1962 Pat left Brian, who moved with Mick and Keith into the infamous Edith Grove flat in Chelsea. After the Rolling Stones became famous, a rift developed between Brian and Mick and Keith. Then, on the morning of 2 July 1969 Brian, aged 27, died under suspicious circumstances in the swimming pool of his home, Cotchford Farm in East Sussex.

33 Brian Jones

34 Cherie Blair

Three days later the Rolling Stones played to a huge crowd in Hyde Park and Mick read a tribute to Brian.

In her autobiography, Cherie Blair [34] says she lived in Weech Road while she was studying for the Bar. The only time her grandmother visited her there she cried her eyes out because conditions were so awful. Cherie wrote: 'The bed-sit was the usual thing for those days: dirty linoleum; peeling paint; windows you couldn't see out of; electric and gas meters into which you put a coin and which would always run out at the worst possible moment. I shared a couple of gas rings on the landing with another girl, and I didn't have a fridge: I kept everything that needed to be refrigerated on my windowsill'.

All Souls' Free Unitarian Church was built on the southwest corner of Weech Road and **FORTUNE GREEN ROAD** in 1903. It closed in 1925, to be demolished and replaced in 1937 by the residential flats of **Weech Hall**. Just north of the junction at No.120, with a crucifix in its gable, is the former St Luke's Hall. Built in 1904 as St Luke's Church Institute, to serve the church in nearby Kidderpore Avenue; in 2015 permission was granted to convert to residential use.

Immediately opposite and opened in November 1876, **Hampstead Cemetery** covers about 25 acres. The laying out and planting of the grounds was carried out by Joseph Fyfe Meston, probably the most important landscape gardener working in London at the time. The twin Gothic-style chapels were designed by Charles Bell, who is buried in the cemetery. The stained glass windows, designed by local artist John Dudley Forsyth (p 125), were added in 1903. In addition to the chapels, 18 monuments have been Grade-II Listed by English Heritage. The railings along the front wall on Fortune Green Road were removed during WWII, the metal intended for recycling as shells and other armaments. They were replaced as part of a Lottery Award that has also financed major improvements to the entire site. The Cemetery gates date from 1950.

Originally there was a large team of gravediggers and full-time gardeners, managed by the Superintendent who lived in the lodge. Greenhouses were built to provide plants for the cemetery, but these were demolished in the 1970s and their site used for the Fortune Green Playspace. Today there are over 60,000 people buried at Hampstead Cemetery and it is the final resting place for many West Hampstead residents. *The Good Grave Guide to Hampstead Cemetery, Fortune Green,* published by the Camden History Society, has biographies of 230 people, of local and international interest, who are buried there. Detailed aerial maps help locate a particular grave. Artists, architects, writers and inventors are all represented, as well as the more unusual, such as a ventriloquist buried along with his favourite dummy, and an inscription in shorthand from a grieving husband. One of the most spectacular graves is the Bianchi Monument [35] which Cesare Bianchi, the chef at the Café Royal, commissioned in 1936 for his wife who died after giving birth to their son.

The Friends of Hampstead Cemetery group was founded in 1994 to speak and act on behalf of all those who care for the cemetery.

The entry lodge (No.69 Fortune Green Road) was also designed by Charles Bell. Just to the south, **Nos.67A-67C** were built by Camden Council, and when the cemetery yard was decommissioned in the 1990s, part of the site was used for two more houses, Nos.65A&65B.

Three of the earliest properties built on Fortune Green Road were owned by stonemasons and stood opposite the Cemetery gates. Underwoods was the first firm to begin trading here and the last to close, in 1961. Several Underwood family members are buried in the Cemetery, where they were responsible for erecting hundreds of monuments. After lying derelict for several years, the site of Nos.122-126 was redeveloped as **Sidney Corob House**, a mental health residential home run by Jewish Care. In 1886, another stonemason, John Cramb, built the highly decorative Greek House (later **No.128**), noted for its Graeco-Egyptian stucco pastiche which was Grade-II Listed in 1974. Beyond are **Burgess Park Mansions**, dating from 1902. Their builder, Mr Pearce, complained to the Vestry in 1905 about one of the nearby stonemasons who was advertising 'funerals provided': he believed the sign was stopping tenants from renting his flats.

The private houses opposite were built from 1911 onwards. The land here was bought by the wealthy Devonshire-born Henry Weech

35 The Bianchi monument

36 Amy Johnson

Burgess (1795-1881). Before settling down in West Hampstead, he had lived in Islington, and in Manchester where in 1835 he purchased the Manor of Ardwick, after which he named his eldest son. In 1838 he built himself a large mansion he called Temple Park, set in extensive grounds that were later covered by Burgess Hill, Ardwick and Ranulf Roads. Henry began developing the property in 1859 by making a start on **BURGESS HILL,** initially a short cul-de-sac off Finchley Road. Six houses had been completed by 1862, with two properties facing Finchley Road.

Henry moved into one of them (the original No.1) and rented out Temple Park. He found the ideal tenant in James Haysman, who needed a building large enough to accommodate his Anglo-French College and space to house his family. On census night in 1871, the mansion was home to 93 people, 77 of whom were Haysman's pupils. By contrast, only six people had been recorded in 1861: Henry and family members plus a visitor and servants. Although Haysman opened a second school at No.339 Finchley Road (p 126), he remained at Temple Park (latterly known as Burgess Park) until 1895, running both academic establishments in tandem. After he left, the house stood empty until it was demolished at the turn of the century.

Dr Edwin Lankester, the coroner for

Middlesex, was living in Melton House, Burgess Hill in 1871. He was a surgeon and public health reformer who played a major role in the control of cholera and was also a close friend of Darwin. He left the area soon after and died in Margate in 1874.

After 1903, when the original cul-de-sac was extended to meet Ranulf Road, permission to name it Belle Vue Crescent was refused.

At the time of her death in 1939, **No.8** was home to Lady Sarah Louisa Blomfield, author, and translator of works on Bahai thought and spirituality. She was also involved in establishing the Save the Children Fund. Lady Sarah had been the second wife of Sir Arthur William Blomfield ARA (d.1899), who served as vice-president of the RIBA and was architect to the Bank of England. The many churches he designed included St James' Church on West End Lane. Lady Sarah shared No.8 with her daughter Mary and her son-in-law Captain Basil Hall. Mary was a dedicated suffragette, who in 1914 threw herself in front of the King and Queen at a Court reception, pleading that the force-feeding of suffragettes in prison be stopped. They ignored her.

No.8 is the only one of the original six 1860s houses to survive. Otherwise, Burgess Hill is entirely 20th-century. **Mackellar House flats** have supplanted Nos.10&12, which were occupied for many years by the Woodlands

School. In the 1930s, it was succeeded by Burgess Hill School, a co-educational primary school. The school left London in 1939, returning to Oak Hill Park in Hampstead about 1948.

The Borough boundary between Camden and Barnet is marked largely by the rear garden walls of houses on the north side of Burgess Hill. **Vernon Court flats**, extending from Burgess Hill to the Hendon Way, were partly in Camden until a boundary change in 1994 placed them wholly in Barnet. When built in 1930 they were advertised as 'labour-saving flats for the discriminating'. One of the earliest tenants was pioneer aviatrix Amy Johnson [36] who lived at Flat 15 from November 1930 until her marriage to fellow pilot Jim Mollison in July 1932. Amy was the first female pilot to fly solo from Britain to Australia and set numerous other long-distance records in the 1930s. In January 1941, while flying a plane for the Air Transport Auxiliary, and blown off course in adverse weather conditions, Amy died after bailing out over the Thames Estuary. Her body was never recovered.

Building in **ARDWICK ROAD** began in 1903, more or less on the line of the carriage drive of Temple Park. Four houses were destroyed on 28 June 1944, and two people killed, when the first of two flying-bombs fell nearby. Fortunately, as most of the properties

were empty, there were no reported casualties when the second V1 landed.

Eric Muir Gamage, who lived at Saltwood, (**No.5**) until about 1930, was the chairman and managing director of Gamages, the large department store in Holborn. It finally closed in 1972 but the Oxford Street branch near Marble Arch which opened in September 1930, only traded for seven months before it went into receivership. Primark currently occupies the site.

Sir Robert Blair lived at **No.19**. After working as a teacher, and inspector, he became London's first Education Officer, a post he held from 1904 to 1924. He was knighted in 1914.

Having rounded a curve at its south end, **RANULF ROAD** strikes north, continuing across the Borough boundary into Barnet, where the house builder Hart who erected many properties in this neighbourhood after 1903, also bought land.

A recent owner of **No.1** put up a plaque commemorating the Short Brothers. The house was once occupied by Mrs Short, whose sons Horace, Eustace and Oswald were famous for their pioneering work in airship and aeroplane construction. Horace survived childhood meningitis, apparently complicated by hydrocephalus, which left him with an enlarged skull. In 1890 he decided to visit his uncle in Australia and en route he met Robert Louis Stevenson in Samoa. He was then captured by cannibals but was spared an unpleasant end when they decided to make him their King. He next became manager of a silver mine in Mexico. In Horace's absence, Eustace and Oswald went into balloon manufacture, eventually establishing a factory in Battersea. In 1908 the three men joined forces as Short Brothers, Aeronautical Engineers, to design and manufacture aeroplanes. Orville and Wilbur Wright contracted them to build six aircraft and the firm opened further factories in Kent and Bedfordshire. The outbreak of WWI meant an increase in production, which by then included bombers, a folding-wing seaplane and airships – Horace is credited with inventing the name 'Blimp'. He died in 1917 but the company continued to grow steadily, diversifying into the building of boats and light-weight bodies for London buses. Eustace died in Maidstone in 1932. He had a heart attack while at the wheel of his sea plane although he managed to land it safely. Oswald (d.1969) lived for a while in Templewood Gardens, and both he and Eustace are buried in Hampstead Cemetery.

The first house to be completed in Ranulf Road was **No.3**, built for the artist Isaac Snowman, (p 82) with a large first-floor studio.

Born in St Pancras in 1873, to Polish émigré parents, Isaac was encouraged by the eminent Jewish artist, Solomon Joseph Solomon to enter the RA Schools, where he studied under some of the most important artists of the day, including local residents Seymour Lucas and Frank Dicksee. Isaac Snowman and his younger brother Emanuel were supporters and personal friends of Israel Zangwill, whose Kilburn home was a regular meeting place for a group of Jewish professionals, and where Zionism took form. Isaac first visited Israel in 1897 and the following year his painting *The Wailing Wall* at Jerusalem was shown at the RA. His portraits included one of the Prince of Wales (later Edward VII), which was made into a postcard and sold thousands of copies. This commercial success enabled Isaac to commission the Ranulf Road house. About 1920 he moved to Palestine, where he lived until the late 1930s. In failing health when he visited England in 1939, Isaac died of heart failure eight years later. His brother Emanuel joined the jewellery firm of Wartski and made regular trips to Russia right up to the outbreak of WWII, to buy items such as Fabergé eggs. This established the firm's reputation for dealing in fine art. Living locally, Emanuel served as a Hampstead Councillor for many years and was twice Mayor.

Another local Councillor and twice mayor of Hampstead was Walter Clifford Northcott, who lived at **No.9**, (see p.82).

After she left her husband in 1947, the novelist Elizabeth Jane Howard spent an uncomfortable few weeks at her father's home, **No.11**, while a flat she was renting was being renovated. 'I didn't get a very good reception at Ranulf Road. I was put into a room which was really somebody else's, which meant there was nowhere to put away clothes. The house was quite large, with a housekeeper on the top floor. It was also clear that I was expected to be in for as few meals as possible. I left the house to sleep in my flat long before it was really habitable'.

At the time of his death in 1960, Australian-born composer and pianist Arthur Leslie Benjamin was at **No.15**. In 1911 he left for London to study at the Royal College of Music, staying until 1915, when he joined up. Arthur was later appointed a piano professor at the RCM, where his pupils included Benjamin Britten. A colourful personality, Arthur was equally at home composing serious works that included five operas, or popular music for films and dance. Such was the popularity of his *Jamaican Rumba* (1938) that he was given a barrel of rum by the people of Jamaica every year. Among his many hobbies was nude sunbathing, in the seclusion of his Ranulf Road garden.

Up West End Lane, again

The east side of the Lane from West Hampstead Underground Station to West End Green, and both sides up to Finchley Road, plus Cannon Hill

Today's **West Hampstead Underground Station** was opened by the Metropolitan & St John's Wood Railway on 30 June 1879. The line was extended to Willesden on 24 November, with a ten-minute service. The station was the first new building between the Railway Hotel on the corner with Broadhurst Gardens, and Canterbury House, a large mansion that stood a little way north of today's Lymington Road. At platform level the station has been remodelled twice, to accommodate successive widening of the track, and to provide a new island platform, in interwar style, for the Bakerloo line, which took over the Metropolitan service to Stanmore in 1939. Forty years later it became part of the Jubilee line. Before the days of automation, there was a staffed barrier and ticket office in the centre of the booking hall, with a few ticket machines to one side. These were eye-height boxes, with the fare displayed on their illuminated tops.

The Victorian composer Arthur Goring Thomas (b.1851) committed suicide at the station in 1892 when he had been staying with his brother in St John's Wood. At West Hampstead the train driver said he saw 'a tall gentleman take one step forward, jump onto the track, and turn his back to the approaching engine'. The train was stopped almost immediately but Mr Thomas was dead when taken out from under the carriages. His compositions included operatic, choral and orchestral works. At the time of his death he was due to write a grand opera for Mr D'Oyly Carte at the Royal English Opera House.

The Metropolitan line was newly electrified when, around 7.45am on 27 October 1907, two westbound trains collided in the station. The noise was tremendous, and people came running to see what had happened. A second train had ploughed into the rear carriage of a stationary train with such force that it lifted the last two carriages high into the air. Given the severity of the impact, rescuers were amazed to find the driver of the second train had survived with only a few injuries, but three passengers in the carriages of the first train were killed and 11 injured. Had it not been for the fact the trains were travelling away from the City, the death toll would have been much higher. It emerged at the enquiry that the line still relied on manual signalling. The signal box was at the south end of the platform and the man in charge was William John Hollis. It was a foggy morning, visibility was poor and he claimed the indictors had shown the first train had departed. In January 1908 Hollis was charged at the Old Bailey with manslaughter but acquitted. Following the Board of Trade Inquiry, the railway company rapidly installed automatic signalling.

In 1879 the estate agents Ernest Owers & Williams opened at **No.106** West End Lane next door to the original station entrance. It remains an estate agent's today. Owers was a land and house agent who recognised the enormous potential the neighbourhood had to offer the speculative investor and developer. Working from his West Hampstead Estate Office, Owers was involved in many property sales locally, and later in Golders Green. To begin with, he used to walk from his parents' home in Shepherd's Bush to West Hampstead every day. After his marriage in 1884, the couple lived at **No.177** West End Lane, almost opposite the business, over a shop a few doors north of Sherriff Road. They later moved to a new house in Finchley Road (p 130). The West Hampstead business was sold to William Charles Williams in 1931, but Ernest continued working for the company. That December he was the victim of a violent attack at the West Hampstead office. Owers had notified jeweller Ernest Phillips that the mortgage on his West

End Lane shop must be paid off. Phillips came to the office, yelled at Owers, 'You are a robber and a thief and I shall put you away'. Then he suddenly threw nitric acid into Owers' face which narrowly missed blinding him. In court Phillips said he was sorry, but the judge said a severe punishment was called for and sentenced him to three years imprisonment. Owers' wife died a few months after the attack and he moved to Brighton where he died in 1938. Owers was an extremely wealthy man: he left £400,790 (worth about £23M today), and most of the money went to hospitals and other good causes. Among his personal bequests was an annuity of £250 (equivalent to about £12,000 today), to the nurse who had looked after both him and his wife in their last illnesses.

In the one-storey terrace north of the tube station entrance, early arrivals were coal merchants John Tims and Spenser Whately, respectively at **Nos.116&118**. These are now a supermarket and watch repair shop. Companies selling coal, the main fuel for heating and cooking, opened offices on both sides of the road. Various firms came and went, some of them trading from the coal depots in the railway sidings.

Across Blackburn Road (p 118), in the late 1950s, **Nos.130&132** (now an estate agent's) became West Hampstead's Post Office. In May 1968, before they realised their mistake, staff started selling presentation sets of decimal copper coins (2p, 1p and ½p), a month before their due release date. The post office closed in July 2014 and relocated to the Sherriff Centre in nearby St James' Church.

At **No.134**, now a minicab business, Miss Elizabeth Elbourne's confectionery shop opened in 1920. A local resident remembered it in its early years: 'the genteel Misses Elbourne sold their hand-made chocolates in a shop remarkable for its cleanliness and fastidiousness'. The shop was still trading in 1978 as El Bourne but closed soon after.

Tower Mansions (Nos.134-136) were built for and owned by Percy and Eustace Sloper (p 118). Newly completed in 1898, the nine flats were comfortable five-room properties, served by a hall porter and a trades lift. Gas and electricity were laid on but there was also a large coal cellar. In 1901, Flat No.5 was occupied by composer Robert Brydges Addison (1854-1920). Having studied at the Royal Academy of Music, and become professor of harmony and composition there, he was later professor and choral conductor at Trinity College, London. He moved on to Sheriff Road, his address at death.

More recently, several musicians have lived at Tower Mansions. In 1975 guitarist Adrian Wyatt moved in. Three years later he went to Australia with a rock band called World, and when he returned he found a whole swathe of new rock 'n roll neighbours. These included, Wilko Johnson the guitarist with Dr Feelgood, Jean-Jacques Burnel the bass player of The Stranglers, Lemmy and Phil Taylor from Motorhead, the singer Billy Idol (p 72) and Steve Strange of Visage. From July 1980 to June 1981 Ade operated the sound system at the Moonlight Club at the Railway Hotel, where numerous punk bands played.

By the side of Tower Mansions, steps lead down to Billy Fury Way (p 118). On the bridge across the Overground, in a run of one-storey commercial premises at Nos.138-146, **No.138** has been an eating place since 1937. Known as the Bridge Snack Bar in 1951, it later changed its name to the more continental 'Café.' Next door, the travel agent's at **No.142** was the Doll's Hospital from 1915, run by Miss Holmes, who also sold toys. Toys were expensive, and many girls took their beloved doll to a specialist 'hospital' like this one to be mended. It was still trading in 1940, but a decade later No.142 had become a wireless and electrical shop. Trading here by 1883 were two more coal merchants: Cannock Chase Colliery at **No.144**, now a barber's shop, and Thomas Lea at demolished No.146. There have been many unfulfilled plans to redevelop this frontage. In 1961, a proposed 8-storey block on the sites of Nos.138-148 was opposed by the Council as being too high and too obtrusive. A proposal in 2004 to move the Overground and Thameslink stations to the east side of West End Lane and install pedestrian subways to link all three local stations, was shelved.

In 2002 permission was granted for the current **Nos.150-152**, a mix of commercial with residential above. It stands on the corner of an access road that originally led to railway sidings and replaced a mid-1950s building occupied by Malacarp Terrazzo until the 1990s. The company, which is no longer trading, had a showroom on West End Lane and a factory on the back land bordering the railway lines, for casting and fabricating concrete, terrazzo and mosaic panels and tiles.

An unlikely survivor, perched at the south end of Thameslink/Midland railway bridge, is the diminutive **No.154**, originally a coal office. For over 30 years, as Nam's Heel Bar, it belonged to shoe and clothing repairer Nam Ho ('Captain Nam'). He had come to London after being released from imprisonment – for 're-education' by the communist regime in Vietnam in the wake of the Vietnamese War. On his retirement in 2015, the shop was to be taken over by his son. In March 2021 it was boarded up and it may close permanently.

At the north end of the bridge, an (unnamed)

access road leads to the Potteries Path (p115). In 1974, all the properties north to No.166 West End Lane were demolished and absorbed into one large new red-brick building, **No.156**. Once containing Camden Council offices, this housed branches of Wickes and Travis Perkins which were empty in March 2021. Vacated by the Council in 2012, the empty floors were briefly squatted, and in 2016 the property became the subject of heated local debate. The proposal to demolish, and build about 160 homes, was contested by the 'Stop the Blocks' campaigners. They argued the proposed development was too bulky and crammed too much onto the site, but Council permission to go ahead with it was granted in 2017. Redevelopment had not begun by March 2021.

The large footprint of No.156 was originally home to several small businesses. Lymington Hall School owned and operated by Miss Topham started here around 1925 in a small building at the then No.156, moving to No.158A by 1928 and then on to Fortune Green Road (p 82), where it became Lymington House School. Miss Topham (by then Mrs Kilmaster) died suddenly in March 1952.

In 1930 the estate agents Leask & Eacott opened in **Nos.158&160**. They were there for many years, and by 1974 they had moved to **No.248**.

Much of the building on the valuable West

End Lane frontage north of this site took the form of commercial premises with flats above. The shops to the corner with Lymington Road, **Nos.166 to 174**, were originally numbered in Lymington Parade with **Canterbury Mansions** above. They were built by Benjamin Smith Boddy and his partner Robert Chapman, who were occupying No.7 and No.9 Canterbury Mansions when they went bankrupt in 1900.

Lola's Bakery is at **No.168** West End Lane, which was originally No.2 Lymington Parade, and opened in 1901 as Poole & Co, hosiers, hatters and shirt tailors. It remained a men's outfitters until the mid-1960s when it became a camera shop. In March 1974 Dave Jacobs opened the Colour Division print shop. After 42 years helping the local community with their printing, he announced that he was closing in September 2016. **No.170** opened as an off-licence in 1899 and from 1912 to the mid-1950s, was 'The Ten Percent Wine Company', written in floor tiles at the entrance. Renamed Finch's Wines, the company went bankrupt in 1996.

No.172 (today's Art 4 Fun, a creative café offering art classes), was the scene of much local interest in November 1962. The singer Shirley Bassey came to West Hampstead and was photographed autographing the sleeve of one of her own records when she opened Shirley's Record Shop here. It was part of her first husband, Kenneth Hume's shop, Books Unlimited, which he opened in 1962. He was a gay film producer, whom Shirley Bassey had married the previous year. The couple separated in 1964 and divorced in 1965, in the wake of the Shirley's affair with actor Peter Finch. In 1967 Kenneth committed suicide and the shop closed in the early 1970s.

The road as far as West End Green and up the hill to Finchley Road originally formed the boundary of three estates: those of *Canterbury House*, Treherne House and West End House (later Hall). Canterbury House was built in the 1860s close to the main road, a little way north of where Lymington Road now runs, at the same time as Sandwell House on the opposite side of the Lane (p 38). The two properties were owned by friends John Marrian and William Greenwood, who later sold their houses to the Midland Railway and moved to Brondesbury. Anthony Lister rented Canterbury House for twenty years until his death in 1896. He was a partner in a large company which manufactured straw hats and bonnets and sold artificial flowers and feathers. Local butcher's son George Cross remembered: 'Every day while he was in residence he drove in state to his offices in Cannon Street, and I often used to wait on purpose to see the iron gates flung open and the carriage and pair come swiftly through,

with the old red-apple-faced, grey whiskered coachman and the upright young footman, in their light-fawn uniforms and cockaded hats sitting high up on the box'. When he died in March 1896 he left £135,000, equivalent to about £15.7M today. Lister and his wife are both buried in Hampstead Cemetery.

Nos. 176-206, north of Lymington Road, were originally numbered in Lymington Parade, with flats above. Some shops were split into two, their doors set at an angle to a single entrance that served both premises. But none of these have survived.

Nos.176-178, now a Tesco Express, was The Pine Shop in the late 1970s. It later expanded into Nos.**180-184** and changed its name to Woods & Woods under the ownership of Damian Pullen. The business closed in February 2008. In 1906, Ellis Stanyon opened his shop selling toys, conjuring tricks and foreign stamps at No.9 Lymington Parade, renumbered as **No.182** West End Lane the following year. He wrote several books about magic tricks and kept the shop until 1919, when he started to sell goods by mail order from his home address in Solent Road (p 57).

The estate agent's at **No.192** occupies what was one of the split shops, now made one. Until around 1987, at **No.192B** was the surgery of Dr Frederick Föbus Jerichower. He was a small, dapper man, who walked briskly

to work from his home in Asmara Road. In common with many GP practices in the 1960s and '70s, there was no appointment system and a queue would start forming long before the surgery opened, with patients dealt with on a 'first come, first seen' basis. Dr Jerichower died in Jerusalem in 2007.

One of the longest-surviving businesses in the parade was Westerns Laundry at **No.198** (now a white goods supply store). The shop was one of a chain, distinguished by a dark blue tiled exterior and a rising sun motif. Towards the end, the manageress would sit behind a long counter with just a few parcels of laundry wrapped in blue paper, waiting collection. The rows of empty shelving bore witness to the fact that this had once been a thriving business. Also long-lived was the Alert Electrical Company at **No.202** (one of the split shops, now reunited as a restaurant), which opened in 1904 and closed c.1983.

Currently a Sainsbury's Local, **Nos.204&206** on the corner with Fawley Road, became the neighbourhood's first chain supermarket when, in the late 1960s, a branch of Pricerite moved in.

Here was the site of the lodge and entry to the carriage drive of *Treherne House*. This took its name from a 4-acre field known as Treherne Croft, eventually transformed into the gardens and grounds of the mansion.

Set well back from West End Lane, it stood south of where Fawley and Honeybourne Roads (p 109) now meet. By 1815, Treherne House was a substantial 2-storey building, complete with a column-lined portico. In 1821, sculptor Robert Shout moved here from High Holborn, but within a year tragedy struck when his wife Lucy died after a long and painful illness. John Samuel Fletcher was the last owner of the property, buying out both his landlord and the owner of neighbouring Canterbury House in the early 1870s. Fletcher renovated and modernised Treherne House, connecting it to the main drainage system and commissioning a stable block from eminent architect George Godwin.

The son of a wealthy Manchester merchant, Fletcher was Hampstead's MP from 1905-18 and was knighted the following year. He was a keen supporter, financial as well as verbal, of many local causes, including saving West End Green and the grounds of the Grange in Kilburn, from the builder. He remained a single man until 1895, when to many people's surprise and at the relatively late age of 54, he married Miss Sara Clark. The couple moved to Virginia Water in 1897 when Fletcher sold both his West End properties. Their development was intimately tied to that of the third and last large mansion on this side of West End Lane.

37 The Miles family, four generations at West End House

The shopping parade north of Fawley Road occupies what was once the main frontage to **West End House**. Set back a short distance from the Lane, this stood immediately opposite Inglewood Road in a substantial 13 acres of grounds. The property extended along West End Lane from Fawley Road behind a high brick wall, past the Green and up the hill, almost as far as Finchley Road. A niche well in the wall provided the villagers with water.

Confusingly, there was another West End House south of the railway lines (p 34). Locals considered the southern to be the older of the two properties, and often referred to the mansion near West End Green as 'New' West End House. John Miles moved here in 1813 with his young wife Anne, and the house remained in the hands of the Miles family [37] for about seventy years. John (1784-1856) was a senior partner in the publishing firm

38 West End House from the garden

Simpkin Marshall & Co. The couple had 11 children and with their architect son Charles, played a leading role in building West End's first school, Emmanuel, on Mill Lane, (p 65). After John's widow Anne died in 1889, West End House [38] was put up for sale. A marketing plan suggested five roads could be built and the land divided into 160 building plots.

The locals waited for a developer to snap it up but instead, the house and estate was purchased by Lieutenant General Charles Craufurd Fraser, the MP for Lambeth North, a distinguished retired soldier. It was reported he paid around £32,000 for the property (equivalent today to about £3.6M), which he renamed West End Hall. Craufurd Fraser

had served during the Indian Mutiny, and was awarded the Victoria Cross for his 'conspicuous and cool gallantry' in rescuing a fellow officer and men from drowning. He was knighted in 1891. His other London home was in Sloane Street and some locals believed he bought the West End property to give garden parties during the season. George Cross (p 42,) remembered them as major local events. 'First came two private bus loads of staff; then follows the band of the 7th Hussars, the general's old regiment, in two wagonettes with all sorts of musical instruments and then more vans, no doubt bringing the ice-cream, the syllabubs, and the champagne cup. Then from a distance we hear the Hussars' band, and the visitors disappear into the park, some to go boating on the lake, and others to wander round admiring the flowers, fruit and vegetable gardens and the hothouses. Before they leave, every dainty lady is presented with a Victorian posy, carefully and skillfully made by the head gardener's wife and beautiful daughter.' Fraser's ownership was a short one as he died at Sloane Street in June 1895. West End Hall was inherited by his brother Keith, whose enjoyment of the property was even briefer, as he died six weeks later.

It was claimed the Lieutenant General had wanted to sell his property to the local authority for £25,000 (well below building

value), if it became a public park. A movement was started to purchase the estate for the public, but in November the local paper reported if no agreement was reached, development would begin after Christmas. The fund-raising Committee managed to get the asking price reduced from £50,000 to £42,500 but could not prevent the house and grounds going to auction in May 1896. The campaign to preserve Fortune Green, running at the same time, diverted support and divided opinion. In the event, the money raised fell far short of the asking price. This failure marked the end of a chapter in West Hampstead's history. Fletcher, the owner of the neighbouring Canterbury and Treherne Houses, had intimated he would sell up and leave if West End Hall fell into the hands of the builders, which is precisely what he did.

By October 1897, Canterbury House and Treherne House had been sold to Mr W Hirsch. He and the owners of West End Hall co-operated to produce an integrated development plan for all three properties, allowing certain roads to cross old boundary lines. Permission was granted in January 1898 to lay down Crediton, Fawley, Honeybourne and Lymington Roads. When newly built in 1903-04, Nos.208-222 West End Lane were named and numbered sequentially as Fawley Parade. Beneath Fawley Mansions, on the corner of Fawley Road, is a branch of a Barclays Bank at **No.208**. It moved here from No.174, replacing the Cameron Irrigation Company which had occupied the premises since the 1950s. The heavily curtained windows gave no clue as to what went on inside their offices. The firm, which made irrigation machinery for farms and golf courses had left for Sussex by 1964.

In 1983 the musician Geno Washington co-owned a basement restaurant at **No.212**. Late in the evening he would entertain diners by singing blues songs such as *Little Red Rooster* and *Got My Mojo Working* to the diners. Born in Indiana, Geno was stationed in England with the US Air Force in the 1960s. In 1965 he was asked by Pete Gage to front a group which became Geno Washington & the Ram Jam Band. They played in all the London blues clubs, including West Hampstead's Klooks Kleek, and had two best-selling live albums.

The Reliable Self Service Grocer was the first self-service store on this part of the Lane at **No.216**, now a branch of Gail's Bakery. It opened in the early 1960s, when the owner simply converted his existing business with little remodelling to the shop interior. No.8 Fawley Parade, later **No.222**, was Debenham's photography studio from 1904 to the mid-1920s. Several members of the family were photographers.

Building along the West End Hall frontage, which began at either end, was only completed in 1927, when the central portion was infilled by Nos.224 to 234, **Queen's Court** (originally Queen's Mansions), flats with shops below, on the site of the old mansion and its front garden.

The charity shop at **No.224** was a butcher's from 1929. George Kingston had moved in by 1951, having previously traded across the Lane at No.263, which was destroyed by a bomb in 1941. Kingston supplied many residents through the years of rationing after WWII. Newcomers sometimes voiced the opinion that they were given inferior cuts, the best stuff being reserved for favoured customers. The shop had sawdust on the floor and a diamond-shaped tile mosaic of a bull's head on the wall. Their other local branch at No.102 Mill Lane closed in 1986.

Currently a flower shop, **No.230** was for many years generally a fruiterer's. From the late 1950s, it was a branch of the popular Sam Cook greengrocery chain. Shopping was a very different experience then. Vegetables like potatoes and carrots were weighed and tipped into the customer's own bag, earth and all. Very occasionally they were loosely wrapped in a bit of newspaper. Fruit was available only in season. The shop sold damaged strawberries by weight, scooping the fruit into a brown paper bag. Great care had to be taken to get this soggy bundle home before the juice soaked through and the fruit fell onto the street.

No.242 was a wet fish shop from 1920 right through to 1989, when R. Rowe & Son closed. Poultry was sometimes sold there as well. Fish was displayed on a large marble slab counter that ran down the middle of the shop, separated by a slippery tiled walkway on each side from another narrow marble counter along each side wall. Customers paid at a cashier's office at the back of the shop, up a short staircase. Since 2003 No.242 has been the appropriately named Wet Fish Café, and the owners have restored the tiled interior which had been painted over.

Joe Palmer, a professional musician, moved his record shop from Midland Parade (p 38) to **No.250**, previously a furniture and carpet shop and now Roni's Bakery. It became a video rental store run by Joe, with a very dark interior. He moved to Spain and ran Sunshine FM on the Costa Blanca.

In 1907, Home & Colonial Stores opened one of its many branches at the newly completed **No.252**. The name reflected the fact the shops sold produce from all over the Empire and Colonies. From a single shop on Edgware Road in 1883, the company expanded to become one of the UK's largest retail food chains. In its final form but after several takeovers and re-brandings, it was absorbed by Safeway in 1982. In the 1950s the West Hampstead store sold loose biscuits which generally weren't very crisp from large tins. Broken biscuits were discounted but you paid more for the chocolate ones. The delicatessen on sale was standard for the time: cheddar cheese, breaded ham, corned beef and spam. The shop closed around 1970. It became a branch of the then popular Wimpy hamburger chain and has since been combined with **No.254** to make a Nando's restaurant.

A narrow entry between **Nos.254&256** leads to a service road called **Elmcroft Mews** running parallel to this stretch of the Lane and lined by garages built in 1928. In October 1996 the Special Branch arrested a man here after the March 1994 IRA mortar attack on Heathrow Airport. The stolen car fitted with mortar tubes used for the attack had been kept in one of the garages and the police had been observing Michael Gallagher for months.

On the corner opposite the Green and where the Lane turned uphill to meet Finchley Road, was a rectangular plot of land that did not belong to West End House. Lewis George Chambers may have begun trading from this site as early as 1861. He was in horticulture all his life, moving up the ladder from under-gardener to owning his own business as a florist and nurseryman at West End. A photo taken in the early 1890s shows him standing in front of his glasshouses shortly before he moved his nursery to Fortune Green Road (p 84). He died in 1909 and is buried in Hampstead Cemetery. The greenhouses and old shops were swept away to be replaced by nine new shops, later **Nos.264-280**, completed in 1901 as Nos.9-1 Central Parade.

Reflecting a different age when a real fur coat was an accepted and aspirational item of clothing, West Hampstead had two furriers in the 1950s: Bodan Furs at No.176, and Penska at **No.266**. Penska advertised themselves as practical furriers offering remodelling, renovations and cold storage. In 1973, this shop was combined with No.264, reopening as a supermarket.

No.270 has been a chemist's shop under different ownership to the present day. It began in 1902 as E R Marsh, which was still trading in 1959 as manufacturing, dispensing and photographic chemists.

From 1958 onwards, **No.272** was Alexis Continental Patisserie, which sold wonderful cakes. Peter Marks took over from his father, who started the business. It closed in 2009, becoming a branch of Dylan's Bakery, and today is Wenzel's.

No.280, now the Feng Sushi restaurant, housed another long-lived business, an Express Dairy branch that opened around 1901. The company had been founded by George Barham in 1864. The name he chose reflected both the source of the milk and the speed of its transport using railways: the Express Country Milk Supply Company. The branches were finished with blue and white tiles. Barham was a Hampstead resident for many years and the Mayor in 1905/06. The West End Lane shop updated its image and became self-service in 1967 but closed in the mid-1970s. For a couple of years, it was used to store sewing machines before becoming a wine bar and then a series of different restaurants.

Leslie David Botibol's short-lived dentist's surgery was over the dairy, at **No.280A**. It opened in 1914, when he advertised that all extractions were painless and cost 1s (about £4.80 today), but the procedure was free of charge if the patient ordered artificial teeth. These cost from 2s for a single tooth to £1 for a set. Botibol had left for Oxford Street by 1919.

West End Green was only preserved as a public open space thanks to the intervention of local people. In 1881 the Hampstead Vestry was approached by John Culverhouse, a local developer who lived in Willesden Lane. He had acquired West End Green some years earlier from the Lord of the Manor. Now he wanted to sell but when the Vestry wouldn't pay his price, Culverhouse disposed of the land to Francis Fowle, a builder in Shepherds Bush. On 26 June 1882 Fowle had the Green surrounded by a wooden hoarding and began to strip off the turf. A few days later angry residents, including a number of Vestrymen (local councilors), held a meeting when feelings ran high. They all knew that the night before, the watchman's hut on the Green had been burnt down. Mr Price, solicitor to Captain Notman (of Cholmley Lodge, p 77) said he trusted no force would be used: 'They were not in Ireland, and it was not worthy of Englishmen to set fire to a man's hoarding'. This was met with derisive laughter, applause and shouts of 'Down with it!' The climax came on the 17 July. At half-past nine that evening, 200 men armed with axes and crowbars converged on the Green by various routes. The solitary policeman on guard, PC Splaine, was taken completely by surprise and the boards were pulled down, chopped up, piled into the middle of the Green, covered with oil and set alight. Bravely, Splaine made a few arrests but was forced to release the men after taking their names and addresses. The blaze was strong enough to defy heavy rain and a crowd of about 2,000 people stood around, cheering. The flames lit up the sky and brought out the voluntary fire brigade and several steam engines, but they couldn't put out the fire. The eight men arrested appeared at Hampstead Police Court and amazingly were found 'not guilty' of any criminal action by the magistrates. The West End Green Defence Association was set up to negotiate with the developers. Local wealthy residents offered money towards the purchase cost. Eventually, in July 1885, the Vestry, with help from the Metropolitan Board of Works and the local pledges, bought the land for £750 and West End Green [39] was secured for future public use.

The Green has undergone several changes over the years. Its area has been reduced and a central pond drained. December 1885 saw its layout and enclosure approved at an estimated cost of some £335 and it was later agreed to

39 Children on West End Green after the hoardings were pulled down, 1882

40 The Cock & Hoop, with E J Cave outside

plant alternate lime and plane trees around the Green as well as along the footpath across the open space. In 1887 an elm to celebrate the Jubilee was planted on the upper part of the Green and in 1903 a Coronation oak was added. The drinking fountain was donated by Anne Miles of nearby West End House. Still in common use as late as the 1950s, today the fountain is dry. The inscription on the base can just be deciphered: 'Presented By Miss Miles /

In Memory Of Her Mother / Who Lived In West End 76 Years / 1897'. In 1919, the Council refused to allow Emmanuel Church to erect a war memorial on the Green, and a proposal two years later to place a captured WWI gun on the open space was never implemented. For many years West End Green was a terminus for the No.159 bus (today's No.139).

Following its original course, West End Lane makes a right-angled turn to climb towards

Finchley Road. For many years, the only building in this upper stretch was a public house on the corner of the Green – the **Cock & Hoop** [40]. The pub dated from the early 18th century and after a fire in 1790, was rebuilt as a substantial brick building. It was closely associated with West End Fair, providing accommodation as well as food, drink and entertainment for the crowds, (p 41). In 1820, landlord Nicholas Kendall unsuccessfully petitioned the Magistrates to allow the Fair to continue. 'I took my present House, for which I paid a considerable sum of money, as it was then stated, and which I found to be true, that the profits upon the receipts of the Fair, would nearly pay my rent and taxes which are heavy, added to which, I was obliged to take by valuation, a very great quantity of extra goods and articles to carry on the business, since which I have had temporary Booths, Marquees, long tables and many other things, to accommodate the numerous parties frequenting the Fair. All which, should the Fair be put down, will be of little or no use and sell for little or no money compared to what they cost.' In 1896 the authorities closed the pub when it was discovered that the named licensee, Mr Robinson, had died some four years earlier. It never re-opened and a brewery plan to redevelop the site as a large hotel was abandoned.

41 Across the Green to Emmanuel Church and Alexandra Mansions

Instead, the Cock & Hoop was sold to Edward Jarvis Cave, who was intending to replace it with flats when he went bankrupt. It was sold on to H A Rayner, who built **Alexandra Mansions** [41] (now No.347 West End Lane), displaying the construction date '1902' and described at the time as 'residential flats of a high-class character'. The 1911 census shows that many tenants had servants but there were no live-in porters.

Mary Benton was renting Flat No.8. She was one of the earliest students at Newnham College, Cambridge and went on to work for the Girls' Public Day School Trust. In 1886, Mary became headmistress of South

42 Jack Bruce in Hamburg, 1972

blues. In 1962, soon after he arrived in London, he shared a flat with jazz trombonist John Mumford on the top floor of Alexandra Mansions. He left in 1964 after his marriage and moved across Finchley Road to Bracknell Gardens.

Today there are estate agents at **No.349** West End Lane. The Delevante Cycle Works opened here about 1890. William Crosland rarely used his first name of 'Delevante,' but gave it instead to his company. There was a boom in the popularity of bicycle riding and William offered lessons and hired machines. He sold several brands besides his own, the 'Princess', said to 'combine advantages of strength, speed and lightness'. The business continued under new ownership. By 1900 the proprietor was Edward Pond, who diversified to include motorcycles and traded here until 1939.

The temptation presented by the 'demon drink' was a source of great concern to Victorians. In an early attempt to counter what the congregation of Emmanuel Church viewed as the malign influence of the Cock & Hoop, the 'West End Coffee House' was opened in August 1884 at **No.351**, after hymn singing and a prayer from Emmanuel's Rev. Davys. From around 1888 Edward Pond's father Frederick was the manager. By 1978 it had become 'Capability Brown', fondly remembered

Hampstead High School, a post she held for 32 years. She encouraged the girls to study languages and the sciences, and under her guidance it became one of the best girls' schools in London. Jack Bruce [42], the bass player and singer with Cream, was classically trained at the Royal Scottish Academy of Music but also played jazz and by critic Giles Coren (in 2012) as a restaurant where the Coren family often went. 'Dream Street,' an antique furniture showroom, opened here in 1993. The police followed the owner for 24 hours a day and then arrested Michael Forwell at his stall in Camden Market. A millionaire marijuana smuggler, he was extradited to America where he was sentenced to 15 years imprisonment.

Lawn and Fern Cottages were built about 1814 on the south side of West End Lane, where it began its climb to Finchley Road. Lawn Cottage was briefly home to Charles Dickens' younger brother, Alfred Lamert Dickens. He was the only one of Dickens' siblings to make something of himself by training as a civil engineer. He worked for several railway companies before coming to London around 1854 where his daughter Augusta was born the following year in Hampstead. Alfred used his civil engineering experience to become a Superintending Inspector appointed to administer the Public Health Act. He rented Lawn Cottage in 1859 and was still living there when he died of pleurisy in Manchester on 27 July 1860. Charles Dickens provided for Alfred's widow, Helen, and their five children. He confided to a close friend, 'Day after day I have been scheming and contriving for them, and am still doing so, and have schemed myself into

broken rest and low spirits'. Charles paid for a house in Kentish Town where his sister-in-law could look after his mother, who was suffering from dementia. She died in 1863, and Helen in 1915.

John Longman Bragg lived at Fern Cottage from 1867-84. He and his wife Deborah worked in his baker's shop in Wigmore Street. She looked after the shop while he baked bread and other products in the basement. About 1860 he introduced his medical charcoal biscuits. These became very popular and were sold in numerous chemist shops and even in Harrods. He died in 1896 but the company continued, and Bragg's charcoal biscuits made to the original recipe, are still on sale today.

Lawn and Fern Cottages were put up for sale in 1900, their sites described as 'well adapted for the erection of flats', which is precisely what happened. Several applications were made on behalf of the Cave family and rejected by Hampstead Council before permission was granted in 1901 to build the four blocks of **Cumberland Mansions** containing 32 flats. Until recently the name appeared on a black slate plaque on the first block north of the Green, a trademark of many Cave developments.

In 1911, Lennox Arthur Patrick O'Reilly, who was born in St Lucia, was renting Flat **No.6**. He was in London training to be a

barrister. He was knighted and became a member of the Legislative Council in Trinidad. He died there in March 1949.

Flat No.9 was the home in 1974 of Graham Arnold, who had been Sales Director for Lotus Cars Ltd, from 1963-1970. It was one of Britain's largest manufacturers of high performance sports cars, started by Colin Chapman in 1952 with its first factory in Hornsey. In the 1960s racing drivers Jim Clark and Graham Hill won the drivers' championship in Lotus cars. After several takeovers, the company is still trading today as part of the Malaysian company Proton.

In 1916, Rikiya Kobayashi was in Flat **No.19**. He was an agent for Mikimoto cultured pearls. Kockicki Mikimoto had first worked out how to grow cultured pearls in 1893 and he gained huge publicity when he presented some to King Edward VII at the Coronation in 1902.

Flora Campbell Patterson was living in Cumberland Mansions when she appeared in court in 1919. She had been arrested while holding up two placards inscribed 'S.O.S' and singing to a queue outside the Apollo Theatre, Shaftesbury Avenue. Flora, who was an actress, composer and singer, claimed she was not begging but drawing attention to the grievances of theatricals, particularly the way British artistes were hired. 'She did not ask for money, but some of the crowd slipped coins into her bag'. She was fined £2 and £1 costs.

In January 1933 the 7th Lord Langford, Clotworthy Rowley was living in Cumberland Mansions. He was taken to court several times for failing to pay maintenance of 40s a week to his wife. He said that he was out of work and had already gone to prison for non-payment. Rowley appeared in court twice in 1944 when he was convicted of obtaining money under false pretences. Born in New Zealand, Rowley was a farmer before working his passage to Ireland. He married Florence Eileen O'Donovan in Dublin in 1922 on the strength of his £3,000 inheritance. But this turned out to be mortgaged and Rowley left her the following year. He had a good voice and was hired to sing Irish songs in Canada where he earned enough to travel first class back to England. Running out of money, he sailed for Australia, where he contracted a bigamous marriage and learned he had inherited the title, and not much else, from his uncle. He claimed it actually prevented him getting a job and once wrote to *The Times*, who published a daily diary of the nobility: 'The 7th Baron Langford of Summerhill, dined last evening at a soup kitchen and slept on a bench on the Thames Embankment'. Following his death in Chelsea in July 1952, the title passed to a distant cousin who died the following year.

Further up West End Lane on the north side,

Buckingham Mansions were built by Cave in two stages, the first three blocks appearing in the 1899 rate book. Mrs Charlotte Singer was living in **Flat No.3** in the corner block at the time of her death in 1923. One of the codicils in her will stipulated that a vein in her arm should be opened after death, presumably to guarantee she was not buried alive.

Diamond merchant Frederic Pelissier lived at **Flat No.6** from 1910-12. His son Harry became a professional entertainer and started Pelissier's Follies, a Pierrot-style entertainment. The six-member group became very popular, combining parodies and skits on opera, Shakespearean plays and current London dramatic and musical successes; Harry called them 'potted' plays.

In the early hours of the morning on 19 February 1944, a high explosive bomb fell outside Buckingham Mansions close to the corner with Cannon Hill. The Dee family – husband, wife, son Michael aged 2 and his nanny – were asleep in their flat; the blast blew the glass out of Michael's window, but he was unhurt. However, their next-door neighbours, Dorothy Fletcher (32) and her six-month old daughter Susan, were killed. They are buried in the Civilian War Grave at Hampstead Cemetery. Many of the flats were empty, otherwise the number of casualties could have been higher.

The remaining two blocks of Buckingham Mansions date from the early 1900s and involved demolishing the large house built by Charles Cannon at the corner of West End Lane and Finchley Road (p 130). Donald Tyerman, journalist and editor of *The Economist* (1956-65), moved from Parsifal Road and was living in **Flat No.41** by 1968. He stayed here until his death in 1981.

On the south side of West End Lane, east of Honeybourne Road (p 109), the residential properties at **Nos.288-304**, were completed by 1918. Following a gap in the numbering, the shops beyond Crediton Hill at **Nos.322-336** were completed in 1907 as Frognal Terrace.

At the time just one of many local shopping centres, they included a general store, butcher's and confectioner's, and a builder/decorator.

Joseph Body, a well-known tenor vocalist was at **No.324A** from 1915 to at least 1940. His career on the London stage began in 1896 and he was a member of the Savoy Chorus.

William George Belham, who worked at the butcher's at No.330, was killed in the 1907 train crash at West Hampstead Station (p 63).

Nos.338-340, along with premises facing Finchley Road around the corner, were built on the site of Hedge Bank, a large house in its own grounds (p 130). The Midland Bank opened at the newly completed **No.340** in May 1928 and remained there until the 1990s.

Today's Manuel Swaden, a solicitor's practice, started in 1989 at No.120 Fortune Green Road, and moved here four years later.

Despite the considerable age of some of the houses, only one ghost story has been discovered for West End and this concerns the Miles property. A woman in old-fashioned clothes was said to appear by the gates to the grounds of West End House, near the junction of Finchley Road and West End Lane. Headless, she walked down the carriage drive rustling her silk skirts, the victim of some dreadful injustice at the hands of a previous owner of the property. It's tempting to think the story provided inspiration for Wilkie Collins when he wrote *The Woman in White*, and described his hero meeting a ghostly figure at the nearby junction of four roads: 'the road to Hampstead, along which I had returned, the road to Finchley; the road to West End and the road back to London'.

Running diagonally between West End Lane and Finchley Road, **CANNON HILL** was, in 1865, the first new street to be laid down in the village of West End. Replacing a footpath, it was the creation of Charles Cannon, a wealthy merchant who lived at nearby Kidderpore Hall (later Westfield College). The intention was to develop the adjoining land, and Cannon chose a moment when building London-wide was on the rise. A large house

was completed at the junction of Finchley Road and West End Lane (p 130), but for some reason 'Cannon Hill Road', as it was first called, remained a track across an open field for the next 34 years.

The road was actually developed by Edward Jarvis Cave. Except for Alexandra Mansions, Cave built all of the flats in the triangle formed by Lyncroft Gardens, West End Lane and Finchley Road. Developer, speculator and eventually bankrupt, Cave was the head of a building operation that employed several family members. His name crops up frequently in these pages, especially in connection with mansion flats. Both sides of Cannon Hill are lined almost entirely by red-brick **Marlborough Mansions**, which first appeared in the rate books for 1899. The 1911 census shows most of the 7-room flats occupied by professional and business men or people of independent means, and almost all had at least one live-in servant. There were five resident hall porters/caretakers.

In 1915, the newspapers recorded the death on 31 May of 19-year-old Flight-Lieutenant Herbert Graham Wanklyn. He lived at **No.10** Marlborough Mansions with his parents and attended University College School in Frognal, where he joined the O.T.C. Herbert entered the Royal Naval Air Service in May 1914 and was

flying his seaplane when it was hit by a German shell. His body was recovered from the sea and buried at Calais. His younger brother Arthur survived the war, as a driver for the French Red Cross.

The 1911 census shows Richard Burrows and his wife Ethel at **No.19**. She gave her occupation as 'suffragette' engaged in working for 'votes for women'. The enumerator crossed through her entry in the 'infirmity' column, used to record a disability such as blindness. Ethel had written 'disenfranchised'.

Edward Jaquet was the author of *The Kennel Club, A History and Record of its Work,* (1905) and when he was living at **No.50** from 1905 to 1912, he was the Secretary. The Club had been founded in 1873 in response to the need for a consistent set of rules to govern the popular new activities of dog showing and field trials, as well addressing concerns for the welfare and health of the animals.

Marcus William Zambra, scientific instrument maker, was living at **No.74** in 1907. He was the grandson of Joseph Zambra, co-founder of Negretti & Zambra who made scientific and optical instruments and ran a London-based photographic studio. Marcus was a director of the firm from 1909 until his retirement in 1935. He died in 1952 aged 74, leaving an estate of just over £43,000.

A blue plaque on the next block uphill

43 Sir
Adrian
Boult,
1923

commemorates Sir Adrian Boult [43], who lived at **No.78** from 1966-77 before moving to Compayne Gardens. Boult was an accomplished conductor, responsible for establishing the BBC Symphony Orchestra, moving from there to the London Philharmonic Orchestra. Under his direction both orchestras set extremely high standards. He championed British music and made many recordings, especially for EMI.

The Coldstream family (p 14) moved to **No.87** in 1937. Sir William Menzies Coldstream CBE (1908-87) lived here until 1961 when he departed for Islington. He was a well-known artist, committed to painting from life. William was a co-founder of the Euston Road School and the Tate has several of his works in their collection. Appointed a War Artist in 1943, on his return to England Coldstream became a teacher, later professor at Camberwell School of Art (1945), and then the principal of the Slade (1949), retiring in 1975. He had been knighted in 1956. After coming out of hospital in April 1984 he moved to Frognal Lodge, a small residential hotel until January 1986. Then he went to a Guinness Trust home in Primrose Hill. He died at the Royal London Homeopathic Hospital in Great Ormond Street in 1987.

Nigel Balchin (1908-70) lived in the first block on the west side at **No.89** for the last year of his life. He had returned from America with pneumonia on 14 May 1970 and died in the Greenaway Nursing home in Fellows Road three days later. His *Times* obituary described him as an intriguing mix of 'skilful novelist and industrial psychologist'. Balchin combined business, namely research in science and industry, with a successful career as a novelist. His earliest published work, under the pseudonym of Mark Spade, appeared in *Punch* and was a series of sketches on business efficiency, or lack of it, which he later combined as a book called, *How to Run a Bassoon Factory*. During WWII he worked as a psychologist in the personnel department of the War Office and as Deputy Scientific Adviser to the Army Council, attained the rank of Brigadier. Balchin adapted his own work and others' for several 1940's films, such as: *The Small Back Room* directed by Powell and Pressburger, and *Mine Own Executioner,* which was a satirical attack on Civil Service burocracy. He is buried in Hampstead Cemetery, where the inscription on his book-shaped tombstone is from the title of his 1947 novel, *Lord I Was Afraid.*

Area 8

East of West End Lane

Roads north of the Jubilee line, bounded by West End Lane and Finchley Road

As previously mentioned (p 96), the last owners of Canterbury and Treherne Houses, and West End Hall, the mansions on the east side of West End Lane, collaborated to draw up a development plan for all three properties. Permission was granted in January 1898 to lay down Fawley, Honeybourne and Lymington Roads, and Crediton Hill.

FAWLEY ROAD runs east off the Lane. **No.4** was known by the occupants as 'Bleak House', from the terrible condition it was in. Numerous jazz musicians lived here in the 1950s and '60s. Colin Purbrook and Brian Lemon were pianists. Tony Coe was a sax player and Jimmy Deucher played trumpet. Colin was 'The Grand Vizier' of parties in Fawley Road, where he lived from 1961-64. When his ex-wife Maureen visited the dying Colin at a Hampstead hospice, she told the consultant that Purbrook was one of the ten best jazz pianists in the country. When she told him what she had said, Colin, by now barely able to speak, croaked, 'Five, Dear, Five'.

In the 1938 Yearbook for Hampstead, Dayan Mark Gollop is shown at **No.13** Fawley Road. During WWI he was in Gallipoli, and he became rabbi at the Hampstead Synagogue in 1930 after being at the Bayswater Synagogue. From 1926 to 1942 he was the Senior Jewish Chaplain to the Armed Forces. He was called up at the outbreak of WWII but retired due to ill health in March 1944; he died on 4 August 1950. He was an enthusiastic minister who promoted the social aspects of congregational life.

The Matheson family moved into **No.21** in December 1901. They had befriended young Henry Walford Davies when his father died, and he lived with them for many years. Henry became a composer and worked as a teacher, broadcaster, choirmaster and organist, including Christ Church in Hampstead, where he was organist from 1892 to 1897. Henry's work *The Temple* was finished while he was living in Fawley Road; his *Everyman* was composed during the winter of 1903-04 and performed at No.21 the following year, with piano, soloists and a full choir in the front hall. His best-known work is the *Royal Air Force March Past* composed in 1918. Walford was knighted (1922) and became Master of the King's Music (1934). He died in 1941 and is buried in the graveyard of Bristol Cathedral.

Except for nine private houses at its south end, **HONEYBOURNE ROAD** is dominated by blocks of flats built by the Cave family. Unlike the Cave blocks on nearby Cannon Hill (p 107), they have no communal gardens.

Yale Court on the east side contains 88 flats. Close to the corner with West End Lane, photographers Leonard (Len) Karstein and Anya Teixeira were in Flat No.14 from at least 1950 to 1980. They formed part of the Hampstead-based 'Creative Photo Group' in the 1960s. Len won a competition at Klooks Kleek jazz club in the Railway Hotel and his photo of the shadow of baritone sax player, Glen Hughes, was published in the *Melody Maker* in 1962.

In **Harvard Court**, opposite, there are 92 flats. In August 1913, Major General George Johnstone Buchanan of the Royal Medical Corps, died from a gunshot wound at his home in Flat No.3. Buchanan had been handing an automatic pistol to his nephew, when it went off. Buchanan told witnesses it was an accident, he was unfamiliar with the gun, believing he had removed all the cartridges.

In 1968, Freda (Freddie) Ross was living in Flat No.6. This was the home of her parents in the 60s. From 1954 she was a publicist for comedian Tony Hancock. They began an affair five years later and married in December 1965. It was a difficult relationship and they were divorced in 1968.

Geoffrey Finsberg, was in Flat No.77 in the 1960s, before moving to Westbere Road (p 25).

Flat No.79 was briefly home to Christina Chute. Her father James Chute married the daughter of actor/manager William Macready senior; the two families dominated the world of nineteenth century theatre in Bristol. In 1906 Christine was running classes in calisthenics and dancing. She had moved to Marylebone by 1911, when she gave her occupation to the census as a 'teacher of physical culture'. She died at her home in Alexandra Road in 1932.

Katherine Gray filled out her census return in 1911, from Flat No.91 Harvard Court. She gave her name, her age (54) and her occupation as a voluntary worker in the slums and no other information. But in common with other campaigners for Women's Votes, she wrote a message on the form: 'As a returned colonist from New Zealand, I resent the position of women in this country, and refuse to supply information to a Government which denies justice to British women'.

Mary Lindsay, who also lived at Harvard Court, was prosecuted in February 1914, for assaulting Lord Weardale whom she had mistaken for the Prime Minister, Mr Asquith. Mary refused to give her name and address when arrested. Remanded for enquiries to be made into her mental state, she went on hunger strike in Holloway. Medical reports concluded Mary was highly strung but not insane. She told the court she fully understood what she had done and refused to apologise, 'I consider men who torture women in the 20th century ought to be thrashed'. Lord Weardale was the joint president of the Anti-Suffragist Society and the Votes for Women campaigners received harsh treatment at the hands of the police and prison warders. The Magistrate ignored her comment and concentrated instead on Lord Weardale: 'Here is a perfectly harmless old gentleman, suddenly attacked by a young woman who hits him on the head with a dog whip – a most offensive weapon'. Mary was sentenced to 14 days in prison or a 40s fine which was paid anonymously.

CREDITON HILL was called Crediton Road until 1914. Many of the houses north of Fawley Road were built by Robert Vernon Hart, a member of a local family responsible for many properties in Hampstead.

No.1 Crediton Hill was York House School from 1929 until 1938, when the fear of bombing raids prompted a move to Rickmansworth. Rev. Cambridge Victor Hawkins had founded the school at No.98 Broadhurst Gardens in 1910. A pupil remembers: 'Their blazers, caps, ties and sock tops were green and mauve. Two women taught the younger boys and administered discipline with the aid of an old gym slipper. The headmaster, Mr Hawkins, a round-faced, bespectacled man, was nicknamed the Owl.'

In 1907, Julius Schnurmann moved from No.67 Hillfield Road to **No.3** Crediton Hill. He was the owner of a large factory in Tottenham which reprocessed scrap rubber. In 1909 two Latvian anarchists stole the wages, and in the resulting manhunt shot and killed a police constable and a young boy. The attack became headline news as the 'Tottenham Outrage'. As the motorcar became more popular, the demand for rubber tyres increased rapidly and Schnurmann's company prospered. In 1917, because of the strong anti-German feeling, he changed his name to James Julius Sherman. He stayed in Crediton Hill until 1933, and then moved to Abercorn Place. He died in his flat at 99 Haverstock Hill in 1948.

Emil and Florence Lifetree moved to **No.23** from Fordwych Road. Their son, Second Lieutenant Ernest Henry Lifetree, was one of West Hampstead's many casualties of WWI. A pupil at University College School, he enlisted in July 1915 in the Honourable Artillery Company. On 21 May 1916 aged 22, he was killed in action on the Western Front. Ernest is buried in Guards Cemetery, Windy Corner Cuinchy, and remembered on the War Memorial outside Hampstead Parish Church. His parents were still at No.23 in 1926. Emil had gone blind and was being cared for by his wife and a male nurse, Charles Anderson. Anderson disappeared from the house that June, taking jewellery and money with him. Found guilty of this and another theft at Bath, he was sentenced to six months hard labour, with a further three months if he failed to pay a fine.

No.27 was home to Edric Connor from 1957. Edric was a pioneering calypso singer from Trinidad who came to England in 1944. In 1951 he brought the Trinidad Steel Orchestra to the Festival of Britain. In 1952 with his band Edric Connor and the Caribbeans, he recorded the album *Songs from Jamaica*. This included *Day Dah Light* a version of which became Harry Belafonte's big hit, *The Banana Boat Song*, in 1957. With his wife Pearl, Edric set up an agency to support black actors and musicians. In 1958 he became the first black actor to appear with the Royal Shakespeare Company in Stratford. He appeared on TV and in 18 films, including *Fire Down Below* with Rita Hayworth and Robert Mitcham. Edric died in Putney in 1968 and Pearl died in 2005.

Fred Gaisberg [44], a pioneer in the recording industry, lived at various addresses in Camden including Fitzjohn's Avenue, 13 Avenue Mansions Finchley Road and finally **No.42** Crediton Hill, where he died in 1951. Born in Washington D.C. in 1894 he joined Emile Berliner at the Gramophone Company. He was sent to London four years later to take charge of its newly opened recording studio in Maiden Lane near the Strand. Gaisberg made recordings of music hall artists such as Dan Leno and Marie Lloyd, and later famous opera singers such as Melba and Patti. But the quality of his 1902 Caruso recordings laid the foundations for the modern record industry, as up to then the gramophone had not been taken seriously. He was a keen judge of musical talent and snapped up the young conductor John Barbirolli in 1927 after he had stepped in at short notice to replace Sir Henry Beecham, and he also helped to launch the

44 Fred Gaisberg

career of Yehudi Menuhin. Fred stayed with the company until he retired in 1939.

In 1904, John Jacoby, a leading lace manufacturer, moved into **No.50** and remained there to his death in 1953. In 1913 Jacoby's wife Sarah took her own life. She had been seriously ill for several years and in constant pain. She wrote several farewell letters and took an overdose of tablets prescribed to help her sleep. The Hampstead Coroner said there was no evidence of Sarah's suffering from any mental instability and the jury returned a verdict of 'felo de se', an old description for suicide. When Jacoby gave evidence to a 1925 Board of Trade enquiry into imposing duty on machine imported lace, he made the surprising statement: 'Our whole trade is useless and I am ashamed of being in it. It is against all my social principles to cater for luxury – and lace is a luxury'. When questioned further, Jacoby said he intended retiring to do something useful such as, 'medical research, intellectual work, anything that makes for progress or enlightenment'. We don't know if this happened, but he remained a leading expert in his field, with a superb collection and giving lectures on the history of lace. Queen Mary, the wife of George V, regularly visited him at No.50. She was an avid collector and it's said antique dealers hid their best items, for if she liked what she saw,

Queen Mary would hint that she expected to be given it as a gift.

Heathburn, the northernmost house on the east side at **No.76**, was built for the Cave family of builders and developers. When Edward Jarvis Cave went bankrupt, the business continued trading in his wife Elizabeth's name and that of other family members.

The actor Eric Thompson (1929-82) moved to Crediton Hill in the 1960s and the road has been home ever since to his actress wife Phyllida Law and daughter Emma. Younger daughter Sophie lived there for many years after her marriage to Richard Lumsden. Eric Thompson was a regular presenter on *Play School* and is best known as the narrator of *The Magic Roundabout*, a children's programme from France for which he wrote the English scripts. His stories made it a cult programme from 1965 to 1977. Phyllida Law, OBE has appeared in many television productions and films and has published several autobiographical books. Actress and screenwriter, Emma Thompson DBE went to Beckford School and then Camden School for Girls. In 1989 she married fellow actor (Sir) Kenneth Branagh. After their divorce, she married actor Greg Wise in 2003. She has had a very successful career as an actor and writer. She wrote and starred in the *Nanny McPhee* films and *Saving Mr Banks*, about the making of Mary Poppins, where she played P L Travers with Tom Hanks as Walt Disney. She has won two Oscars for *Howards End* and *Sense and Sensibility*. Greg has appeared in the TV dramas *Cranford, Trial and Retribution*, and *The Crown*. His recent film work has included, *Johnny English* and *Effie Gray* (with a screenplay by Emma Thompson).

Their neighbours are husband and wife actors, Jim Carter OBE and Imelda Staunton CBE. Jim is passionate about cricket and was the Chair of Hampstead Cricket Club. Although he is now best known for his role as the butler in *Downton Abbey*, he has had a very successful career which included The *Singing Detective, Brassed Off* and *Red Riding*. He met Imelda Staunton in 1982 when they appeared together in Richard Eyre's National Theatre production of *Guys and Dolls*. She won Best Actress at the Venice Film Festival for her role in Mike Leigh's *Vera Drake*, and Best Actress in a Musical, when she appeared with Michael Ball in *Sweeny Todd* (2013) and as Mama Rose in *Gypsy*, (2016). She has also appeared in two of the *Harry Potter* films.

Charles Chilton MBE and his wife Penny moved to Crediton Hill about 1986. He joined the BBC as a messenger boy aged 14, later working in the record library. He produced 'Journey into Space', 'Take It From Here' and several episodes of the 'Goon Show' and was awarded the MBE in 1976. In January 2013 Charles died in the Royal Free Hospital aged 95.

York House School (see above) was on the corner of **LYMINGTON ROAD**, at the western end of which, above shops at the junction with West End Lane, are **Lymington Mansions**. In 1962 Gus (Angus) Dudgeon, recording engineer and producer, was in Flat No.2, where he stayed until his marriage in 1965. The blues singer Long John Baldry slept on a bed in his hallway. When he left school Gus had had several short-term jobs before he was employed as a junior assistant at Olympic Studios in Baker Street. In 1962 he managed to get a job as an engineer at Decca Studios in Broadhurst Gardens, where he worked on numerous records until he left and set up his own company. Gus later lived at Kings Gardens at the Kilburn end of West End Lane. By 1970 he was recording with Elton John and many other artists. He and his wife Shelia were tragically killed in a car accident in July 2002.

Gwladys Cox lived with her husband Ralph, a barrister, in Flat No.6, Lymington Mansions. She kept a diary of her wartime experiences in West Hampstead which is now in the Imperial War Museum. When the couple returned home after a visit to her sister in Guildford, they found that an incendiary bomb had damaged their top floor flat on 1 October 1940. They managed to rescue their cat Bobby, but their antique furniture and Ralph's collection of books and records had been destroyed and Gwladys' jewellery had been looted. They moved to No.59 Cholmley Gardens, where Ralph died in 1958. Gwladys died in Kingston upon Thames in 1972.

Some of the backland behind today's No.156 West End Lane was used for a tennis courts. In the 1930s it was the Mayfair Tennis Club owned by Debenhams, the Oxford Street department store. The land was still undeveloped as late as the 1950s when, derelict and overgrown and with the trace of an allotment or two, it was a playground for children living in the houses on the south side of Lymington Road. Though strictly forbidden by parents, it was easy to climb over the low garden wall and enter the jungle.

The houses in Lymington Road were all built by Boddy and Chapman, as far as No.21 (north side) and No.30 (opposite), where for many years the road ended at the boundary with Maryon Wilson land.

Ken Livingstone lived at **No.9** from 1977-80. In 1978 he won a seat on Camden Council where he served for four years, becoming Chair of Housing. In May 1979 he stood for Hampstead in the General Election but was beaten by the incumbent MP, Sir Geoffrey Finsberg (p 110). Livingstone later became Mayor of London.

Sculptor James Nesfield Forsyth was at **No.18** in the mid-1920s. He studied at Paris and the Royal Academy Schools and worked with his father James Forsyth (p 125). Nesfield went on to specialise in portraiture. His sculpture *Age* was shown at the RA in 1901 and is now in the Lady Lever Art Gallery, Liverpool. He was also responsible for a bronze bust which has long since been stolen, but originally crowned the family grave of architect Banister Fletcher in Hampstead Cemetery.

In retirement, James 'Pasha' Wilson lived at **No.19**. He died in 1906 and is also buried in Hampstead Cemetery. His Grade-II Listed memorial, in the form of an Egyptian temple in pink granite protected by a winged disc intended to ward off evil, is appropriate for a man who was employed by the Egyptian Government for 44 years as a civil engineer. Born in Renfrewshire, Wilson was first apprenticed to Napier and Sons, Glasgow, and later worked for the Cunard Steamship Company. In 1857 he went to Egypt as chief engineer of the Nile Steam Towing company, moving to the service of Ismail Pasha a year later. He worked to improve agriculture and other industries and was appointed Chief Engineer by the Egyptian Government (1875-1901) when he was primarily responsible for increasing sugar production. He received the title of 'Pasha' in 1895, the last of a long line of honours.

On the corner of Crediton Hill, Lionel Harris and his Spanish born wife lived at **No.21** from at least 1902-20. The house was demolished and rebuilt as flats in the mid-1970s. Harris founded the Spanish Art Gallery in Mayfair and was responsible for importing most of the important works of art which came from Spain in the years before and after the First World War. Lionel died in 1943. His son Tomas was born in Lymington Road in 1908. He became an artist and sculptor and then worked with his father as an art dealer. During WWII he joined MI5. His greatest achievement was as the case officer of the agent known as Garbo, and the most successful double-cross operation of the war which misled the Germans about the Allied invasion of France in 1944. For his work he was awarded the OBE the next year. Harris died in a car accident in Spain in 1964. His superb collection of Goya etchings is now in the British Museum.

No.21 was home to comic actor Sidney James from 1953-56. A focal point was Sid's bar - which occupied a complete room of his flat - with plain white-wood furniture and wall to wall deep scarlet carpet. The walls were covered in just two kinds of decoration - a cluster of framed photographs of Sid in his film and stage roles, and scores of miniature liquor bottles. The shelves, as Sid informed any new guest, he had built himself. He left West Hampstead for Gunnersbury Avenue.

Sid also lived in Compayne Gardens.

Novelist and journalist Edmund Clerihew Bentley was at **No.28** from at least 1911-26. He invented the clerihew, a four-line humorous verse about a famous person. He was a school friend of G K Chesterton. Clerihew worked on several newspapers, including the Daily Telegraph. His detective story, *Trent's Last Case* (1913) was very highly praised. He was president of the Detection Club (1936-49) and wrote several crime stories which were broadcast in the 1930s.

Warwick House School, founded in 1883, moved to **No.30** around 1939. Errol Brown, one of the founders of the band Hot Chocolate (p 74), went there in the 1960s. 'When I was 14, we moved to West Hampstead, and my mother – who was my greatest inspiration – sent me to Warwick House. That was the major move in my life because secondary moderns didn't encourage you to have any ambitions at all beyond being a manual worker. They made out that you didn't have the brain power. When I went to the private school, everyone wanted to be doctors, lawyers and account-ants. There was a completely different mindset about what you could achieve in your life, and how you could better yourself.' In 1963 the headmaster resigned after parents withdrew their boys when they found that two teachers had prison records. It continued, as

'Lymington School', until at least 1975.

Lymington Road ended here at the boundary with Maryon-Wilson land, until it was eventually continued to Finchley Road in 1902, replacing a rough and ready track. From 1877 this had led from Finchley Road to the **Hampstead Cricket Club** (HCC) who leased five acres here, described by a club member as, 'a cultivated arable field with growing crops of turnips, mangold wurzel, potatoes'. It took a great deal of hard work to create the first pitch. The club was very successful and gained wide recognition when on 3 August 1886, a match was played at Hampstead between HCC and the Stoics. At the time no declarations were allowed, and Andrew Ernest Stoddart batted for just over six hours, making 485 runs, the highest individual score ever recorded at the time. For many years before and after WWI, matches were played here to raise money for charity. The teams were made up of musicians, actors and writers who were very well-known in their time. The club visitors' book shows the names of many famous people including W G Grace and J M Barrie. To celebrate the club's 150th anniversary, in May 2015, a bronze statue of Stoddart was unveiled by former England cricket captain Andrew Strauss.

The cricket club grounds border on the west side of **ALVANLEY GARDENS**, approval for

which was granted in May 1914. The first names suggested were Hall Oak Avenue or Gardens. The alternative of Lymington Gardens was put forward, but rejected by the LCC, who countered with Alvanley. WWI intervened, and building work was put on hold. In 1916 a vacant site bounded by Alvanley Gardens, Lymington Road and Finchley Road was used as allotment gardens by council employees for the duration of the war.

North of the HCC, the west side of the road is lined by the grounds of the **Cumberland Lawn Tennis Club**. The Club moved here in 1903 and bought the freehold in 1922. In 1960 it applied to build 14 houses on its courts, but Hampstead Council refused permission. Six would have fronted the road with a further eight in a cul-de-sac. Since then the Club has expanded to include squash, and in the 1970s it provided practice space in the run up to Wimbledon, for tennis aces such as Guillermo Vilas and Bjorn Borg.

Many of the twenty houses on the eastern side were built after 1923 by the Cave family. In 1963, classical violinist Raymond Cohen was living at **No.6** when he was named in a libel action. An article to which he contributed had alleged that orchestral conductor Herman Roderick Lindars was incompetent and unfit to have accompanied the Royal Philharmonic on a recent tour of Russia. Lindars won a substantial sum in damages. Born in Manchester into a musical family, Cohen first took violin lessons from his father and then won a scholarship to the Manchester (now Royal Northern) College of Music. After WWII he became a Professor at the Royal College of Music and for six years he was leader of the Royal Philharmonic Orchestra. In 1953, Cohen married the pianist Anthya Rael. They had two children: Gillian, a violinist, and Robert, a cellist. In 1993, the family was featured in a BBC radio programme called *The Musical World of Raymond Cohen.*

Sir Archibald Montague Gray died at his home, **No.7,** in 1967. He had moved to West Hampstead around 1954. Gray initially studied obstetrics and gynaecology but went on to specialise in dermatology. He was a talented clinician and administrator. Gray headed departments at University College Hospital and the Hospital for Sick Children, Great Ormond Street, and served on the board of many medical and educational organisations. In 1963 the British Association of Dermatology established the Archibald Gray Prize and Medal.

Walter Zander, a lawyer, scholar and writer specialising in Israel and its international relations, lived at **No.16** from 1957 to the late 1980s. He had emigrated from Berlin to England with his family in 1937. His son,

Michael Zander QC, is Professor Emeritus of Law at the London School of Economics & Political Science and the author of several highly respected books on legal matters. In 1961, Alvanley Gardens was Michael's address when he was legal adviser and appeal treasurer to Tony Benn, in his battle to remain in the House of Commons.

Maria Martha Saran (1897-1976), known as Mary Saran, was a writer and journalist. A left-wing activist in the years leading up to WWII, she escaped from Germany with her 12-year-old daughter Rene in 1933, travelling to France and then to England. Mary wrote in her autobiography *Never Give Up* (1976) that in 1941 she moved into an evacuated house in Alvanley Gardens with a group of friends. The house was a meeting place and the centre for the Socialist Vanguard Group. Mary went on to become a teacher, journalist and active Labour Party supporter.

The 1902 extension of Lymington Road followed Hampstead Council's purchase of 3½ acres of land between the Cricket Club grounds and the Hampstead Junction Railway tracks, at a cost of £18,000. Part was used as a new municipal depot for vehicles and materials, which needed proper road access. During WWI the yard was used by the 138th Heavy Battery, Royal Garrison Artillery, nicknamed the 'Hampstead Heavies', to store

equipment and stable over 150 horses collected from all over London.

The Hampstead Council depot closed in the 1970s and the site was redeveloped by Camden Council for housing. Officially the **Lymington Road Estate**, it is familiarly known as the 'Potteries', in view of the names chosen for the new roads: **Wedgwood Walk, Spode Walk, Beswick Mews, Worcester Mews, Minton Mews, Doulton Mews, Crown Close** and **Dresden Close**. Running westward alongside the Overground line, and linking the Estate with West End Lane, is a public right of way known as the **Potteries Path**.

East of the former Council depot, off the north side of Lymington Road at No.27 was a drill hall for the Queen Victoria's Rifles, 9th London Regiment. It ended its life as a car showroom before the site was redeveloped as part of JW3 (p 128). Opposite, there was a short run of commercial premises with living accommodation above. Here, No.66A was one of several flats occupied locally by the artist David Bomberg (p 15). On the site today are the **Pulse Apartments** (No.52), part of a major development off Finchley Road (p 126) that was completed in 2004.

Off the main road, to the south, Lithos and Rosemont Roads were built on a landlocked triangle of land, created in the 1860s when the Hampstead Junction Railway (Overground) railway tracks were carried over those of the Midland Railway (Thameslink). In 1871 the site was used for dumping rubbish and making bricks. In 1880 Hampstead Vestry bought two acres at the apex of the triangle, to be used as the parish 'stoneyard', where rubbish was taken, and road repair materials and carts were kept. In 1881 permission was given to create **LITHOS ROAD** as a permanent link from Finchley Road to the stoneyard.

In December 1892, Hampstead Vestry decided to open its own electricity power plant here, run by a private municipal company. Just three years previously, it had argued against adopting any supply scheme for Hampstead on the grounds that 'the science of electricity is not at present sufficiently developed'. The buildings were constructed by Yerbury & Sons of Kilburn and the two chimneys, 130ft high, became a local landmark. On the evening of 1 October 1894, the electricity was switched on and an enthusiastic crowd in Finchley Road watched 22 street lamps light up simultaneously for the first time. The Vestry found a new site for their stoneyard depot, in Lymington Road. The Lithos Road plant ceased generating in 1922 but remained in Hampstead's control until nationalisation in 1948. It was replaced by new offices for the London Electricity Board (LEB), opened in 1975 and demolished only eight years later when a new

depot was opened in Islington. An electricity substation remains.

In the surviving terrace of Victorian houses in Lithos Road, **No.37** was the home in October 1940 of Cora Nellie Roder, the first woman ARP warden to be killed in WWII. She was on duty when a high explosive bomb damaged the Hampstead Central Library on the corner of Arkwright Road (p 126). Cora was buried under debris and a heavy beam. She spoke to her rescuers but was unconscious when finally dug out and died from her injuries. She is buried at Hampstead Cemetery.

Properties in Lithos Road became run down in the 1960s and '70s, and some were squatted. Lithos and Rosemont Roads were included under the Central Hampstead redevelopment plan, which underwent several revisions but essentially involved rehabilitating or demolishing many of the properties and building new houses. Much of the north side of Lithos Road has since been rebuilt.

In 1991 the stoneyard area was redeveloped as the **Lithos Road Estate**. All the block names have a common 'tree' theme: Laurel, Sandalwood, Iroko, Banyan, Rosewood and Ebony Houses on the north side of the road; Hornbeam, Jacaranda, Sequoia, Mahogany and Juniper to the south.

Permission to redevelop **Nos.32&34** was given in 2005. The original properties here

were called Gainsborough House and Claremont House. About 1902 the artist Allan Davidson moved into Flat No.1, Claremont House. Specialising in nudes, genre scenes, portraits and interiors, he had 25 works exhibited at the Royal Academy. Flat No.6 was home in 1911 to Waldemar Sommerfelt, a Norwegian-born composer and pianist. He died in 1919, aged 34, during the Spanish flu epidemic. In January 1993 it was announced that the West Hampstead Housing Association was to demolish fourteen houses, Nos.2-28, and replace them with **PETROS GARDENS**, new homes built round a courtyard.

South of Lithos Road is **ROSEMONT ROAD**. In 1893, after a couple of refusals, Edward Jarvis Cave was given permission to build what was described as 'a mews between Finchley Road and Lithos Road', which provided stabling with living accommodation above, later adapted to the needs of small industries or used as garages. In 1911, the census showed most men living here were employed as coach drivers, chauffeurs or in the horse trade. Some of the now modified first-floor hayloft doors may still be seen at **Nos.2-6**.

At one time, many premises were occupied by jobmasters Taylor & Lown [45]. The firm was started by in 1888 by Joseph Taylor and William Lown, transporting goods and hiring out horses and carts. The two men probably

45 Taylor and Lown stables

Rosemont Road. Taylor & Lown were occupying eight premises there in 1904, and fifteen in 1926, by that time providing cars and chauffeur services.

Premises were later adapted to the need of small industries or used as garages. In 1905, Joseph Rogers was in court. He traded from Rosemont Road as the 'German Laundry Company'. Several of his female employees were kept at work all night and despite Rogers' claiming they were just helping him out, he was fined for making them work excessive hours.

In 1951, Nos.16-26 were being used to make Dorlon Chocolates. Production had moved to Nos.30&32 by 1970, the year the company went bankrupt. After several attempts, permission was obtained in 1998 to redevelop these properties with mews-style houses (**Nos.16-28**) and to use the land behind, known as the Rosemont Embankment, for a gated housing development with some commercial space (today's **Nos.30-72**).

North of Lithos Road, and running parallel to the Overground tracks, is **Billy Fury Way**, a footpath linking Finchley Road and West End Lane. In the 1950s and '60s the gloomy walk, through an area crisscrossed by railway lines and sidings, was often referred to as the 'Black Path' (not to be confused with a namesake off the other side of West End Lane, p 69. Local

moved to Rosemont Road when their previous premises in Canfield Place were partly demolished by the Great Central Railway to build their line to Marylebone. An earlier advert for stabling in 1894, had promised a 'magnificent opportunity for jobmasters' in children also called it 'Granny Stairs'. The footbridge that carried it over the Midland line had damaged planks with large gaps; it shook as the trains passed below and clouds of steam and smoke rushed up through the cracks, to the delight of children standing above. A door in a brick wall provided West Hampstead residents with a short cut to the LEB offices in Lithos Road to pay their electricity bill, without walking round via Finchley Road. That pedestrian access to Lithos Road is still in place, emerging there beside No.34. Back in 1927, the name Sportsway had been suggested for the footpath, as there was a sportswear shop near each end. The path remained officially unnamed until 2010, when after a poll it was decided to name it after rock 'n' roll star Billy Fury, who had recorded at Decca Studios on Broadhurst Gardens. A large mural of his face was painted at the top of the steps leading down to the path from West End Lane but was graffitied and has since been painted over.

Billy Fury Way is joined by a second footway running south to Broadhurst Gardens, with a footbridge to carry it across the Underground tracks. This replaced a much older path, on a different alignment, which once crossed the fields between Abbey Road and West End Lane. En route it crosses **BLACKBURN ROAD**.

Although there seems to have been a plan to carry it through to Finchley Road, until quite recently it remained a vehicular cul-de-sac off West End Lane, ending at the boundary of the Midland Railway's land, tracks and sidings. Though approved in 1869, it was not made a public road until the turn of the 20th century. In the meantime people took advantage of the quiet surroundings to illegally dump rubbish. Inadequate lighting made it hazardous at night while the building of the Metropolitan line caused further problems.

George Cloke was living in Brondesbury in 1911 and made his money from recycling. In 1921 he advertised 'pulverised London house refuse' as the best substitute for horse manure, price 5s a ton from Railway Wharf, Blackburn Road. A year later Cloke said the material had been used by farmers for years but the price had been reduced to 2s 6d and in 1923 he was offering potential purchasers a free truckload.

The four surviving houses at the western end were built in 1886 for Richard Pincham, developer and the publican at the nearby Railway Hotel. In 1893, John Aitchison of No.1 (now **No.9**) asked the Vestry to intervene, stating 'that cartloads of carpets were brought into that road by sweeps, who beat them in the roadway, smothering the adjoining houses with dust'.

From at least 1974-83, **No.3** (as Kingsbury House) was home to the Institute for the Study of Drug Dependence, a charity established in 1968, providing information on drugs and drug use and now known as DrugWise.

Joseph Sloper built the Tower Royal Works, **No.11**, in 1872. Part of the small 2-storey factory was still standing in March 2021, backing onto Billy Fury Way. Sloper started out as a house decorator and builder but there was another side to the man, that of a creative inventor. During the Victorian period businesses were plagued by thefts of postage stamps and cheques from company stocks. Because these could be stolen and resold, dishonest employees found them an attractive target. Sloper invented a perforating machine which punched the name of a firm onto cheques. After his death in 1890, the factory continued under the management of two of his sons, Eustace and Percy. The employees working on the ground floor made machines for perforating metal (including photo frames), felt (ventilating felt hats was specifically mentioned) and paper (including patterned stationery products). After Percy died in 1933, the business was sold to Reginald Theodore Firminger. During WWII the factory, where staff worked 12-hour shifts, mainly produced spare parts for aircraft. In 1991 the business was taken over by Checkpoint Security

Systems Ltd, who transferred all viable operations to Reading.

After the Blackburn Road factory shut, the renowned sculptor Phillip King (p 85) used the building as a studio. The Maak Gallery was built to the right of the old factory building. The Israeli-born artist Zadok Ben-David was there until 2015, when the owners applied to redevelop the entire site, including King's studio. Permission was granted in 2017, for new housing, artists' studios and gallery space, but had not been implemented by March 2021.

By 1926, the Imperial Hard Courts, part of the Imperial Sports Ground, were at the end of the cul-de-sac, beyond Sloper's works. The owner was Alexander Forbes of Fairfax Road. As well as sports equipment, he sold leather goods, wireless sets and aerials which he installed. Offering table tennis on two evenings a week, the pavilion-cum-dancehall was in a ruinous state by the 1950s.

In the late '50s the General Post Office used the land to build a service centre with a large car park; their successors, British Telecom (BT) were to remain here till the 1990s. The building, No.13, was renamed Asher House after the founders of the Accurist watch brand, who occupied part of the building as offices. In 2014, permission was given to convert from commercial to residential use. In 1986 Accurist had been appointed as the first official sponsor of BT's Speaking Clock, hence the name chosen for the new flats: the **Clockwork Factory Apartments**. In 2020 an application was registered to demolish the Apartments and replace with three mixed use blocks arranged round a new open space. A car repair garage had been built on part of the BT car park, but in 2011 permission was obtained to redevelop and the private student hall of residence named **Nido House**, with office space beneath called **Blackburn House**, were completed in 2013.

On the south side of Blackburn Road, Express Dairy opened their distribution depot at **No.14** in the mid-1950s. It was a familiar sight to passengers on the southbound platform at West Hampstead Station, who could see into the yard and hear rattling glass bottles being loaded onto the small electric powered milk floats. Although in 2004 permission was given to redevelop the site for mixed residential and commercial use, it was occupied by a builders' merchant in 2021.

Beyond Nido House is the O2 centre, where two large premises now lying under the car park were once reached via Blackburn Road. The first was the Canadian Building originally occupied by the Canadian Government in the 1930s. The aim of adverts issued by the Director of Canadian Trade Publicity from this address was to encourage everyone to buy Canada's 'pure food products'. In 1931 housewives who wrote to Blackburn Road would receive a free copy of *The Maple Leaf Canadian Recipe Book*. Retailers could take a Maple Leaf Tour of Canada. A pension department was located here in 1944 and it became the Canada House Business Centre.

Cadbury's (later Cadbury Fry) opened their distribution depot next door in 1932. This was part of a new initiative to make more use of rail freight (in this case, a daily train consisting of 11 wagons) and the depot provided significant local employment. A contemporary news report commented: 'thousands of Easter eggs were brought direct from Bournville in a special train yesterday formally to open the new distribution depot at West Hampstead. The new centre contains offices, stores, and loading banks and is capable of dealing with 500 tons of chocolate and cocoa a week. About a hundred people are employed, and a canteen has been built for them'. The purple lorries were a familiar sight in West Hampstead until in the 1980s Cadbury's moved out. In 1988 the building was being used as a specialist store, selling Art Deco and Arts & Crafts furniture.

Today, Blackburn Road provides emergency vehicle access to the O2 Centre, with a permanent pedestrian link.

Up the Finchley Road

North from Finchley Road Underground Station
to the corner of the Hendon Way. (For the section
southward to the Westminster boundary, see
*Streets and Characters of Kilburn & South
Hampstead*.)

Colonel Henry Eyre was the owner of a valuable St John's Wood estate. It took him four attempts before an 1826 Act of Parliament allowed him to lay down the line of Avenue Road and Finchley (New) Road. His main opponent was Sir Thomas Maryon-Wilson, who saw no benefit to his property or to Hampstead. He did manage to insert a clause in the Bill, stipulating that the road had to be built southwards from Finchley, to ensure it wouldn't be abandoned. Opened in 1829, the Finchley New Road was little used and patrols were needed to protect travellers from robbers. It was still a country road in 1857; lacking drainage and with a surface below that of the neighbouring fields, it was prone to flooding. Building progressed slowly northwards and the 1860s OS map shows houses on both sides from Boundary Road as far as Fairfax Road and the North Star pub (opened in 1850). Beyond, the road crossed open fields until it reached the small hamlet of Child's Hill. The only buildings encountered en route were Finchley & Frognal railway station (on the west side), and the six villas of New West End (east side) north of the village of West End.

As the neighbourhood developed, Hampstead Vestry recognised the importance of **FINCHLEY ROAD**, and in 1890 reported it had been 'planted with sycamore, elm and plane from the Public Baths (at No.177, now Iceland) to the boundary of the parish at Child's-Hill. It is probably the longest and promises to be the most imposing avenue or public highway near London'. In 1932 it was still described in glowing terms: 'with its fine shops and many artistic modern houses standing back in their own private gardens, Finchley Road must be considered one of the finest of the great main arteries leading out of London'. All this changed when in the 1960s it was widened to six lanes of traffic. On the works' completion in 1969, the Royal Institute of British Architects commented, 'the road has become a dirty, cold and fume-laden tunnel'.

The numbering of the road is complex, and we have tried to order the text roughly to reflect the positions on the ground.

Finchley Road Underground Station

opened on the Metropolitan line & St John's Wood Railway in 1879 with its entrance on Canfield Gardens. The station was rebuilt in 1914 and again in the 1930s ahead of the arrival in 1939 of the Bakerloo (now Jubilee) line.

Built above the new station entrance, to a design by Frank Sherrin, was **Canfield House,** where the tropical medicine specialist Sir Robert Hammill Firth was living in Flat No.4 at the time of his death in June 1931. At street level, **No.219a** was part of a run of shops. In 2019 it was combined with adjoining premises, Nos.219, 219b and 219d, and opened as a Pret A Manger sandwich shop. In 1971 Gary Nesbitt and colleagues opened The Tape Revolution at 219a. This was the beginning of a chain of shops which became Our Price Records in 1976. Ten years later the company was bought by WH Smith for £43M, and then it was taken over by the Virgin group in 1998.

The modern church opposite the station is **Holy Trinity Church** which began life as Trinity Church, in a temporary building on Belsize Lane. The site for a permanent church in Finchley Road was donated by Sir Thomas Maryon-Wilson and consecrated in August 1872. Holy Trinity School took over the old church until 1876, when it moved to its present site in Trinity Walk. The first vicar was Rev. Henry Sharpe, who took up the cause of improving conditions for the navvies building the Midland Railway in the 1860s. 'A great many would get Mr Sharpe to mind a part of their wages, so that it was impossible for them to spend the whole in drink as some of them did.' The vicar gave the men tea in his church: 'some of the navvies would say, look at our dirty clothes, Sir. Mr Sharpe would reply, never mind your clothes, come as you are.' He did, however, provide washing facilities. On the spiritual side, he took the church to the navvies, preaching to them in the Belsize tunnel, 60ft underground. He remained in post until his death in 1900. The church was demolished in 1976 and replaced two years later with a smaller building. The original cupola survives as an ornament in Gainsborough Gardens, Hampstead. In 2017, Camden Council approval was obtained to replace the church with The Lighthouse, a 6-storey building with a striking circular motif on the main façade to Finchley Road. The proposal includes a 450-seat auditorium, as well as commercial units, residential space and worship areas.

North of Holy Trinity, **Lief House** is part of the British College of Osteopathic Medicine.

Based since 1954 in nearby Netherhall Gardens, this had been founded in 1936 by the pioneer naturopathic osteopath Stanley Lief. The modern block is officially No.3 in the short cul-de-sac called **Sumpter Close**.

Beyond, along the east side of Finchley Road, the Optimax laser eye clinic at **No.128** occupies handsome premises built for the National Provincial Bank. At **Nos.130-150**, past steps leading up to Netherhall Gardens, is a parade of late-Victorian shops built by Edward Jarvis Cave, called Fitzjohn's Esplanade, or simply 'The Esplanade'. Fitzjohns (no apostrophe) was a Maryon-Wilson family property in Essex. The old parade name has recently been revived for property marketing purposes.

The modern **Holiday Inn Express** covers the site of No.154-156. In 1910 No.154 housed a shop of the suffragette Women's Social & Political Union (also p 123). From 1912 to 1915 they were at No.178 when Daisy Solomon (p 58) was the Hampstead branch secretary.

North of the Tube station, on the west side of the road [46], another parade of shops and flats was built by Cave and known initially as Fitzjohn's Promenade. The properties were soon renumbered as Nos.223-253 Finchley Road, but many businesses continued to use 'Promenade' in their address, presumably because it promoted an upmarket image.

46 Finchley Road looking south towards Finchley Road Underground Station

No.233 (as No.6 Fitzjohn's Promenade) was occupied by Thomas Fall from 1889 until 1895, when he moved to No.180. An important photographer, he specialised in portraits of dogs and worked extensively for Crufts.

Early occupants at Nos.11-13 The Promenade – dubbed 'The Louvre' – were Symmons Brothers, 'drapers, hosiers, silk merchants, and ladies', gentlemen's & children's outfitters'. They went bankrupt in 1894. Their successors were Green & Edwards, drapers and house furnishers, who went on to occupy seven consecutive shops, Nos.241-253. A resident in the 1930s remembered: 'They were a splendid draper's emporium with an elegant gentleman shop-walker to welcome you and guide you to whatever department you wanted.' Although the shop was smaller and less glamorous than the nearby department store of John Barnes, there were good bargains to be had.

A group of addresses once housed nightclubs, including the El Toro Dance Club (c.1957-66) at No.251, which became London's first licensed folk club in 1964, and the Low Profile which was here in 1983. Next door, No.253 was the Moulin Rouge Dance Club (c.1956-64), and Les Élite discothèque nightclub in 1970s and '80s. No.263B was La Côte d'Azur Dance Club in 1964.

There was nothing lavatorial about the intriguingly named South Hampstead Toilet Club Ltd, at No.265 in 1893. Advertising 'handsome spacious saloons for ladies, gentlemen and children', it offered hairdressing, manicure and chiropody, and the ironing of hats. The premises later became the registered office of an unusual company. Juan de la Cierva established Cierva Autogiro Co in 1926, to develop his idea of the small 'autogiro or windmill flying machine'. Ultimately this led to the first practical helicopter designs. The company assembled machines at Hanworth Aerodrome where it also opened a flying school. A 1934 advert said: 'The Autogiro cannot stall or spin, is under perfect control at all air speeds and can descend vertically and land without forward run'. In 1951 the company was taken over by Saunders-Roe who later took over Rotocraft to become Cierva Rotorcraft Ltd, of No.265 Finchley Road. An autogyro featured in the 1967 James Bond film, *You Only Live Twice*.

Today, all the former Nos.239-279 lie under the O2 Centre. In 1963 a more extreme plan proposed the demolition and redevelopment of the entire 50-acre block enclosed by Finchley Road, Lymington Road, West End Lane and the back of properties in Broadhurst Gardens. The intention was to build a concrete raft over the railway lines, with shops and housing for more than 6,000 people above parking. Residential blocks were suggested for the northern perimeter, some as high as 20 storeys. The site was to include an amphitheatre, library, dance hall, tennis and squash courts, with a clinic, crèche and a new school. A single circular, 20-storey tower was planned on Finchley Road.

Although covering a much smaller area than that envisaged in the 1963 proposals, the site of the **O2 Centre** stretches back almost as far as West End Lane. The back land largely comprised derelict railway sidings and there had been several proposals how best to redevelop it. Buildings on Finchley Road were demolished in the early 1990s but problems with planning permission led to construction being delayed. The original £15m budget was exceeded by early 1997, causing a further delay until additional capital investors could be found. The O2 Centre, owned by Land Securities, finally opened in 1998. Besides shops and eateries, the indoor shopping complex includes a Vue cinema and a gym. In January 2021 Landsec who own the land, issued a consultation about their plans to demolish Sainsbury's, the O2 Centre and build 2,000 new homes, a park and town square between Finchley Road and West End Lane. Camden Council asked for public comments by 6 April.

Beyond the access road to the O2 car park

is the triangular site of the Finchley Road station of the Midland Railway, which opened in 1868 and passed under Finchley Road to enter the Belsize Tunnel en route to St Pancras. Finchley Road & St John's Wood Station stood immediately north of the O2 centre. The name lingered on although officially shortened to 'Finchley Road' after just seven weeks. In 1906 the Midland created new access with steps down to platform level, through an arched entrance framed by the six shops of Midland Crescent. Owing to low passenger numbers, around only 18 per weekday in 1922, the station closed in July 1927. Concealed behind a hoarding for some years, the Crescent buildings survived until 2003. In 2005 permission was granted for a commercial use building. In 2015 a residential element was agreed. By March 2021 no building had commenced.

There were a number of companies selling coal from small offices near the Midland station. One of them was Samuel Buston, a Kilburn Ward vestryman in 1893-95. A few doors away, the future was unfolding. Around 1892, the London & Hampstead Battery Company built a plant at No.287 Finchley Road. Electricity was supplied to householders using overhead wires, in direct competition with Hampstead's own underground municipal supply. In 1898 the Battery

Company was bought by the Hampstead Electric Supply Co. Ltd, who also acquired the adjacent No.2 Rosemont Road with the intention of using it as a base for charging electric vans. In 1901 it was re-named as the North-West London Electric Supply Company which remained at No.287 until 1905.

A run of properties on Finchley Road opposite Midland Crescent was redeveloped in the 1930s as shops with flats above. Next door to **Midland Court** is **Warwick House,** on the site of a small 240-seat cinema at No.158 Finchley Road (originally No.156B). The Frognal Bijou Picture Palace opened here in April 1910. Leopold Vieyra, the manager until 1914, was arrested as a German spy and sentenced to death in 1916. But this was commuted to ten years penal servitude, and with remission for good behaviour he was released in 1924 and returned to the Netherlands. From 1925 the picture house was known as the New Frognal Cinema. In 1927, Frank Beard and Horace Joseph Johnson bought the remaining 19 years of the lease. They traded successfully until September 1929 but their landlord obstructed attempts to create two emergency exits required by the LCC. The cinema lost its licence and the business went into receivership in July 1931.

The shops beneath **Frognal Court** flats are

still numbered as **Frognal Parade,** and the Finchley Road numbering resumes at **No.160**. In the 1920s, this two-storey building with oriel windows was a dance hall, variously named over time as the Hampstead Palais de Danse, Odett's, and the Casino de Danse.

In October 1993, over eight days, the IRA left a series of Semtex bombs in various London locations. Three bombs exploded in Finchley Road, including one outside the branch of Domino's Pizza at **No.166**, on the corner of Frognal. Luckily nobody was killed but six people were injured by flying glass. Later, Derek Doherty (23) and Gerard Mackin (33) were found guilty of planting the bombs and jailed for 25 years.

Nos.166-200[1] were originally Nos.1-18 in (The) Grand Parade, another Cave development.

Before and during WWI, **No.178** was the base of the Hampstead branch of the Women's Social & Political Union, whose organising secretary by 1913 was the notable suffragette Daisy Solomon (p 58). In 2020, it was suggested that the site of Nos.166-200a needed refurbishment or redevelopment, while retaining the Victorian frontage to Finchley Road.

In 1966, **Nos.202-204** was Parkway House where Autair (later Court Line Aviation) opened their North London Air Terminal, with coaches running to Luton Airport. By 1968 Clarksons, who offered cheap package holidays, was operating from the site. But in 1972, Clarksons like many other travel companies suffered huge losses and were sold to the Court Line for just a £1. In August 1974 Court Line went into liquidation and the collapse has been called, 'the most spectacular failure in package holiday history'. Ultimately, the Government stepped in to cover the losses and the 100,000 people whose holidays had been paid in advance eventually had their money returned. The Terminal closed in 1974.

The Gallup company, who conduct social surveys and polls, were at No.202 by 1972. They had moved across Finchley Road to No.307 by 1992. Currently the ground floor of the renamed Meridian House at Nos.202-204 is occupied by the Allied Irish Bank with residential accommodation above.

In 1890 the local paper announced that Mr Cave was about to build another run of shops across the road, after an earlier plan to erect a hotel on the site was abandoned. The shops, Nos.14-1 Fitzjohn's Pavement, were later renumbered as **Nos.289-315** Finchley Road.

No.307 was first occupied by baker and confectioner William Hill. '1891', the date of its completion, is displayed on the side of the building along with a terracotta decoration, depicting intertwined letters 'W, H & S',

standing for William Hill & Son. The business was started in 1784 by Hill's great grandfather David, at a time when bread making was tough physical work. Men sweating profusely and stripped to the waist, bent over huge troughs to knead the dough. William's new shop was called a 'Hygienic Bakery' to distinguish it from such concerns. Hill used machines to make dough in a well-ventilated bakery where cleanliness ruled. William died in 1919 but his company continued to prosper

and amalgamated in 1934 with the Aerated Bread Company (ABC). William's son Oliver Falvey Hill (b.1887) became an architect and garden designer. Influenced by Edwin Lutyens, he produced Arts & Crafts-style houses and built the Midland Hotel in Morecambe. Hill's bakery continued to trade at No.307 until 1925.

At the same address, from at least 1966-83, was the popular Purple Pussy Cat Club and discothèque. In 1981 it advertised 'great sounds', with opening hours from 9pm to 3am.

47 The Aylesbury Dairy and Finchley Road & Frognal Station

In December 1897, the Aylesbury Dairy Company opened a depot at **No.317**. The firm had been founded in 1865 by George Mander Allender, at the time when milk was often adulterated or poorly stored. His company did much to promote a good-quality product and the Finchley Road premises were advertised as 'specially designed for the reception and distribution of milk, cream and other dairy produce'. The building [47] was conveniently located next door to Finchley Road & Frognal Station, to which milk was delivered by rail. The depot closed soon after 1915 and the company was absorbed into United Dairies in the 1920s. In strange circumstances, Allender was murdered while on a visit to Monte Carlo in 1894 and his killers were never caught.

A wine bar opened at No.317 around 1965; by 1969 it had become the Burgundian public house, later renamed, first as The Carney Arms and then as O'Henery's. The actor Michael Elphick's daughter, Kate, remembered the Burgundian: 'Dad was very friendly with the landlord and his wife and sometimes used to help out behind the bar when they were short-staffed'. Michael had previously worked there when he was student, and he would give Kate pennies to play the fruit machine. In 2015 permission was granted to replace the empty building with flats, superseded in 2016 by a taller block, **Skylark Court**, with an even bigger footprint. The 10-storey block by architect Amin Taha featured a particular load-bearing stone structure. The pub buildings have been demolished, but the site had not been redeveloped by March 2021.

On 2 January 1860, the Hampstead Junction Railway was the first to open a station on Finchley Road. It arrived well in advance of any houses or potential passengers; the *Illustrated London News* published a drawing of the new station sitting among fields and hedgerows, with sheep grazing the slopes of Hampstead hill. Later renamed **Finchley Road & Frognal**, the station is now a stop on the London Overground.

In 1878-9 sculptor James Forsyth commissioned a house and studio to be built adjoining the station. **Ednam House** (No.327, and later No.337) is still standing: a well-proportioned, 4-storey villa with granite pillars flanking an imposing entrance once lit by a suspended gas globe. The property was bought by Camden Council and permission to use it as a hostel for single mothers was granted in 1984. After the Council sold the property in 2009 it was converted into residential flats. Forsyth's studio and workshop (later No.325 and eventually No.335) were to the rear and side of the house and their site has been redeveloped. James Forsyth was known for large monumental works: stone was delivered by rail and a crane capable of carrying 20 tons was built into the yard. The firm also made smaller works such as busts and medallions, while many commissions were for church or cemetery furniture. The studio space was shared by Forsyth's sons, James Nesfield and John Dudley, who worked in stained glass. James senior's career took off when he acquired a wealthy patron, William Ward who was created the first Earl of Dudley in 1860. He inherited a vast fortune of £80,000 a year (worth about £7.6M today). His wealth came from iron works, coal mines and 30,000 acres of land in Worcestershire as well as plantations worked by slaves in Jamaica. The Earl decided to convert his Worcestershire home, Witley Court, into a palace. James Forsyth produced the amazing 20-ton Perseus and Andromeda Fountain (1862), depicting Perseus on his horse rescuing Andromeda from a sea monster. It was described in the contemporary press as, 'probably the largest piece of sculpture in Europe'. The figures stood 26ft above the water, and the centre jet could reach 120ft into the air, producing a deafening noise. The whole work, including an extensive and complicated plumbing system, cost over £20,000 (equivalent to about £1.9M today). The mansion was left a shell after a fire in 1937 but is now owned by English Heritage and the fountain was restored in 2017.

Forsyth kept the Finchley Road workshop/studio but left Ednam House for Goldhurst Terrace around 1893. He died, aged 83, in 1910 and is buried alongside his second wife in Hampstead Cemetery. His son John Dudley did some attractive stained glass for the consecrated chapel in the Cemetery. His windows for the Baltic Exchange, commemorating members killed while serving in WWI, were badly damaged by a terrorist bomb in 1992. After restoration they were put on display at the National Maritime Museum in Greenwich.

By 1908, the area behind the studio was occupied by the Finchley Road Garage Ltd. The business expanded into the studio building and the site remained in the hands of the motor trade until its redevelopment in the early 2000s. In September 1978, Astrid Proll, one of the most wanted members of the Baader-Meinhof terrorist gang was arrested at the North London Vehicle Repair Shop, behind the Finchley Road premises. She had answered an advert to teach car maintenance in a government-financed training scheme. The manager said she had all the necessary qualifications: 'she had an accent and we knew she was foreign but she was very good at her job and all the lads liked her'.

The railway station and Ednam House were the only buildings along this stretch of Finchley Road until the opening in July 1885

of the International College at No.329 (later No.339). Owned by James Haysman, it stood on the corner of what would become Lymington Road, and was designed by local architect, Banister Fletcher. The hall, with its Chappell organ, could seat 700 and a central tower was fitted with a revolving celestial telescope. The position of the College at the bottom of a steep hill caused problems: in 1895 Haysman reported the fifth and most serious accident to his property involving a runaway horse. It had galloped out of control down Arkwright Road and careered across Finchley Road: 'his two daughters were at needlework in the recess of the window when the horse's head came through, accompanied by a shower of bricks, and only the strength of the heavy window frame saved the young ladies, who could only escape by crawling over the debris'. Haysman had opened his first Hampstead college in 1867 at Burgess Hill (p 90) and until 1895 when the lease there lapsed, he ran both academic establishments in tandem. He put No.339 up for sale in 1906 and moved to Finchley, where he was running another school in 1911. Haysman died ten years later, and there is a window dedicated to the memory of him and first wife Elizabeth in Hampstead Parish Church. After Haysman left Ednam House, it was divided into three units. In the 1990s, the largest of these was rented

to the Hampstead Bible School and the Victory Christian Centre, an evangelical group who left and took over the old Grange Cinema in Kilburn in 2001.

Nos.321-339 Finchley Road (and Nos.52-68 Lymington Road) were sold by Camden Council. The subsequent redevelopment, completed in 2004, comprises ground-floor retail units, affordable housing in **Hatstone Court**, eight mews-style houses, **Turner House** flats (in Dresden Close, to the rear), a community hall, and the Pulse Apartments (p 115). The complex wraps around Ednam House.

Opposite, **Arkwright Mansions,** also built by Cave, lead up to Arkwright Road. The building on the north corner, first opened in 1897 as Hampstead Central Library, was badly damaged in October 1940 by a high explosive bomb, and even more seriously by a V2 rocket that landed behind it on 17 March 1945 [48]. About 1,000 properties were affected. The library moved to Swiss Cottage in 1964 and a year later the Grade-II-Listed building became Hampstead, later **Camden Arts Centre**. The sites of Nos.210&212 Finchley Road, destroyed by the V2, now form part of the centre complex.

Flanking the junction with Langdale Gardens are **Langland Mansions** and **Leinster Mansions**, further blocks built by the Cave family. On 1 Oct 1940, a bomb killed

48 Hampstead Central Library, Arkwright Road, after the V2 rocket attack

Helen Durrant and May Durrant, both living at Flat No.6 Langland Mansions.

In 1903, on the west side of Finchley Road, a one-acre site immediately north of Lymington Road was proposed as the site for a new Town Hall for Hampstead. Instead a terrace of shops, Nos.341-359, was built. Located at No.343 from 1906-1941 was Langfier Court Photographers, a firm founded by in 1895, in Bond Street, by Louis Langfier. Albert Edward Elsy was appointed general manager at the Hampstead branch in 1912. After WWI broke out, Langfier offered a free photograph to any man in uniform. When Albert was called up, his wife Ethel took over running the studio until he was demobilised. Langfier Ltd went into voluntary liquidation around 1940, following Albert's death from a stroke the previous year. The firm's huge store of negatives was sold at auction in 1941 and dispersed. His daughter Mary Elsy (d.2013) became a teacher, editor and writer of children's TV shows in the 1950s.

Albert Elsy also managed Hampstead Art Gallery, next door at No.345, which opened on 1 October 1919. The first two exhibitions of paintings featured works by Alfred Wolmark and Walter Bayes, both South Hampstead residents. There was also a tiny cinema where children photographed by Elsy could watch Felix the Cat and Mickey Mouse cartoons.

Prior to demolition, Nos.341-359 were progressively taken over by car dealers Alan Day Ltd. The fronts were remodelled but the interiors were simply knocked through, retaining parts of ceilings and other decorative features from the earlier shops. In 2005, demolition and replacement of the properties (and No.27 Lymington Road) with flats and retail units was authorised but not carried out. Instead, in 2009 the Jewish Community Centre for London's plans for a new 3-storey arts, culture and community centre were approved, and **JW3** was opened in October 2013. The development also includes a 9-storey residential block, **Nos.353-359**.

The red-brick Hampstead telephone exchange, **No.361**, opened about 1932 and displays the Royal Arms of reigning monarch George V at first-floor level. At the time, every caller had to speak to a switchboard operator, who would connect them by plugging a cord into another line. The exchange still had 110 employees when it shut in January 1985, to be replaced by automated systems. It is still operational.

The two houses at **Nos.385&387** were once differently numbered, first as Nos.357&359, and then as Nos.357A&357B. Completed by 1906, they stood alone on this stretch of Finchley Road until the late 1920s. They are now sandwiched between two of three blocks of flats, in very different architectural styles, that were subsequently built along the frontage here. **Mandeville Court**, marketed by estate agent Ernest Owers in 1935, comprised 2- or 3-bedroom properties serviced by liveried porters. In 1935-39 Dame Grace Hay Drummond-Hay was living in Flat No.23. She was a pioneering journalist who worked for the American Hearst organisation, and was the first woman to fly around the world in the Graf Zeppelin in 1929. During WWII she was interned by the Japanese in Manila. She died in the Lexington Hotel, New York in 1946.

After fleeing Austria in October 1938, the artist Oskar Kokoschka (p 129) and his future wife Olda Palkovska, lived in several Hampstead addresses before moving into Mandeville Court in January 1941. On 16 April, they watched incendiary bombs falling on the City from the roof of the building. In the winter of 1946/47 the couple moved to Eyre Court in St John's Wood, where a blue plaque commemorates his tenancy. In 1953 they left for Switzerland, where Kokoschka [49] founded and taught at the International Academy of Fine Arts. He died in Montreux in 1980. The Tate Gallery held solo exhibits of his work in 1962 and 1986.

Dunrobin Court was first shown in the local directory for 1930. In 1959, the freehold sold for around £100,000 (today worth about £2.3M), when the property was described as,

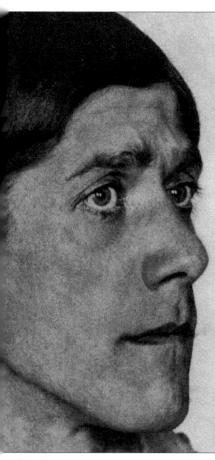

ar Kokoschka

'a first-class block of 18 superior family flats'. Marketed by Owers in 1934, **Hillside Court**, beyond, included smaller flats with bed-sitting rooms and a 'bed alcove'. There was a billiards room and restaurant for the benefit of residents, the latter also open to the public.

Across the road, Robert Newman who started the 'Proms', lived at **No.246** Finchley Road from 1914 until his death in 1926. The son of a jobmaster in Regent Street, Robert had a good bass voice and, after studying music in Italy, returned to London to sing professionally and work as a concert agent. In 1893 he became the lessee and manager of the newly opened Queen's Hall in Langham Place. Newman wanted to widen the appeal of classical music. 'I am going to run nightly concerts and train the public by easy stages – popular at first, gradually raising the standard until I have created a public of classical and modern music.' He approached a young organist called Henry Wood to conduct the orchestra, and their first concert took place on 10 August 1895. It was a great success and began a partnership which lasted 32 years. Tragically, in 1916 Newman's son, Robert junior, a member of the Royal Flying Corps, was killed when his plane crashed in an accident near Thetford. Father and son are buried together in Hampstead Cemetery.

Beyond the flats of **Alvanley Court** and of **Palace Court**, and on the corner of Frognal Lane, is **St Andrew's Frognal** Grade II listed, with its distinctive green spire. Designed by Pite and Balfour and built in Kentish ragstone, the church was completed in 1903. It became United Reformed in 1972, when the Presbyterian and Congregational churches merged. On the closure six years later of Lyndhurst Road Congregational Church in Belsize Park, its few surviving worshippers moved to St Andrew's.

In retirement, film director and producer Aida Young lived at **Osprey Court, Nos.256-258a**. Born Aida Cohen in the East End in 1920, she was the daughter of a watch repairer. She overcame the prejudice against women in the film industry to enjoy a long and successful career. Aida became a role model for young female film-makers and helped to open up employment opportunities for women in the industry. She had a long association with Hammer Films including their break-through film *The Quatermass Xperiment* (1955). Then she worked in television, producing programmes such as *Danger Man*. She returned to Hammer and produced *She* (1965), featuring Ursula Andress and *One Million Years BC* (1966), starring Raquel Welch. Aida also worked on the *Dracula* films with Hammer, before switching to EMI to make movie versions of *Steptoe and Son* (1972), and *The Likely Lads* (1976). She eventually suffered a stroke and died from pneumonia at the Royal Free Hospital on 12 August 2007.

A large house called Hedge Bank, later **No.461** Finchley Road, stood in ½ acre of grounds at the southern corner of the main road and West End Lane. Built about 1885, it was probably designed by its first occupant the architect Francis William Tasker. His wife was Maria Louisa Negretti (p 131). The purchase of Hedge Bank by Hampstead Council in 1925 was prompted by the need to widen the footpath at the junction. The remaining land was sold and developed as shops (**Nos.457-463**) with residential above, and two houses in Alvanley Gardens (Nos.23&24).

On the opposite corner stood another large property, built by Charles Cannon with a frontage to West End Lane and Finchley Road. Completed in 1870, it had a short life. Originally called Kidderpore Lodge, and then West Lodge, it was again renamed as Wellesley House by Rev. Frederick Stammers who rented the house in the 1880s. Ernest Owers purchased the property in 1902 and sold it on to the Middlesex Building Company, which was owned by the Cave family. The site was used to complete Buckingham Mansions (p 106) and build **Nos.465-489** Finchley Road, shops with living accommodation above, initially numbered in the first Frognal Parade

(cf. a later namesake, p 123.

Beyond the shops, the blocks making up **Avenue Mansions** are separated by the Finchley Road junction with Cannon Hill. Cave began building here in 1897, advertising the flats on the 'Avenue Estate' as 'high-class, substantially built, fitted and decorated in the most modern style, with floods of light'. The date '1897' appears near roof level on the corner block with Cannon Hill. By 1909 Margaret Sibthorp was renting Flat No.7. A writer and journalist, she was editor of the pioneering women's periodical *Shafts* from 1892-99. Covering feminist issues and related causes, it struggled financially. From 1895 it was published from Margaret's home at No.11 Westbere Road and ceased soon after this. Margaret died in 1916 at her home in Hampstead Garden Suburb.

On 1 January 1902, the London & South Western Bank opened a branch on the ground and basement floors of Nos.35 Avenue Mansions, later **No.503** Finchley Road, on the corner with Cannon Hill. In 1918 the L&SW was taken over by Barclays Bank, a branch of which remained here until December 1989. Permission was given in 1990 to remodel, as commercial and living space and later for residential use only.

Early on the morning of 25 October 1890, the body of 18-month old Phoebe Haslope Hogg, familiarly known as 'Tiggie', was discovered

lying face down in a bed of nettles in a field at the corner of Cannon Hill and Finchley Road. She was the daughter of Phoebe and Frank Hogg but Frank had been continuing his relationship with an old flame, Mary Pearcey. Phoebe suspected her husband and went to visit Mary at her Camden Town home, wheeling Tiggie in her bassinette perambulator. The women argued, and Mary took a poker and shattered Phoebe's skull, then set about cutting off her victim's head, which was left attached to the body by a thin section of skin and muscle. The body of 31-year-old Phoebe was found in Crossfield Road near Swiss Cottage. Mary Pearcey was convicted of the double murder and hanged on 23 December 1890. Frank Hogg sold the pram and other items to Madame Tussaud's and on 27 December, just four days after the execution, they went on display in the Chamber of Horrors.

North of Lyncroft Gardens, a short row of shops **Nos.509-517** was at first known as Avenue Parade. Beyond, **Kings Court** flats stand on the site of Heathfield at No.523, a substantial house of seventeen rooms. It was located in the rural part of Finchley Road when merchant Edward Meyerstein moved in. He had been forced to quit Broadhurst Gardens when the Great Central Railway Co. acquired and demolished a run of houses, to build their line into Marylebone. Meyerstein was at Heathfield from at least 1895 until 1912, when he left for even more rural Kent. A philanthropist, he later gave a £¼ million to the Middlesex Hospital to establish the Meyerstein Institute of Radiotherapy. His son Edward Harry Meyerstein became a poet, biographer and novelist and is buried in the graveyard of St John's Hampstead. Fellow novelist John Wain described him as a disconcerting friend with some strange habits, such as reusing Christmas cards.

Across Finchley Road is **Studholme Court**, a low-rise social housing estate on the site of New West End. This 1840s development of six large houses was the first new build in the neighbourhood but if it was intended to encourage other speculators to follow suit, this did not happen for many years. The still rural, and sometimes perilous, nature of the neighbourhood was illustrated in April 1888, when Mrs Phillips of No.2 New West End (later No.288) contacted the Vestry. She asked, 'whether bulls were allowed to graze in fields across which there is a public footpath', and alluded to her own experience recently in crossing the fields between Oak Hill Park and Finchley Road'. Around 1902, Ernest Owers (p 93) moved into No.288 and stayed for thirty years. He left West Hampstead following his wife's death in 1932.

Builder James Gibb was at Holly Lodge No.3 (later No.290) from 1900 to his death in 1930. He was responsible for building hundreds of local houses. James is buried in Hampstead Cemetery with his widow Hellen, who died at Finchley Road in 1946.

Henry Joseph Paul Negretti, who lived at No.6, Dovedale (later No.296) for a few years from the mid-1880s, was the co-founder of Negretti & Zambra, scientific and optical instrument makers. He later moved to Frognal, where he was living at the time of his death in 1919. His daughter lived across the road at Hedge Bank.

In the early 1950s, several houses were demolished and by 1956, had been replaced by the flats of Studholme Court. The development's name recalls its famous neighbour, the actress and singer Marie Studholme (1872-1930). In 1906, she was photographed in her 'pretty new residence', Croftway, later **No.298**, which stands well back from the main road. It may have been designed by architect Edward Maufe and took its name from an old footpath that ran along its side wall, and which still leads to Ferncroft Avenue. Born in Bradford as Caroline Maria Lupton, Marie Studholme [50] started her stage career in 1891, singing in the chorus at the Lyric Theatre, London. Her fortune was made after she caught the eye of George

50 Marie Studholme

Edwardes who owned the Gaiety Theatre. She was petite and beautiful; the main requirements for a Gaiety Girl, and her face sold thousands of postcards. Rumour said she charged 6d to autograph a card, donating the money to charity. Marie toured widely for Edwardes at home and abroad, ending her career in the music hall. After retiring in 1916, Marie lived quietly at Croftway. She died there from heart failure in March 1930 following a severe attack of rheumatic fever. Her funeral service was held at nearby Emmanuel Church. In 2012 a blue plaque in Marie's memory was unveiled at No.298 by the Music Hall Guild of Great Britain and America.

No.527 is a single building occupying a large site at the corner of Parsifal Road. The building dates from 1887 as Hackney Theological College, a training college for nonconformist ministers founded in Hackney in 1802 that moved here from the East End. In 1924 it amalgamated with New College, Swiss Cottage; their College Crescent building was demolished in 1934, leaving the Parsifal Road site, where a rear extension was added. Assuming the New College name, it continued as a divinity school of the University of London for the training of Congregational ministers. The Open University took over the building in 1977, as its London Regional Centre, renaming it Parsifal College. Since 2005 it has been the London campus of

ESCP Europe, a business school with premises in other European cities. Established in 1819, it is the oldest business school in the world.

Now a residential property, No.527A Finchley Road started life as the West Hampstead Congregational Chapel, established with the help of the College next door. The architect Henry Spalding designed the octagonal building in red brick and terracotta with good acoustics. Built in 1894, it seated over 1,000 but the number of worshippers was always well below capacity. They had dwindled to just 30 by 1939 and it closed the following year. The Chapel was bought by the **Shomrei Hadath Synagogue** in 1946. In the 1980s, permission was granted for remodelling the interior to create flats, **The Octagon**, completed by 1992, while the Synagogue has a new building (of 1989) to the rear.

A final terrace of shops ends this stretch of Finchley Road, to its junction with Fortune Green Road. Burgess Parade was built in the early 1900s and later renumbered as **Nos.551-575**. There was accommodation over the shops and three flats in Burgess Parade Mansions. In 1911 the occupant of Flat No.3/563, 45 year old widow Alice Edith Hall, was another local resident who added a comment on her census form, *I wish to protest against my voteless condition.*

In 2021, planning permission was granted

to restore traditional shop fronts and roof details for **Nos.551-557**.

Grocer William Dimond began trading in Fairhazel Gardens around 1881 and by 1904 his son also named William, was at the newly built **No.559**. In the 1930s, the family sold off all the shops, but a business trading in the name of Dimond continued here until the mid-1960s. From the end of 1936 to the following October, Benjamin Britten lived over No.559 with his sister Beth, who was running a dressmaking business.

The parade wraps around the corner into Fortune Green Road with an attractive turret over **No.575** on the corner, today's Balthorne Safe Deposit Centre. By 1921 it was a bank and in the 1980s it became the Hampstead Safe Depository owned by Safe Deposit Centres Ltd (SDC). On the afternoon of 2 June 2008, it was one of three SDC premises simultaneously raided by armed police as part of Operation Rize, the Met's biggest ever operation against money laundering at privately owned safe depositories. 6,717 boxes were opened and of these, 3,549 were seized. Police found evidence of gun crime, child pornography, human trafficking, multi-million-pound tax evasion, drug dealing and ivory trading. Two directors of the company received jail sentences and according to Detective Superintendent Mark Ponting, Operation Rize disrupted the activities of 32 organised crime gangs and led to 146 arrests and 30 convictions.

Opposite, all the houses north of Croftway as far as Platts Lane, **Nos.300 to 338** were taken over by Westfield College, University of London, who left the site for Mile End after the creation of Queen Mary & Westfield College in 1989. King's College London took over the entire campus that extended back and across Kidderpore Gardens. Much was demolished in the 1990s to create **Westfield**, a luxury apartment development including **Sycamore House** (No.300). The sites of Nos.328-338 now form part of **Kidderpore Green**, a development of new blocks and refurbished houses, including a home for the Hampstead School of Art. Today it is difficult to imagine how imposing the remaining Finchley Road properties once were, as successive road widenings have removed their front gardens.

Beyond the junction with Fortune Green Road, the semi-detached houses at **Nos.577-615** were built soon after 1904. Some suffered severe damage from two V1 flying bombs in 1944, one landing in Ardwick Road and the second behind the Finchley Road properties. Nos.587-607 were rebuilt.

In 1911, Phyllis Barker was at **No.603** with her widowed mother and sister. She was a beautiful actress from the Gaiety Theatre. On 27 July 1917 she was returning to England from the USA on the Cunard liner *Laconia* when it was torpedoed without warning by a German U-boat. There were 292 persons on board; Phyllis was among the survivors, but 12 passengers and crew died. She told reporters, 'We found everything we wanted in our boat – food and drink enough for a long voyage and plenty of brandy should we need it'. One of the stewards entertained the passengers by imitating Harry Lauder, the famous music hall performer of the time, until a rescue boat approached. Phyllis concluded, 'We suddenly and truly sang with heart and soul the National Anthem'.

Influential journalist and author Alfred George Gardiner (1865-1946) was their neighbour at **No.613**. His pen name was 'Alpha of the Plough'. Gardiner left school aged 14 to work as an apprentice shorthand writer and reporter, and from 1902-19 was editor of the *Daily News*, the oldest Liberal newspaper. Gardiner opposed privilege, despised imperialism and hated corruption. In 1922 he left No.613 for Balham.

In 1933, the sites of No.617, and of the end house in Burgess Hill, were redeveloped as a garage. Recently demolished and undergoing redevelopment, the Tower Garage was in Camden until a 1994 boundary change exiled this northernmost tip of West Hampstead into Barnet.

The Hendon Way, originally known as the Watford By-Pass, was needed to relieve the already heavily congested stretches of the Great North Road and Edgware Road, with an eye to increased traffic levels in future. With the opening of the Hendon Way in 1926, the appearance of this section of the Finchley Road was irrevocably altered, and its tranquillity lost forever.

Sources

Books and pamphlets

Aston, Mark. *The cinemas of Camden*. L B Camden, 1997

Bebbington, Gillian. *London street names*. Batsford, 1972

Booth, Charles. *Life and labour of the people of London*. Macmillan, 1892-97

Cherry, Bridget & Pevsner, Nikolaus. *London 4: North*. Penguin, 1999 (*The buildings of England*)

Clunn, Harold. *The Face of London*, new ed. rev. by E R Wethersett. Spring Books, 1962

Colloms, Marianne & Weindling, Dick. *The Good Grave Guide to Hampstead Cemetery, Fortune Green*. Camden History Society, 2000

Colloms, Marianne & Weindling, Dick. Images of England. Kilburn and Cricklewood. Tempus, 2001

Colloms, Marianne & Weindling, Dick. *The Greville Estate, the history of a Kilburn neighbourhood*. Camden History Society, 2007

Colvin, H M. *A biographical dictionary of British architects, 1660-1840*, 4th ed. Yale UP, 2008

Pevsner, Nikolaus. *London, except the Cities of London and Westminster*. 3rd ed., Penguin, 1973 (The Buildings of England)

Galinou, Mireille. *Cottages And Villas. The Birth of the Garden Suburb*. Yale University Press, 2010

Richardson, John. *A history of Camden*. Historical Publications, 1999

Swenarton, Mark. *Cooke's Camden. The Making of Modern Housing*. Lund Humphries, 2017

Thompson, F.M.L. Hampstead. *Building a Borough, 1650-1964* Routledge & Kegan Paul, 1974

Walford, Edward. *Old and new London*, Cassell, 1878

Weinreb, B & Hibbert, C (eds). *The London encyclopaedia*, 3rd ed. Macmillan, 2008

Weindling, Dick & Colloms, Marianne. *Kilburn and West Hampstead Past*. Historical Publications, 1999

Also many individual biographies and institutional histories, in printed form or digitised

Maps

Rocque 1746; Greenwood 1834; Stanford 1862; Ordnance Survey 1871 & later; Bacon 1888; Booth's poverty maps 1889/98; LCC bomb damage maps

Periodicals & Newspapers

Camden History Review
Camden History Society. *Newsletters*
Camden New Journal
Hampstead and Highgate Express
Hampstead Record
Kilburn Times

Other records

Census returns, 1841–1911
Conservation Area Statements (L B Camden)
Goad insurance plans, 1880s & later
Hampstead Vestry & Council Minutes
Licensed Victuallers Recognizances, 1723 & 1760
London County Council/GLC street lists
London County Council: Education Committee & Housing Committee reports
Local Street Directories for Camden, Brent, Hendon and St Marylebone
Post Office London Directories (Kelly & Co.)
Registers of Electors

Websites

Numerous online resources, including websites of extant local institutions, and also:
Ancestry (www.ancestry.com)
British History Online (www.british-history.ac.uk)
British Newspapers Archive (www.britishnewspaperarchive.co.uk)
L B of Camden: Planning (www.camden.gov.uk/planning)
Discovery: The National Archives (www.discovery.nationalarchives.gov.uk/)
Deceased Online (www.deceasedonline.com)

Find A Grave (www.findagrave.com)
FindmyPast (www.findmypast.co.uk)
Grove Music Online (www.oxfordmusicoline.com)
Historic England: Listed Buildings (www.historicengland.org.uk/listing/the-list/)
London Picture Archive (www.londonpicturearchive.org.uk)
London Pubology (www.pubology.co.uk/)
Music Hall & Theatre History (www.arthurlloyd.co.uk)
Old Bailey Online (www.oldbaileyonline.org)
Oxford Dictionary of National Biography (www.oxforddnb.com)
Pathé News (www.britishpathe.com)
Times Digital Archive 1785-1985 (www.gale.cengage.co.uk/times.aspx)
Wellcome Library (www.archives.wellcome.ac.uk)

Archive centres
British Library
Brent Local Studies & Archives Centre
Camden Local Studies & Archives Centre
Guildhall Library
London Metropolitan Archives
Powell-Cotton Museum (www.powell-cottonmuseum.org)
RIBA

Index

Streets included in the survey are indicated in boldface, as are the main entries for these and other selected subjects

* = illustration

PH = public house

142